D0079230

DUE DATE

JAN 2 6 1999		
MAY 2 1 2004		
- 8 MAY 2006		
201-6503		Printed in USA

Revisiting Blassingame's
THE SLAVE
COMMUNITY

Recent Titles in
Contributions in Afro-American and African Studies
SERIES ADVISER: Hollis R. Lynch

Revisiting Blassingame's
THE SLAVE
COMMUNITY
The Scholars Respond

Edited by Al-Tony Gilmore

CONTRIBUTIONS IN AFRO-AMERICAN AND AFRICAN STUDIES, NUMBER 37

GREENWOOD PRESS
WESTPORT, CONNECTICUT • LONDON, ENGLAND

Library of Congress Cataloging in Publication Data
Main entry under title:

Revisiting Blassingame's The slave community.

(Contributions in Afro-American and African
studies; no. 37 ISSN 0069-9624)
Includes index.
1. Blassingame, John W., 1940- The slave
community—Addresses, essays, lectures. 2. Slavery in
the United States—Southern States—Addresses, essays,
lectures. 3. Plantation life—Southern States—
Addresses, essays, lectures. I. Gilmore, Al-Tony.
II. Series: Contributions in Afro-American and
African studies; no. 37.
E443.B553R48   975'04'96073   77-84765

Library of Congress Catalog Card Number: 77-84765
ISBN: 0-8371-9879-8
ISSN: 0069-9624

First published in 1978

Greenwood Press, Inc.
51 Riverside Avenue, Westport, Connecticut 06880

Printed in the United States of America

10 9 8 7 6 5 4 3 2 1

This volume is respectfully
dedicated to
Earl E. Thorpe
Scholar, Teacher, Independent Thinker, and Mentor of Historians

Contents

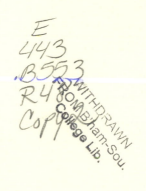

AL-TONY GILMORE
Introduction

Most scholars of the slavery experience will agree to varying degrees that John W. Blassingame's *The Slave Community: Plantation Life in the Antebellum South* (*TSC*) represents one of the more novel approaches to and important discussions of slavery to have appeared. Although released without the benefit and advantage of an exhaustive promotional campaign or the fanfare surrounding other recent books on slavery such as Robert Fogel and Stanley Engerman's *Time on the Cross,* Eugene Genovese's *Roll, Jordan, Roll,* or Herbert Gutman's *The Black Family in Slavery and Freedom, The Slave Community,* as the essays in this volume demonstrate, has left an indelible mark on the writing of slavery.

Clearly the most significant methodological contribution of *TSC* lies in its sharp break with historiographical tradition by focusing on the institution of slavery *from the perspective of the slave.* The first major study of slavery to employ that methodology full-scale, it was based primarily on an innovative use of the autobiographies of ex-slaves and bolstered with traveler reports, agricultural journals, and a wide range of other secondary sources, including the use of psychological theory. *TSC*, in brief, argues that the pressures of slavery with its accompanying planter power and coercion was not, in most instances, strong enough to infantilize slaves to the point of being sambos; to force slaves into total identification with their masters; or to prevent slaves from developing and sustaining their own cultural norms, value system, and world view. Much of this,

TSC continues, was because considerable aspects of slave life were largely free from planter control. The net effect of "relative freedom" within slavery was the creation and fostering of cultural mechanisms among slaves that enabled them to transcend and cope with their bondage.

Long before the publication of *TSC* a wide-spread opinion among black people was that they were best qualified to speak for themselves, particularly on matters relating to their condition. *Freedom's Journal*, America' first black newspaper, opened its initial edition in 1827 with the statement: "We wish to plead our own cause. Too long have others spoken for us. Too long has the publick [sic] been deceived by misrepresentation, in things which concern us dearly."[1] Indeed, an ex-slave carried this further when in 1929 he insisted to an interviewer from Fisk University that "if you want Negro history, you will have to get [it] from somebody who wore the shoe, and by and by from one to the other you will get a book."[2] Richard Hofstadter recognized the implication of that statement for the academic community when he admonished scholars that "any history of slavery must be written in large part from the standpoint of the slave."[3]

Why then, one might ask, did it take such a long time for a serious synthesis of slavery to be written with critical consideration given to the slaves' point of view? This question becomes more interesting when one considers the several collections of slave letters and documents, the thousands of interviews with ex-slaves conducted by the Works Progress Administration, and the numerous ex-slave autobiographies.[4] Admittedly, given the political climates and social contexts in which most of these documents were written, it must be conceded that they—like many other historical sources—have presented more than a few problems for the historian but not nearly enough to escape confrontation with them as indispensable sources for the writing of slavery.[5] Still, equally important considerations in dealing with the above question are the political climates and social contexts in which historians write history. U.B. Phillips, for example, whose book *American Negro Slavery* published in 1918 and until recent years ranked by "scholars" as the authoritative work of Afro-American slavery, held such a derogatory view of black people that he was blindly obscured from giving any meaningful consideration to slave sources as reliable and legitimate documents. Phillips, a molder and mirror of his times, felt assured that black people were biologically inferior to white people—nothing more and nothing less. The impact of his book on subsequent slavery historiography and its confirmation of widely held beliefs about black people cannot be dismissed lightly. Perhaps no book has been more influential in the stacking of the historiographical deck in favor of the slave owners.

Kenneth Stampp's *The Peculiar Institution* appeared in 1956 and replaced Phillip's study in some liberal quarters as the best general work on slavery. He, too, was also convinced that because there were "few reliable records of what went on in the minds of slaves," one could only gauge their "thoughts and feelings from their behavior, that of their masters and the logic of the situation."[6] Though Stampp clearly did not harbor the same racist view of Phillips, he, perhaps unwittingly, continued to promote a methodology that for all but practical purposes excluded the slaves' point of view. A few years following Stampp a neo-Phillipian view of slave personality was presented by Stanley Elkins in *Slavery: A Problem in American Institutional and Intellectual Life.*[7] Elkins concluded that Phillips was wrong about slaves being innately inferior. Rather, he surmised, they were "made" sambos. The argument is patently academic but casts revealing light on Elkins' inability to grasp the need for a sophisticated use of slave-based sources as legitimate documents. Thus George Rawick's claim in 1972 that the "masters not only ruled the past in fact" but also "rule its written history" marked one euphemistic way of saying that a white man's word carried more historical weight than that of a black man. Until the appearance of *TSC*, that statement could only be strengthened with a reading of the major studies on slavery. Fortunately, in recent years this situation has begun to change, especially in the area of slavery.[8]

To be sure, Blassingame was not the first scholar to suggest the potential of slave-based sources nor was he the first to use them for critical documentation.[9] However, *TSC* was the first comprehensive study of slave life to use them as the bulk of its primary material and, to date, the *only* survey history of American slave life based essentially on ex-slave autobiographies. Thus, *TSC* in essence represents a reshuffling of that deck stacked by Phillips and others. Still, the need to distinguish the difference between the merits of a methodology employing slave-based sources and psychological models to construct an "inside-out" view of slavery and the extent to which *TSC* achieved success and experienced failure in that area cannot be overstressed. More to the point, an endorsement of the basic aims of *TSC*'s methodology is not tantamount to an endorsement of all or, for that matter, any of its conclusions. And the reverse is equally true. Those are delicate but separate issues and are appropriately treated as such in this volume as both *TSC*'s methodology and conclusions are subjected to criticisms ranging from mild rebuke and strident rejection on one hand to warm praise and enthusiastic applause on the other.

Although there is a tendency for most essays in the collection to criticize and evaluate *TSC* from a number of angles, the major and more imaginative thrusts of each and the similarities of several are worthy of mention. George Rawick's "Some Notes on a Social Analysis of Slavery" examines the conservative manner in which *TSC* treats slave culture as a political force and charges the work with male chauvinism for its omission of a well-defined female slave perspective.

"Toward a Psychology of Slavery," by Eugene Genovese, and Earl Thorpe's "Studies of Slavery Need Freud and Marx" both agree with Blassingame's utilization of psychological theory as a vehicle for the probing of the mind of the slave but insist that a closer look at the teachings of Sigmund Freud, rather than those of Harry Stack Sullivan, might have yielded firmer results. Leslie Howard Owens' "Blacks in *TSC*" raises important questions on the limits and dangers of Blassingame's use of psychology and proceeds to point out areas and issues he considers to have been conspicuously overlooked and misunderstood without advocating alternative psychological models. Of particular interest are Owens' comments on Blassingame's discussion of sambo as a slave personality-type.

Ralph Carter's "Slavery and the Climate of Opinion" and James Anderson's "Political and Scholarly Interests in the 'Negro Personality' " weigh the factors of public opinion on scholarly research on Afro-Americans in general and slavery in particular. Tracing the writings of slavery from U.B. Phillips through *TSC*, Carter demonstrates how the theories that underpin those studies "display a strong proclivity to the racial and social mood of the country at the time of their appearance." He then calls for the creation of new theories and methodologies that divorce themselves from the trappings of the old. Anderson's essay, following the line of reasoning advanced by Carter, measures the significance of *TSC* against comparable studies that influence social policy.

Stanley Engerman's "Reconsidering *TSC*" weighs Blassingame's study against subsequent studies of slavery that now "provide us with more information and detail" that have increasingly become "necessary complements to, supplements of, or replacements for his [*TSC's*] chapters." Issues relative to aspects of *TSC* where quantitative methods may have proved advantageous are also raised by Engerman.

It is interesting to note that Engerman, like Rawick, Genovese, Carter, and to some extent Thorpe, views *TSC* as a reactionary response to the framework and rules of debate offered by Elkins' 1958 publication, *Slavery*.

John Henrik Clarke's decidedly favorable critique, "*TSC* and the World Community," underscores the importance of the perspective of the slave for studies on slavery and in that area judges *TSC* as a methodological contribution of major importance. He also augments *TSC*'s discussion of the Atlantic slave trade by providing along the way—like all of the essays in this volume—valuable insights from his own research.

The more specific criticisms of *TSC* from each contributor are dealt with by Blassingame in his "Redefining *TSC*: A Response to the Critics."

This volume grew out of a session based on *TSC* held at the 1976 Chicago meeting of the Association for the Study of Afro-American Life and History (ASALH). The session proved to be one of the largest in the history of the annual meetings of the ASALH, with nearly five hundred people in attendance. Participants were Mary Frances Berry, Herbert Gutman, Leslie Howard Owens, George Rawick, and Earl Thorpe. A written critique of *TSC* was prepared by Eugene Genovese and distributed in advance of the session. John Blassingame also responded to the critiques but due to communication difficulties was greatly handicapped by having received some of them only minutes before the session. This collection of essays has provided him with ample time for his reply, "Redefining *TSC*: A Response to Critics."

For this volume James D. Anderson, Ralph D. Carter, John Henrik Clarke, and Stanley Engerman have also contributed critiques. Mary Frances Berry's "Review of the Reviews" is also included, and an article on using ex-slave testimony by Blassingame has been reprinted with the permission of the Southern Historical Association. The reprinting of that article seems proper considering that it represents Blassingame's most detailed response to the unusual amount of criticism surrounding *TSC*'s use of certain slave-based sources and its exclusion of others, while offering guidelines on the use of slave-based sources as historical documents. The variety of perspectives on *TSC* and the writing of slavery in general as contained in these essays is impressive. A reading of *TSC* is, of course, recommended as a prerequisite for a full appreciation of this volume.

Perhaps the single greatest lesson to be learned from any collection of this sort is that the institution of slavery was much too large, endured far too long, and drew too many people into its web to be definitively captured by a single scholar or, for that matter, a single discipline. However, this does not preclude the need for more studies aimed at exploring well-defined aspects of slavery within the limits of the disciplines and the methodologies employed. The puzzle of slavery is a difficult one, and an assessment of *TSC*'s place in the total picture is the purpose for *Revisiting Blassingame's THE SLAVE COMMUNITY*.

My debts are to many who assisted in putting this volume together, but to none do I owe more than the contributors who took the time from their demanding schedules to write the essays of this collection. Both Mary F. Berry and George Rawick offered invaluable suggestions and encouragement in the early stages of the project. Stanley Elkins, Carl Degler, Robert Fogel, Nell I. Painter, Willie Lee Rose, Henry Suggs, Arnold H. Taylor, and Peter Wood, all offered advice on the selection of contributors. I wish to thank the Association for the Study of Afro-American Life and History, for whom I served as Program Chairman in 1976, for the support given in the organization of the session on which this collection is based. Gratitude is also offered to Mrs. Beatrice Youngblood, my co-worker, and my wife, Beryl, for understanding my concern about *TSC* and the issues that it raises.

Al-Tony Gilmore
University of Maryland
College Park, Maryland

NOTES

1. "To Our Patron," *Freedom's Journal,* March 16, 1827, p. 1.
2. Fisk University, *Unwritten History of Slavery: Autobiographical Accounts of Negro Ex-slaves,* ed. Ophelia Settles Egypt, J. Masuoka, and Charles S. Johnson (Nashville, 1945, unpublished typescript), quoted in Lawrence W. Levine, *Black Culture and Black Consciousness: Afro American Folk Thought from Slavery to Freedom* (New York: 1977), p. 443.
3. Richard Hofstadter, "U.B. Phillips and the Plantation Legend," *Journal of Negro History* 29 (1944), p. 124.
4. John Blassingame's recent *Slave Testimony* (Baton Rouge, 1977) and Robert S. Starobin's *Blacks in Bondage, Letters of American Slaves* (New York, 1974) are excellent collections of documents written during slavery by slaves. The most outstanding compilation of interviews with ex-slaves is the Slave Narrative Collection of the Federal Writers' Project of the Works Progress Administration taken during the years 1936-1938. These are currently being edited and published by George P. Rawick in his multi-volume study *The American Slave: A Composite Autobiography* (Westport, Connecticut). Rawick also uses a smaller collection of interviews from the project conducted at Fisk University in the late 1920s and 1930s. In addition to *TSC* a good list and discussion of slave autobiographies is contained in Charles H. Nichols' *Many Thousand Gone: The Ex-slaves' Account of their Bondage and Freedom* (Leiden, Holland, 1963).
5. The appendix of this volume contains a discussion by Blassingame on the approaches to and problems of using these sources.

6. Kenneth Stampp, *The Peculiar Institution: Slavery in the Ante-Bellum South* (New York 1956), p. 88.

7. Stanley Elkins, *Slavery: A Problem in American Institutional and Intellectual Life* (Chicago, 1958).

8. George Rawick, *From Sundown to Sunup: The Making of the Black Community* (Westport, Connecticut, 1972), p. xiv. This study by Rawick is based primarily on slave interviews from the WPA slave narratives.

9. See Frederick Bancroft, *Slave-Trading in the Old South* (New York, 1931); Charles S. Johnson, *Shadow of the Plantation,* (Chicago, 1934); and John B. Cade, "Out of the Mouths of Ex-slaves," *Journal of Negro History* 20 (1935), pp. 294-337. Since the publication of *The Slave Community,* several excellent studies have utilized slave-based sources with sophistication. Most notable are Eugene Genovese, *Roll, Jordon, Roll: The World the Slaves Made* (New York, 1974); Leslie Howard Owens, *This Species of Property* (New York, 1976); and Herbert Gutman, *The Black Family in Slavery and Freedom* (New York, 1976).

Revisiting Blassingame's
THE SLAVE COMMUNITY

MARY FRANCES BERRY

The Slave Community:
A Review of Reviews

In the six years since *The Slave Community* was published, it has continued to receive critical acclaim from scholars and students alike as one of the most important books on slavery. It was, until the publication of *Time on the Cross, Roll, Jordan, Roll,* and *The Black Family in Slavery and Freedom,* "the most important discussion of American slavery since Elkins." Even after the publication of these three works, it remains one of the most important books on slavery published in the 1970s. The most significant contribution of Blassingame's book is that it was the first book-length treatment to make a departure from Stanley Elkins' *Slavery* and to provide a slave's perspective on the institution. No prizes or awards resulted from its publication in 1972, as were accorded to Genovese's *Roll, Jordan, Roll;* and Blassingame, unlike Fogel and Engerman and Gutman, was not invited to appear on *The Today Show.*

But *The Slave Community* was not ignored. It was reviewed as widely as is usual for historical monographs, and it has been discussed in most college and community circles. But one essayist's view that *The Slave Community* avoided the sensationalism and controversy engendered by *Time on the Cross* because the early 1970s' intellectual climate reflected pro-black, pro-slave, and anti-slavery comments is probably wrong. On the contrary, *The Slave Community* generated comparatively little public comment or notice because the early 1970s were largely an anti-black, white-blacklash period in American history.

The public at large, fed up with the Great Society, riots in the cities, affirmative action, and told by their leadership that blacks should stop asking for special treatment, approved of Fogel and Engerman's view of slavery as an economically efficient and rational institution—morally evil, yes, but not so evil as previously supposed. The controversy that swirled around the book resulted from white and black liberal efforts to submerge the original acclaim Fogel and Engerman's conclusions received. To the lay public Blassingame's book most likely was a militant voice for black self-determination crying in the wilderness at the tag end of the Johnson era of domestic social reform. Blassingame's voice, to this public, insofar as they heard it, was that of just another young, self-serving black raging against the injustices of slavery.

But *The Slave Community* did inspire a number of perceptive reviews in newspapers and magazines, as well as the usual scholarly journals. Considering its reception by the reviewers, the book should hold its own in succeeding generations of university and college circles, and it remains the most exhaustive discussion in book form of slavery from the viewpoint of slaves.[1]

The Slave Community received its fair share of favorable notices in *Choice, The Library Journal,* and local newspapers. Most of these, even when making slightly negative comments, asserted the overall effectiveness and value of the book.[2] But a few newspapers and magazines made harshly critical comments. One reviewer wanted to know that if "most slaves hated and were suspicious of all whites," as Blassingame asserted, why during the years of the Civil War "so many slaves protected otherwise helpless families consisting of white women and children."[3] One possible answer, of course, is that most is not all, and one could as easily point to the large number of slaves who killed their masters or ran away and joined the Union army to defeat their masters in the war.

The most incisive newspaper criticism of the book was provided by reviewers in the *Washington Post* and the *Times Literary Supplement.* Historian Carl Degler, writing in the *Post,* praised the book as coming "closer than any previous study to answering the question 'what was it like to be a slave?'" Degler complained, however, that the discussion of modern psychology in the book was not integrated with the historical materials. Furthermore, Degler emphasized that the author failed to tell the reader that the most likely reason why the autobiographies he used stressed the stable family life of blacks was that the abolitionists who edited or supervised the writing of these autobiographies wanted to persuade readers of the stability of slave family life. Degler's own analysis, however, remains conjecture. The fact that abolitionists wanted to emphasize stable black family life does not necessarily mean that the autobiographers did not perceive stable families.[4]

The Slave Community's most critical newspaper reviewer became involved in a "tempest-in-a-teapot" when it was discovered that he published the same review in two different places, one signed, the other unsigned. In any case, the reviewer endorsed Blassingame's major conclusions but complained that the book was "fragmentary and uneven and shows many signs of hasty compilation." Furthermore, the reviewer asserted, "most if not all of Professor Blassingame's contentions have been reached by other commentators in recent years, and work on all of the subjects treated so briefly here is still proceeding." Blassingame, according to this reviewer, was too preoccupied with refuting Stanley Elkins' thesis of slave docility, which few scholars had accepted without reservations. Blassingame also erred, according to him, in basing his treatment of slave resistance largely on Herbert Aptheker's pioneering, thorough, methodologically sound work. Therefore, Blassingame added little to present knowledge of the subject, and his work should be supplemented by Gerald Mullin's "thoughtful study." The reviewer also faulted Blassingame for failing to use the "remarkable collection of narratives of surviving slaves which were assembled by the Federal Writers Project during the New Deal . . . ." Therefore, the book is a beginning, but we must "await the outcome of more sustained academic labors in the still fertile field of American Negro slavery."[5]

It is fair to say that only one of these negative assessments of *The Slave Community* seems justified. Perhaps stung by the frequent criticisms, Blassingame has explained elsewhere, after the fact, the problems involved with relying on the slave narratives, but he could have avoided this criticism by including the narratives in his bibliography and critical essay on sources used in the book. The *Times Literary Supplement* reviewer's remaining criticisms would be better characterized as a difference of perspective. Although many scholars did not accept the Elkins' thesis without reservation, large

numbers included references to it in their own work without criticism; students in history courses throughout the country were
reading it as the last and latest word on slavery; and sociologists
were incorporating its findings into their own work. It is fair to say
that *The Slave Community* helped to lay the Elkins' thesis to rest,
just as Herbert G. Gutman's long essay in the *Journal of Negro
History* helped to lay *Time on the Cross* to rest.[6]

The reviewer's disdain for Herbert Aptheker's work on slave
resistance and his preference for that of Gerald Mullin reflects, perhaps, his own biases. As I have pointed out elsewhere, Mullin's
work purports to be a study of slave behavior, but it is based almost
entirely on sources generated from the masters and should most
appropriately be called the master's perception of how slaves be-
haved. No matter what the criticisms of Aptheker's methodology
and work have been, it is fair to say that he did not restrict himself
to sources generated by the master. It is also clear that Blassingame's treatment of slave resistance is not based entirely on the
work of Aptheker, even though he reaches a similar conclusion that
slaves were not docile and did engage in acts of resistance and rebellion.[7]

A reviewer in the *Economist* shared his *Times Literary Supplement* colleague's critical assessment of Blassingame's book. The reviewer bowed to Blassingame's concentration on the slaves, their relations with each other, their roots, and culture, but he regarded
the psychological theory contained in the book as a "parade" and
suggested that serious historians could skip it. He also pointed out
that Blassingame did not explain away successfully the failure of
slaves to begin an insurrection during the Civil War. He found the
book to be a "healthy adjustment of perspective and a cool corrective for the myths that had been accepted concerning slavery."[8]

On the contrary, Bernard Weisberger, writing in *American
Heritage,* described Blassingame's work as a valuable assessment
that recognized it was not the final truth about slavery. He saw it as
shedding new light on the perceptions of slaves about their experiences. In general, he categorized it as an example of the perspective
of different persons about the same events in history—providing a
valuable lesson that could be learned from the study of history in
general.[9]

A number of journals included rather bland assessments of *The Slave Community.* In the *South Atlantic Quarterly,* Robert F. Durden found it to be an important book that did not become an "overt, point-by-point refutation of the work" of Stanley Elkins but that demolished Elkins' thesis about American slavery. Durden thought the book stood on its own merits and found only one generalization to complain about—Blassingame's statement that "most slaves hated and were suspicious of all whites." This he regarded to be in conflict with the general thesis of the book, that there was a great variety of slave attitudes.[10]

In the *Journal of Political Economy,* Stanley Engerman, who might have been expected to write a critique that would compare the book with *Time on the Cross,* simply reviewed it as a study not written for economists that makes limited use of economical analysis. He regarded it as a rather traditional, historical account. He did not regard Blassingame's use of psychological theory as a new approach and criticized the failure to even mention the 2,000 WPA interviews. He did believe that Blassingame effectively explained the difficulties with Elkins' thesis.[11]

Jarritus Boyd, in reviewing Blassingame's study, successfully contrasted it with Robert Manson Myers's *The Children of Pride.* She saw these books as showing the two communities of the antebellum south: *The Children of Pride,* picturing the slave-owner society comfortably well-off, educated, and cultured; and *The Slave Community,* showing the struggle of slaves for existence, self-identity, survival, and freedom. She thought that Blassingame effectively described a community of interest between master and slave and the accommodations between blacks and whites and their interactions on the plantation. Commending his use of the slave narratives and the slave autobiographies, she found his use of contemporary records and sociological and psychological materials on personality groups convincing. Boyd was apparently not disturbed by the focus on the Elkins' thesis that seemed to perturb other reviewers.[12]

In 1973 Keith Polakoff ecstatically expressed the opinion that "only with the publication of Blassingame's work do we obtain for the first time a detailed examination of the daily lives of the slaves on large plantations, with some intelligent speculation about the forces to which they were subjected.'' Unlike some other reviewers, Polakoff believed that the book was strengthened by the use of the illustrations interspersed at appropriate places throughout the text. His reaction may very well have been influenced by the fact that the journal in which he wrote is directed toward teachers who might find the illustrations useful in their courses. Other reviewers in scholarly journals, knowing that some of the illustrations were done after the Civil War and that others were well-known, found them a useless detraction from scholarly concerns.[13]

David Goldfield raved about Blassingame's book as the most impressive and balanced attempt to date to understand the slave's responses to plantation life. He knew that Blassingame did not use the WPA narratives, but that did not detract from the book's importance. Goldfield saw plantation slavery in Blassingame's treatment as analogous to black experience in the twentieth century. The city and the plantation can be regarded as similar battlefields; there is an urban cottonpatch where blacks are dehumanized and buffeted by prejudice as in the master/slave relationship. But as in the ghetto, the urban slave-quarters, the modern black finds the same strength and group solidarity that slaves were able to find on the plantation. Goldfield inferred from this analysis that ''the plantation and the modern cities stand more as monuments to the resilience of the black man than to the brutality of white society.''[14]

The most critical reviews of *The Slave Community* were found, naturally, in the historical journals. The historians selected to prepare these reviews were almost uniformly scholars who possessed some expertise on the institution of slavery and were, therefore, in an exceedingly good position to review Blassingame's work. Most of them found much to complain about but something to praise in the book. Uniformly they were unhappy with Blassingame's failure to use the WPA narratives, and some did not like his emphasis on resistance. Others were simply disturbed by the brevity of the book, believing, perhaps, that a long book is somehow more significant than a short one and that important ideas must be expressed at great length.

Kenneth Wiggins Porter found Blassingame's emphasis on the many different slave personality types, ''Sambo'' being only one, to be not a new departure from but rather close to the work of Eugene Genovese. He regarded Blassingame's dependence on printed sources as a major weakness in the study. Although Blassingame stressed the reliance on autobiographies, plantation records, and other such materials, and the bibliography lists some fifty manuscript materials, he found that the footnotes indicated the use of not more than a half dozen. Porter was perturbed by the fact that many items were mentioned in the footnotes but not included in the select bibliography and that Frederick Law Olmstead's very important travel accounts were absent from the travel-account section. Only about a third of the figures and illustrations could be identified by reference to a library or other collection, and Porter was disturbed to note that, even when identified, some were either "childishly crude" antebellum illustrations or twentieth-century artistic reconstructions. Overall, Porter found the tone of the book to be more of a high-school text than that of a scholarly work but was impressed by the thoroughness and judicious spirit of the study that did permit some masters to seem less than evil. Overall, Porter assessed *The Slave Community* as a "sober and sane treatment of an aspect of Negro slavery which has usually been neglected or distorted."[15]

Walter B. Weare described *The Slave Community* as an important transitional volume in the third round of historiography on American slavery, but not free of fundamental blemishes on a number of points. He stressed the absence of original interpretation in some of Blassingame's narratives. For example, according to Weare, his chapter on "African Survivals" added nothing to the work of Melville Herskovitz done thirty years before, and the chapter on "Plantation Realities" did not extend the discussion beyond the work of Kenneth Stampp or U.B. Phillips. Uniquely, Weare was impressed primarily with the methodology employed by Blassingame that made a book created from traditional sources a relatively sophisticated study, "steeped in the social sciences with an eye toward quantification." Although his study may strike some as "less than a dramatic breakthrough," Weare believed Blassingame did more than anyone else to penetrate the life and minds of the slave community. The book, Weare explained, addresses Elkins, even though he is only mentioned twice, once in a footnote, and once in the bibliography, but "like Banquo's ghost, he shows up in all but name in virtually every page in some chapters." Therefore, some sophomore reading the book might be puzzled until someone told him that it was an attack on the Elkins' thesis and told what the Elkins' thesis was. But most importantly, Blassingame's suggestion that gold brickers in American prisons or the army might provide better parallels to slavery than Elkins' use of the German concentration camp is weak, Weare believed, because planters never saw their slaves as soldiers or convicts. They saw them as grown-up children who might engage in devastating mischief. Weare suggested that perhaps someone, without using Elkins' assumptions, ought to look at a comparison between slavery and child-rearing as the next stage in analyzing master/slave relationships.[16]

Willie Lee Rose welcomed Blassingame's book for its intrinsic worth in describing slavery as it must have been for the slaves and for its contribution to scholarship on the institution of slavery. She applauded him for using the autobiographies but complained that his explanation of their value is marred by his neglect of the WPA narratives. Rose introduced one other "mild demur," which should "be entered against what is otherwise an entirely sucessful work:" Blassingame's quotation from fragments and secondary works of some available primary sources rather than from the sources themselves. She found that this tendency sometimes misled him, since he did not have the entire piece before him to analyze. Rose regarded these as minor irritants in a book that displayed that Blassingame "is in complete command and has written a book all American historians could read with profit."[17]

The mildness of Willie Lee Rose's criticism was perhaps a palliative to the strong views expressed by Gerald Mullin toward the book. Mullin, whose own book on slave resistance in Virginia received high praise from some of Blassingame's critics, regarded Blassingame's work as an essay in the original meaning of the term, "an effort that falls short of its goal." He found that the book relied too heavily on one kind of evidence and left unanswered too many important questions about the black community before the end of slavery. Mullin explained that even in using the narratives and autobiographies Blassingame fought old battles in arguing the importance of slave personality and behavior in the quarters. Blassingame was so distracted by battling with Elkins that he paid little attention to analyzing perceptively the real issues raised by the very experiences he described in the book. *The Slave Community*, explained Mullin, is impressionistic in that Blassingame inferred behavior too often from what people said. For example, in one chapter Blassingame asserts that there is evidence of black resistance to bondage and of an undying love for freedom among the slaves but does not provide enough examples of actual behavior to prove this point, relying instead on generalizations. Mullin would have preferred more evidence of specific behavior and more analysis of motives and action.

Mullin found Blassingame's quantitative use of non-narrative sources persuasive. Examples are the examination of Virginia divorce petitions to describe the incidence of miscegenation and the use of marriage certificates of freedom to show the extent to which owners broke up slave families. But he concluded that many of Blassingame's opinions, particularly about docility and infantilism exhibited by slaves, were based not on plantation records or on seminal interpretations made since Elkins' 1959 work but on work by scholars, such as Genovese, that provides evidence on these issues. The major problem for Mullin was what he called Blassingame's "uncritical use of evidence"—for example, many of the writers of the autobiographies were elitists, whose work should be discounted.

The indispensable variables for delineating the slave community are, according to Mullin, "terrain, demography, work, the extent of urbanization and planter absenteeism, and, most important, regional differences in crops and stages of development." Therefore, instead of praising Blassingame for using psychological theory in a new way or for providing a new methodology, Mullin regards his work as "reducing slave behavior and culture to a question of roles and psychological characteristics." What this means for Mullin is that an "E.P. Thompson for the American Black community during slavery is still off-stage," and that we still need a social or economic historian to write persuasively about the slave experience.[18]

If believers in Blassingame's thesis and his work were somewhat dismayed by reading Mullin's review, they were probably even

more disconcerted when they read the critique published by Marian
DeB. Kilson in *The American Historical Review*. Kilson began
mildly enough, explaining that Blassingame's aims were "imperfectly realized" because he "lacks a clear analytical perspective."
She helpfully suggested that he should have arranged his chapters
in a different order and that he should have discussed the plantation and the system before discussing African survivals, the slave
culture, and resistance so that the book would provide a systematic
institutional framework more to her liking. Furthermore, the
reader would have been able to determine more easily "the significance to slave life of the topics discussed in the first four chapters."

She found his discussion of slave personality-types "fascinating," liked his concluding historiographical essay, and believed
that "his methodological aims are important if not systematically
pursued." But many of Blassingame's assertions she believed
would be better considered as hypotheses for further study. For example, before accepting his description of slave militancy, one
would have to see what the prevalence of "Sambo" personalities
among house slaves and on small plantations might be. Essentially,
Kilson found his overall contribution to the understanding of slave
life "frustratingly uneven."

Kilson discovered what she regarded as a number of serious sub-
stantive weaknesses in Blassingame's description of slavery. One is
that he underplayed the coercive role of blacks in deference to a
focus on resistance to slavery. Like one newspaper reviewer, Kilson
complained that Blassingame mentioned only indirectly the role of
African blacks in selling slaves, which makes it impossible to
understand the origins of slavery and the slave trade. She also explained that he does not deal at all with the social and psychological
complexity of the black driver's role, although he does refer to the
driver as part of the authority system. The fact that he does not
treat this coercive role of blacks distorts his portrayal of the life of
slaves. She was intrigued by his promise to utilize a trifocal perspective on slavery involving the discussion of the slave, the planters,
and even the views of travelers in the South but found that promise
largely unfulfilled. Blassingame's suggestion in his preface that
scholars have rarely used slave autobiographies to understand
slavery she regarded as "disingenuous" in view of E. Franklin

Frazier's seminal paper in 1930 on "The Negro Slave Family," which was based on slave autobiographies. Furthermore, other historians had used slave autobiographies.

Blassingame failed in his analysis, according to Kilson, because "his intellectual integration of social and psychological orientations has yet to be fully achieved." In addition she concluded that his study was weakened by his "attempts to satisfy a variety of audiences from scholarly peers to students in introductory Black Studies courses." Although Kilson apparently believes that these two objectives are irreconcilable, others might believe that they are not and that Blassingame should be applauded for attempting to bridge the gap between scholars and students interested in Black Studies and Black History.[19]

Other scholars also found reason to criticize *The Slave Community* negatively but none with the vehemence of Mullin and Kilson. Robert Reinders recognized Blassingame's successful refutation of Elkins' concentration-camp thesis and his persuasive discussion of slave culture but pointed out the "inexplicable" failure to cite Frederick Law Olmstead's travels, "without question, the finest travel account of the ante-bellum South." According to Reinders, Blassingame ignored the role of free Negroes as an influence on slaves but somewhat compensates for this by his discussion of the little-known subject of American Maroons, demonstrating that the Seminole War resulted more from a fear of Maroon society than from any concern over Indian raids.[20]

Thomas P. Govan found that *The Slave Community* provided a valuable description of slavery as experienced by the slave that is sharply corrective of previous writers but which, on the whole, confirms the findings of those few historians who tried to describe the lives and experiences of slaves using the same and other sources.[21] Govan criticized Blassingame for trying to present particular circumstances and events as general truths and covering too long a period of time. He also quarreled with the lack of attention paid to small farms, since more slaves lived on small farms than the larger plantations. Govan recognized that Blassingame is interested in African cultural survivals, family lives, and slave patterns of behavior, and that on these matters he has "supplied much useful information and some new interpretations."[21]

The rather mild criticisms of Reinders and Govan were somewhat jarred by Orville W. Taylor's analysis in the *Journal of Negro
History*. Taylor liked Blassingame's "lively and readable" writing
style that did succeed in drawing "a portrait of the Southern plantation slave which is very close to life." But Taylor believed that
whether the book is the most important discussion of American
slavery since Elkins, only time will tell. He found the book to be
conventional in its explanation that the typical slave was no "indolent, faithful, humorous, loyal, dishonest, superstitious, improvident person." Taylor pointed out that Blassingame does not
indicate that Kenneth Stampp made almost exactly the same point
in demolishing Elkins' "Sambo" thesis at a meeting of the
Southern Historical Association about two years before *The Slave
Community* appeared. Taylor does not tell us whether Blassingame
was aware of Stampp's unpublished assessment. Taylor expressed
extreme unhappiness with Blassingame's "unsubstantiatable claims
to originality and uniqueness." Disconcerted because Blassingame
asserts that historians "never" have systematically explored the life
and experiences of American slaves, Taylor pointed out that his
"Master, Charles S. Sydnor" and other historians have looked at
the slave experience extensively. He regarded this as an example of
Blassingame's tendency to overgeneralize. *The Slave Community*
he assessed as a good book despite its weaknesses, which would
probably become a standard work on the history of slavery.[22]

The most concentrated attention to the contribution of Blassingame's book to historical methodology did not come until 1974
when William Issel published an essay in which he paid close attention to Blassingame's use of psychological theory. Issel focused on
Blassingame's assumptions concerning conflict in the affairs of
human beings as contributing to progress as opposed to the importance of order.[23]

As we have seen in this consideration, *The Slave Community* was
not received with "almost unvarying praise" by scholars. There
were some rather pointed criticisms made of it, and we should consider why it did not receive the wide discussion and emphasis in the
public press accorded to *Time on the Cross* that might have
generated a large amount of royalties to the author and
disseminated its ideas more widely. If the ground on which it fell

had been as fertile as the anti-black, white backlash ground on which *Time on the Cross* fell, perhaps *The Slave Community* would have received the same publicity. Despite, or because of, its public reception, Blassingame's study will stand the test of time among scholars, and his study will remain a classic long after less imaginative interpretations have been erased from the public mind.

NOTES

1. Thomas J. Presley and Harvey H. Chamberlin, "Slavery and Scholarship, Some Problems of Evidence," *Pacific Northwest Quarterly* 66 (April 1975), pp. 79-83; Robert Fogel and Stanley Engerman, *Time on the Cross* (Boston, 1974); Eugene G. Genovese, *Roll, Jordan, Roll* (New York, 1974); Herbert G. Gutman, *The Black Family in Slavery and Freedom* (New York, 1976).

2. *Choice* 349 (April 1973), pp. 652-53; *Library Journal* 97 (November 1, 1972), p. 3583; *St. Louis Post Dispatch,* February 4, 1973; *Columbia Missourian,* September 25, 1972; *Times-News* (Erie, Pa.), December 10, 1972; *Union Leader* (Manchester, N.H.), January 12, 1973; *Nashville Tennessean,* May 27, 1973; *Press-Telegram* (Long Beach, California), March 30, 1973; *Greensboro Daily News,* April 18, 1973; *Wisconsin Magazine of History,* Spring 1973; *Long Beach California Independent,* March 30, 1973; *West Africa,* April 16, 1973, pp. 501-02; *New Society* (London), February 8, 1973; *Charleston* (S.C.) *Post,* November 24, 1972; *Kansas City Times,* October 10, 1972; *Richmond News Leader,* November 1972; *Kirkus Reviews,* July 1, 1972; *America,* May 4, 1974.

3. *The Progress Index* (Petersburg, Va.), February 8, 1973.

4. "Bookworld," *The Washington Post,* October 15, 1972.

5. *Times Literary Supplement* (London), March 2, 1973; *Journal of American History,* June 1973; pp. 131-33. *The Virginia Quarterly Review,* Winter 1973, p. iv, also finds the book, as a whole, "somewhat shallow" and not "the final word" on slavery. Gerald Mullin, *Flight and Rebellion: Slave Resistance in Eighteenth Century Virginia* (New York, 1972).

6. Any number of reviews pointed out the failure to use the WPA narratives; *The Georgia Review,* Spring 1974; *Journal of American History,* June 1973, pp. 131-33; *Journal of Southern History,* May 1973, pp. 293-94; *Journal of Negro History,* June 1974, pp. 470-71; *The American Historical*

Review, October 1973, pp. 1132-33; Herbert G. Gutman, "The World Two Cliometricians Made: A Review of Essay of F plus E = T/C" *Journal of Negro History,* January 1975. *Societas—A Review of Social History,* Summer 1974, pp. 241-43, also complains that "Blassingame's abundant reference to the Elkins's thesis appears a bit overdone." (p. 242)

7. Mary F. Berry, "Slave Behavior in Eighteenth Century Virginia," *Reviews in American History* 1 (June 1973), pp. 192-95.

8. *The Economist* 246 (January 27, 1973), pp. 90-91.

9. *American Heritage* 23 (October 1972), pp. 110-11.

10. *South Atlantic Quarterly* 73 (Spring 1974), pp. 273-74.

11. *Journal of Political Economy* 81 (November/December 1973), pp. 1476-77.

12. "The Two Communities of the Ante-bellum South," *The Maryland Historian* 4:1 (Spring 1973), pp. 65-68.

13. *The History Teacher* 6 (August 1973), pp. 638-39.

14. *Agricultural History* 47 (July 1973), pp. 227-78.

15. *Journal of Southern History* 39 (May 1973), pp. 293-94.

16. *Civil War History* 19 (June 1973), pp. 176-78.

17. *Journal of American History* 60 (June 1973), pp. 131-33.

18. *William and Mary Quarterly* 30 (July 1973), pp. 513-16.

19. *American Historical Review* 78 (October 1973), pp. 1132-33; Jack Leland, *Charleston* (S.C.) *Post,* November 24, 1972.

20. *The Americas,* October 1974, pp. 423-24.

21. *Maryland Historical Magazine* 69 (Spring 1974), pp. 106-07.

22. *Journal of Negro History* 58 (October 1973), pp. 470-71.

23. William Issel, "History Social Science and Ideology: Elkins and Blassingame on Ante-bellum American Slavery," *The History Teacher* 9 (November 1975), pp. 56-72.

GEORGE P. RAWICK

Some Notes on a Social Analysis of Slavery: A Critique and Assessment of *The Slave Community*

A new literature about the experience of American slaves has begun to appear, a literature that has not been greeted by much public discussion and notice outside professional circles. It includes, in my view, the work of Herbert Gutman, Leslie Owens, Peter Wood, Gerald W. Mullin, Sterling Stuckey, Julius Lester, Vincent Harding, and my own work, among others. It builds upon the solid base created by such scholars as Benjamin Quarles, John Hope Franklin, Carter Woodson, W.E.B. Du Bois, C.L.R. James, Philip Foner, and Herbert Aptheker. It is a literature not usable by the guardians of the American status quo for their ideological purposes, so it has made its impact quietly, usually without the aid of special awards, large-scale government-financed conferences, and editorials of praise in the nation's newspapers and magazines. It is a literature that is a direct result of the ferment produced by the civil rights movement and the black revolution of the 1960s.

At its fullest these works have the following general thesis, although not all of the authors agree with all of it. It asserts that the source of black culture and black struggle is the black community itself. The autonomous development within American society of a black community was made possible by the actions in their own behalf of those who were slaves. Black culture and struggle under slavery come not out of imitating or twisting or turning or internalizing the world made by the slaveholders. They come from the slaves themselves, taking what they themselves had in their minds and memories and from their social relations with each other and forging, against great odds and difficulties, a life space for themselves that both preserved human life and was the source for the creative energy out of which has come almost four hundred years of struggle virtually unparalleled in human history. Black people in America created a humane civilization that all the forces of official society have struggled to crush. They did this not because they internalized the Protestant Ethic and the Spirit of Capitalism, nor because they accepted the hegemony of the ideas of the slaveholders. They did this out of their own resources, those that they had brought with them in their minds and memories from Africa and those that they found or forged in the New World. Slaves were not dependent children, dehumanized and deculturalized, although everything possible was done to try to make them such. Nor were they clever adolescents simply turning master's bag of tricks against him. They found ways of achieving their own adulthood and left a record that inspires all those willing to look, a record that offers a more firm model of a just and ethical society than do the actions of their oppressors who have for so long masqueraded as the creators of a great civilization.

John Blassingame's *The Slave Community* is basically part of this historiography. Whatever we say in criticism of that work must be understood as criticism of a work that is "ours" rather than "theirs." I would hope that I would be equally capable of well-deserved criticism of my own earlier efforts at writing the history of slavery in America.*

Blassingame's book was one of the first works on American slavery to break away from the deadening historical convention that there is no way to get at the slave's experience of slavery. Indeed, leading historians to this day publicly deny that the antebellum slave narratives, the letters from ex-slaves in the Freedman Bureau's papers and elsewhere, the post-Civil War narratives, and the over 25,000 pages of interviews with ex-slaves done at Fisk University and by the Federal Writers' Project in the 1930s are as useful for historians as such sources as planter's letters, planter's

---

*Editor's Note: See George P. Rawick, *From Sundown to Sunup* (Westport, Conn.: Greenwood Press, 1972).

diaries and journals, and articles in *De Bow's Magazine*. For example, that was the argument of Kenneth Stampp, the author of an important mid-1950s study of slavery, at a conference at the University of Mississippi in the fall of 1975. Stampp believed that the slaveholder's autobiographies were more reliable because they could be checked against the slaveholder's diaries and letters and other contemporary writings. Blassingame's work is one of the few recent books that demonstrates the inadequacy of Stampp's assessment.

But while all that is true, our intention is not to bury or to fulsomely praise a particular book but to further a common task and a common body of work. Having stated that John Blassingame's work is one of the handful of books on slavery worth serious consideration, it is time to raise certain concrete questions about that work.

My overall criticism of John Blassingame's work on slavery is that it tends to mute the essentially accurate and important views it expresses, presenting them in a relatively conservative framework. Out of what may have been strategic and tactical considerations, Blassingame tends to limit the impact of his argument by both too many careful, modifying terms and by at times spending too much time restating and seemingly half-absorbing for the moment views that he clearly does not share. However, I note with approval that he ends the main body of the text rejecting all of the Sambo thesis, by describing the slaves as rebellious, although rebellious is modified by "occasionally," which we really need not be told, as none of us believe that the slaves were always on the barricade. (Parenthetically, Herbert Aptheker has been falsely accused of making this assertion in the most extended treatment we have of black revolt under slavery—his *American Negro Slave Revolts* (New York, 1943)—but a careful reading will demonstrate that he makes no such claim.)

The problem with the overly muted tone of Blassingame's work is that it leaves readers, including myself, with some doubts; for example, how much of the statement of the general thesis about slavery that I developed above would he accept? I know, certainly, that his work is part of the study that has gone into the development of this point of view, but I am genuinely uncertain whether to state that Blassingame's work does itself develop much of this thesis. He leaves us, I believe, with a certain ambiguity about his views on the historical development of an independent black community.

The opportunity to assess an important work requires that we try to further its basic line of analysis without blaming the author for not having accomplished everything in his initial work. For example, Blassingame's work touches on but does not fully develop an analysis of the internal occupational and status hierarchy—not class, all slaves were of the same class, even slavedrivers—in the slave community.* It is not an accident that a leading neo-apologist for slavery, William Scarborough, has devoted a major work to the slavedriver, one that greatly exaggerates, in my view, the importance and independent power of slaves who acted as foremen or drivers. Genovese in *Roll, Jordan, Roll* (New York, 1974) offered an estimate of the percentage of the slave population who worked under black drivers that was somewhat lower than that of Scarborough, but essentially he agreed with the latter's estimate of the importance of these functionaries. Fogel and Engerman virtually make the achievement of such an "honored" status the goal of their mythical, upwardly mobile, achieving slave population, miraculously "making it" within the capitalist plantation economy. We need to pay serious attention to this question both quantitatively and qualitatively. Otherwise we will once again have an historiography that shifts the burden of the development and maintenance of slavery to the slaves themselves, following the well-known tactic of blaming the victim, just as, of course, the masters of racist historiography have tried for years to pin the onus of the slave trade primarily upon Africans themselves. Blassingame, unfortunately, has remained vague on this subject.

Moreover, we need an internal analysis of occupational and status hierarchy among slaves for many other reasons. For exam-

---

*Editor's Note: In a recent article Blassingame critically analyzes slave status and social structure and concludes that "occupation represented only one among a multitude of status creating factors."—From "Status and Social Structure in the Slave Community," in Harry P. Owens, editor, *Perspectives and Irony in American Slavery* (Jackson, Miss.: University of Mississippi Press, 1976), p. 151.

ple, a careful analysis of slave skills almost certainly will indicate that the lack of skills economically useful in a capitalist economy might not be due to slavery—not all ills can be blamed on slavery, as Gutman has now so magnificently demonstrated—but to further workings of a racist society that pushed blacks out of skilled jobs. Those of us who develop the analysis of an autonomous slave community must be very careful to separate out, as Professor Gutman has done, what it is in the contemporary black community that we can attribute to slavery and what clearly comes from later activities. If Du Bois's assertion, that with the thirteenth amendment slavery ended and racism began, is useful, as indeed I believe it is, then it implies that while both are obviously very related, the oppressions of black people in post-slave society are not simply an extension of slavery but ought in crucial ways to have manifested new techniques for the social control of black people. John Blassingame and most of us who have been studying the slave community have not been careful to make this distinction.

We desperately need work that depicts and analyzes the lives of black women under slavery. We have had very largely a male-dominated literature about slavery. Blassingame, unfortunately, does not help us at all in this task. He writes virtually exclusively about men—"slaves" mean men for him, it seems, unless he specifies women, as he does very rarely. His book is marred with many revealing and male-chauvinist phrases, such as "The Africans retained enough manhood to rebel . . .," (p. 39) "a few masters were so brutal . . . that they could crush the slaves' every manly instinct," (p. 166) and "the typical slave . . . preserved his manhood in the quarters. . . ." (p. 216) He finds in tales of sexual conquest positive ways of preserving "manhood in the quarters," (p. 44) ignoring that if there is a conquered, there is a conqueree. He discusses slave games as if virtually the only games were male games. He discusses marriage among slaves from a totally and exclusively male perspective, and we learn nothing about how it affected women. He cites as an example of lucky slaves those whose masters refused to intercede in family affairs, "even when they beat their wives." (p. 92) Is that really "lucky"? And, above all, he almost exclusively talks about slave women as lovers, wives, and mothers and spends virtually no time talking about women as

workers or as central figures in the struggles of the black community. Why must we always use Nat as the name for the rebellious
slave? Why not Harriet? The women's liberation movement has for
some time used a poster that reproduces an image of Harriet Tub-
man with a long rifle. I think that might be a good symbol for all
black struggle.

I believe that the brilliant essay by Angela Davis on black women
in slavery, emphasizing the dual role of slave women as field-,
yard-, and house-workers, where virtually no task that men performed was not regularly performed by women, and as mother,
wife, and cook is an excellent alternative to Blassingame's views.
The Federal Writers Project's interviews with ex-slaves, as well as
other slave narrative sources, are rich sources for a history of the
heroic struggles of black women on behalf of themselves and of the
whole black community.

Blassingame is aware of the ways slaves utilized African cultural
forms in the New World and developed a new syncretic culture, but
he often is very conventional in his analysis and therefore does not
get through to the basic depths of the experience. Blassingame
basically sees all black cultural forms in a much too exclusively de-
fensive way. He wrote: "As long as the plantation black had cultural norms and ideals, ways of verbalizing aggression, and roles in
his life largely free from his master's control, he could preserve
some personal autonomy, and resist infantilization, total identification with planters, and internalization of unflattered
sterotypes calling for abject servility. The slave's culture bolstered
his self-esteem, courage, and confidence, and served as his defense
against personal degradation." (p. 76) It seems to me that the
slaves, from Blassingame's view, never ever took the offensive
other than in a few revolts.

This view of black cultural forms does not, for example, get us to
the point where we can see crucial aspects of slave religion as rebel
religion, as an expression of politics wrapped in religious robes. For
example, Blassingame is led to analyze the spirituals, which he
declares were "songs of sorrow and hope rather than of protest."
That may not be an adequate view, even within the terms of Blassingame's concrete discussion of some of the spirituals. I find it interesting that he avoids coming to grips with the analysis of

spirituals in Miles Mark Fisher's *Negro Slave Songs in the United States* (Ithaca, N.Y., 1953), which suggests much more of a political reading of spirituals. The spirituals expressed a world view and a desire fundamentally different from and opposed to that of the masters.

We have in the slave narratives a good source for an analysis of the religion of the fields and the hollows, the religion of the illegal prayer meetings, in which the black community was literally created and re-created. Utilizing symbols of African origin, slaves met each other for prayer, gossip, discussion, and re-creating social bonds in a fellowship that transcended their daily oppression. I miss in Blassingame's discussion of slave religion the rebellious metaphors of such former slaves as Carey Davenport, a black Methodist preacher born in 1855: "Sometimes the culled folks go down in dugouts and hollows and hold they own service and they used to sing songs what come agushing up from the heart."[1] Or that of Richard Carruthers, born in Memphis in the mid-1930s: "Us niggers used to have a prayin' ground down in the hollow and sometimes we come out of the field, between eleven and twelve at night, scorchin' and burnin' up with nothin' to eat, and we wants to ask the good Lawd to have mercy. We put grease in a snuff pan or bottle and make a lamp. We take a pine torch, too, and goes down to the hollow to pray. Some gits so joyous they starts to holler loud and we has to stop up they mouth. I see niggers git so full of the Lawd and so happy they draps unconscious."[2]

Images of late-night meetings with the people "scorchin' and burnin' up with nothin' to eat," asking the Lord for mercy or of "songs what come a gushing up from the heart" does not lead to a religion of quietude, of pure solace. While these late-night meetings were prohibited and their participants were often severely whipped when caught, we have virtual universal reports of their occurrence. I usually find nothing very politically hopeful about expressions of religion. Indeed, they often seem to be ways of inculcating the docile spirit of "pie in the sky in the sweet by and by." Only when they become linked with the struggles of the oppressed in this world do they become impressive to me. I think some slave religion was eminently that, and yet that view seems muted in Blassingame's treatment. I believe Blassingame would have developed a more fruitful view of slave religion if he had focused upon the fact that on many occasions slaves marched out of the late-night meetings—and into battle with the masters and their hirelings. The masters were not afraid of such prayer meetings out of pure paranoia. If we look at accounts of the three most important slave revolts in North America, we find that two of their leaders, Gabriel Prosser and Nat Turner, were exhorters both claiming descent from African religious leaders and that Denmark Vesey's second in command, Peter Poyas, was also a slave exhorter or preacher. Moreover, these revolts began with such night-time prayer meetings.

The slaves, I would contend, created a community of struggle and did so because no other form could adequately express their needs. Any collectivity that does not really express the fundamental needs of people is not really a community; it is simply an aggregate of people, a crowd, a mob, perhaps an aggregate or crowd or mob that even makes it easier to exploit people.

While the term community is all too often filled with a crippling romanticism and a related banality of conceptualization, it need not be. It can simply refer to a group of people who both recognize specific common links and treat these common links as having very special life-giving attributes, usually ones that resist exploitation and mistreatment. And American slaves did have such a community because it expressed their primary need of daily struggle against their brutalization, exploitation, and treatment as sub-humans. That community is not in sharp focus in Blassingame's *The Slave Community*.

The weakest part of Blassingame's work is, in my opinion, his discussion of "slave personality types." His first major error lies in adopting the very questionable deterministic social psychological role theories associated with such writers as Irving Goffman and Henry Stack Sullivan. What fundamentally is wrong with this model, which is similar enough to the one used by Stanley Elkins although Blassingame comes up with opposite conclusions, is that it parodies the basic complexity of the "psychology" of the oppressed who simultaneously view themselves in socially negative terms while struggling against that view of themselves and their behavior. In Hegel's dialogue of the master and the slave, the central point is that the slave struggles with himself in order to free himself from the master. This point of departure offers a much better source from which to view slave personalities than either the determinism of behaviorism or that of Freudianism. The slaves fought against the masters by wrestling with their own internal conflicts—conflicts that were in them because they lived at the center of a conflicting social environment. The wills of the masters and the wills of the slaves both appear as contradictions within each slave. In order to survive, the slave is forced to struggle for some resolution of these contradictions and in the process discovers that these contradictions are in fact not basically within him but within the social relations in which he finds himself. He must struggle to overturn these social relations if he is not to be ripped apart. In order to see and understand social struggle, such a view is necessary.

I suggest, in common with a very rich sociological tradition, that the way to deal with the question of "slave personality" is to turn to a nondeterministic social understanding of people. We must see people in conflict not as fixed entities but as individuals caught in a web of contradictory and exploitative social relations and biological experience, seeking their own fruitful solutions. One does not have to resort to Freudianism with its theological underpinning of a trans-historical, even trans-biological, tragic fate of man. Having spent some time trying to tie Freudianism to a sociological study of slavery, I now believe it offers no more of an answer than does behaviorism. Although it is very fashionable to talk about psychohistory, to me it seems to be the way toward self-confusion and leads to an analysis that can never further the struggles of the oppressed and exploited.[3] Without the elaborate behaviorist argument, I contend, Blassingame would have come to the same conclusions that he arrived at with it, because the historical evidence as seen through an unadulterated commitment to the struggles of the slaves and an equally uncompromising hostility to the masters would have led him there. And his views would then be presented in their own right, rather than as answers to the views of Stanley Elkins.

It is about time that we stopped fighting with the ghost of a confused book—Stanley Elkins's *Slavery* (Chicago, 1959). Only by being mired in academic excess do we come to think that the tortured analysis of Elkins is some sort of landmark for us. Why not

start with the lives of those who were slaves, the place where Blassingame started, without this excursion into abstraction?

John Blassingame's work has come in for some sharp criticism in
this essay. Yet that should not obscure the fact that his book was of
such merit as to warrant spending our time criticizing it four years
after its publication. Yet, like many good books, it should have
been better. More importantly, the needs of people today for intellectual clarity on these issues require that we engage in this task
of what is both criticism and, if you will, self-criticism. We have
not accomplished what we must unless we have provided strong
shoulders upon which those who follow us can stand.

NOTES

1. George P. Rawick, *The American Slave,* Volume 4: Texas Narratives,
Part 1, p. 282.
2. Ibid., pp. 198-99.
3. At one time I took Freudian terminology, particularly in the revisionist terms of the early work of the left-wing disciple of Freud, Wilhelm
Reich, more seriously. Today Freudianism seems to me to be so laden with
an attempt to explain away the tragic consequences of racism and of
capitalist civilization by an appeal to a static view of human nature, and
with an arrogant male chauvinism, as to have no proper appeal for
historians attempting to understand the past. Freud makes his subject the
ahistorical understanding of the human personality. Humanity is doomed
by the necessities of "civilization and its discontents" to learn to accept a
world in which the only significant activities according to Freud are what he
means by "work"—the Capitalist Ethic—and "sex"—the male ethic. I
had used the Freudian-Reichian categories as metaphors, not as transcen-
dent categories in earlier work, as guides to the discontent of the oppressed
in a specific form of human society that since the fifteenth century has
attempted to dominate all human societies. But the fundamental need is to
demystify that society, not to switch from one language of mystification to
another. And the roots of Freudian theory in an acceptance of all the ancient oppressions does not qualify it under any possible reworking for such
a task of demystification. I would rather look to the history of the concrete
struggles of real human beings for that clear understanding that is necessary.

EUGENE D. GENOVESE

Toward a Psychology
of Slavery: An Assessment
of the Contribution
of *The Slave Community*

Blassingame deserves congratulations and warm appreciation for his unusually thoughtful, well-written, and provocative book. More important, he deserves the engaged criticism that provides the only genuine tribute one scholar can offer another. Accordingly, I shall pass directly to our disagreements and, specifically, contest his psychological model; in so doing, I shall take for granted that this paper will be understood as an attempt to probe the limits of the contribution made by an illuminating book and not as an attempt at a balanced critique of the book as a whole.

Blassingame sprinkles sensitive and suggestive insights into slave behavior throughout *The Slave Community*, and his overview of folk culture commands particular admiration. Yet his ill-advised, not to say dreary, psychological apparatus obscures more than it illuminates and does not do justice to that sensitivity to human nuance which informs the best parts of the book. He candidly lays out his assumptions in Chapter VII, and a critic ought to lay out his own with equal candor. He follows Sullivan and the interpersonal school, whereas, as those who know my work must surely have noticed, I prefer Freud.[1] Now, I am sure that Blassingame will join me in appreciating the absurdity of two historians quarreling over theoretical matters deriving from a discipline in which neither has had formal training. Yet, absurd or no, every historian must interpret people's behavior in order to make any statement at all and, whether consciously or mindlessly, must bring to bear a set of assumptions about human behavior. Thus, the debate over *Time on the Cross* revealed that Robert W. Fogel and Stanley L. Engerman, while properly insisting upon the greatest care in the delineation of the economic theory implicit in any historical analysis, failed to reflect adequately on the content and consequences of the psychological theory into which they had inadvertently slipped. Blassingame, on the contrary, has enormously advanced the discussion, as Stanley M. Elkins did before him, by offering an explicit theoretical statement.

At first blush, it might be thought that since Blassingame and I project different psychological models, his conclusions should emerge largely at variance with mine; and that since he projects a psychological model similar to that of Elkins as well as Fogel and Engerman, his conclusions should emerge largely in conformity to theirs.[2] Yet, a comparison of our books would show that he and I agree much more than not, whereas we both generally disagree with Elkins and with Fogel and Engerman, who themselves arrived at radically different conclusions in their respective books despite a common adherence to behavioral psychology.

Should we then not bother with an explicit statement of psychological theory? Does it have any relevance? Should we not dismiss it as an afterthought or an exercise in academic pretension? Hardly. True, up to a point, the relevance remains cloudy. Not one of us, thank God, has been so idiotic as to study psychology and then "apply" some theory to our data. If we were to do so, we should probably never agree on anything but would nonetheless share the dubious honor of erring on most important matters. For the most part, occasional pretenses notwithstanding, we are forced to use psychological theory essentially as we use a good novel: to heighten our sensitivity to the contradictory facets of human behavior and to help us order our approximation of the reality under examination. Thus, the finest parts of Blassingame's book, including those that explore psychological terrain, are precisely those in which he either forgets his Sullivanian psychology or finds that it merely restates in its own terms interpretations readily available in other forms. In short, the case for Blassingame as an arresting historical psychologist of the slave rests on an appreciation of his talent for artistic reconstruction. And I do intend this judgment as a compliment: contrary to current fashion, I have a poor opinion of the prospects for a "scientific" history.

Blassingame's formal model cannot, however, be brushed aside as merely a matter of taste, for *The Slave Community* does indeed show the influence of Sullivanian psychology and of Behaviorism, to which it is a shame-faced cousin. In this respect Blassingame follows rather than challenges Elkins, much as Fogel and Engerman and such recent writers as Herbert Gutman have done. These and other historians and social scientists have nonetheless arrived at different conclusions, since, apart from the different degrees of talent and sensitivity they have brought to the subject matter—and clearly Blassingame offers much greater theoretical sophistication and historical imagination than most recent writers do—they pursue somewhat different versions of their common Behaviorist psychology, yielding significant differences in their results.

Consider those "slave personality types" in Chapter VII. One of the great strengths of Blassingame's book, both on its own and in comparison with many others, lies in its underlying appreciation that the lives (the history and culture) of blacks and whites emerged thoroughly intertwined. Blacks—slave and free—forged a culture distinct from that of the whites they lived with, as Blassingame well shows in some of the most eloquent parts of his book. But that cultural distinction necessarily arose at the margin, albeit a wide margin, as a vital variant of the larger southern culture to which blacks contributed so much. To pretend that the discretely black cultural development may be understood as an autonomous process—that whites in general and slaveholders in particular made no great positive impact on black culture—is to descend into mystification, not to say nonsense. And, ironically, such a view inadvertently denigrates the black achievement by implicitly denying the extraordinary power of the black contribution to the white community, for cultural penetration cannot simply work in one direction. By eschewing such ideological distortions during a period in which they have been recurring with great force, Blassingame makes a major contribution toward the proper delineation of one of our most difficult historical problems.

As Blassingame demonstrates so well in his sympathetic treatment of white preachers—a bit too sympathetic for my taste—this question of cultural interpretation arises outside ideological disputes and yields to overwhelming empirical evidence as well as to elementary logic. Whites and blacks, masters and slaves, intersected on all levels of material life and consciousness. The remaining questions quickly expose ideological differences among historians: for example, to what extent and in which ways was the intersection "good" or "bad," however those terms may be defined? Did the specifically black component of Afro-American Christianity create a difference of essence or of emphasis from the Christianity of the whites? These and other unavoidable questions become ideological, at least in part, because they do not lend themselves to strictly empirical investigation: Too much depends upon their specific and value-ridden formulation. And the question of a psychological model—or less pompously, of the psychological assumptions informing our work—emerges, contrary to all claims of scientific precision and objectivity, as preeminently ideological.

Although Blassingame ranks among our most sensitive writers on the white-black, master-slave dialectic, he runs aground in his discussion of slave personality-types, not because he makes some empirical errors or questionable judgments—everyone does—but because his sensitivity to nuance and human complexity seems to desert him. What really has deserted him, however, is his Sullivanian psychology, which has never been worth much in dealing with the inevitable problem of "the father."

For "the father" haunts the discussion. Nothing so thoroughly demonstrates the hegemony exercised by Stanley Elkins during the last decade and a half. Love his book or hate it, no matter—Elkins's questions have prevailed, and so, regrettably, has much of his psychological apparatus. Blassingame errs most grievously in this very respect, for he stays too close to Elkins's questions and categories, responds too much to Elkins's exaggerations and errors, and, above all, slips into the trap of Elkins's psychological theories, even while turning them against Elkins's conclusions. His performance nonetheless reminds us that Elkins did write a brilliant book; did ask burning questions; did compel every serious writer after him to come to terms with a richer historical reality—and did err in most of his conclusions. If, however, at the psychological level, Elkins's book has had a salutary effect, the reasons lie outside his Behaviorist and Sulli-vanian models. For old Freud entered the discussion through the back door, notwithstanding Elkins's attempt to hustle him into the basement. Hence, the question of the father.

How does Blassingame handle this question, which no ideological gyration or paroxysm of militant rage can exorcise? First, he must be congratulated for having insisted on its importance in the face of predictable widespread hostility. Few subjects evoke such mindless outbursts and misunderstanding. Some people, upon hearing words like "father" or "paternalism," assume—or for polemical purposes pretend to assume—that Ole Massa is getting another coat of whitewash and that blacks are once again suffering insult. Such readings are nonsense. At issue, as Blassingame demonstrates in terms appropriate to his own model, is the existence of an authority figure in the larger society and of the tendency inherent in all human beings to identify with it.

The strength of Blassingame's presentation relative to that of Elkins's lies in asserting (a) a more flexible application of the notion of "significant others" to demonstrate that the negative force of the authority figure in the society (the master) was in part offset by the existence of an authority figure in the immediate family (the real father or black male surrogate); (b) that the psychological impact of the real father often proved more powerful than that of the master since the formative period of personality lies in those years in which the real father, despite relative feebleness in the larger society, exercises the greater direct power; (c) that, nonetheless, to some extent the master could usurp the father role and create grave psychological tensions in all concerned, including, let it be noted, the masters themselves. All except the most willfully obtuse must recognize that these relationships, including the projection of the master into the role of surrogate father—that is, recognition of his objective existence as an extraordinarily powerful authority figure—have nothing to do with whitewashing Big Daddy, who could have been and often was a monster. And it cannot possibly denigrate those blacks whose social circumstances drew them into such relationships, for at this point in the analysis the description of their condition represents no more than a special case of the human condition. If they are thereby denigrated, so are we all, including the late Great Helmsman, Chairman Mao, who in his brilliant political career demonstrated a genius for understanding this problem and turning it to revolutionary purposes.

And now to the quarrel. At the beginning of his discussion of personality types Blassingame makes a statement that left me gasping until I remembered that it reflects the entire liberal and reformist ideological bias of the Sullivanian and Behaviorist schools and thereby should have been expected once Blassingame had unwisely committed himself to their path. He writes: "The person's first, most important, and most enduring concept of himself develops during childhood as a result of his parents treating him as a unique, thoroughly lovable individual." (p. 185) Blassingame assumes that, at least initially, normal parents respond to their helpless infant affectionately and lovingly. For the sake of the little sanity remaining in this insane world, we may have to proceed as if we share that assumption, although, as Blassingame undoubtedly knows, much contrary evidence fills the pages of journals of psychology, not to mention reports of the police and courts. But even with that assumption, made holding our breath, the conclusion Blassingame wishes to arrive at does not follow logically or empirically.

Under the best of circumstances parents can hardly be expected to provide love and affection without some elements of resentment, fear, or discomfiture. Still, if we could suspend all disbelief and envision a pure parental love, unencumbered by ambivalence or ambiguity and undiluted by any qualifications, the problem would remain. For, under any circumstance, the child experiences much more than the parents' loving intentions. Even Sullivanians, with their roseate view of a liberal psychological and social order, dare not go so far, and I doubt that Blassingame will choose to defend his assertion in its present form. But the sentence is no slip, and no qualifications will save it. When, for example, Blassingame speaks of "the dominant-submissive, hate-love axes," he introduces the complexities of subsequent interpersonal relations but still bypasses, as Sullivan did, the essential Freudian challenge.

We come into the world in terror. Is the initial cry of a newborn child an expression of joy at the experience of love? It is not necessary to accept all of Otto Rank's work on birth trauma or all of the implications of Phyllis Greenacre's outstanding reformulation to recognize the depth of the basic insight. The newborn child lives, has sensations, and experiences the world. What else, then, can that first projection of a sensate but as yet unreasoning being into the unknown be except traumatic? All the love and affection provided by the wisest and most loving parents cannot, either at that critical moment or for long thereafter, wholly draw the fear and terror from the child's being. And this pattern—this confusion of love with danger and pain—grows sharper as parents assume responsibility for saving a growing child from the folly of its inquisitive and rebellious ways. Love continues to accompany pain, anger, and discord. Black people during and after slavery surely knew this well: How many mothers and fathers had to punish severely children they loved so as to instill in them the do's and don'ts of a hideous power system in which a mistake could cost lives?

Blassingame's model, as its creators intended, leads him away, from a confrontation with the tragedy of life and with the struggle of opposites inherent in its relationships, including those relationships within the mind of the individual. The child's first and most lasting experience of parents, especially of the father, concerns love and succor less than the sense of being subject, for good or ill, to another—the experience of fear and awe in the face of power. By extension, I cannot agree with Blassingame when he writes, "A person may identify with the dominant person either because of affection or fear. In the latter case the identification or internalization of the ideals of the dominant person is directed toward avoiding punishment and is on a rather shallow level." (p. 187) Identification with a dominant person must rest on fear and must therefore always introduce some element of self-denigration, unless we assume that one person can experience the power of another as unrelieved joy. Certainly no child could experience parents that way, especially at the earliest stages of life, during which he or she cannot communicate verbally and must suffer intense frustrations.

Blassingame surely errs in asserting that identification based on fear reflects only the wish to avoid punishment and "is on a rather shallow level." (p. 186) From Anna Freud's pathbreaking analysis of identification with the aggressor and from the large and expanding literature on *anorexia nervosa* and suicide, we know that fear

provokes vast psychological ravages far beyond anything accoun-
table for by the wish to avoid punishment. Quite the contrary,
anorexia nervosa and suicide, both of which stem from the deepest
fears, suggest the opposite: the wish to impose the harshest punishment on the self, the former slowly and the latter in a stroke. This
contorted process of self-extermination hardly implies a shallow
level of internalization.

These preliminary considerations point toward the specifics of
slave behavior, toward the historical problem. Blassingame applies
Sullivanian and related theories too mechanically when he con-
fronts the problem of deference. His analysis lacks that sensitivity
to the contradictory nuances—to the dialectics—of the master-
slave relationship that may be found in so many passages
throughout his book. Only once in these pages does he approximate
his best form: "In practically all interpersonal relationships, the
subordinate has some independence, some power, some resources
as long as he possesses something valued by the superordinate,
whether it be labor or deference." But, suggestive as this passage is,
it falls far short of Hegel's famous discussion on lordship and
bondage, which it echoes. For Hegel, in a manner Freud might
have been delighted by if he had chosen to pay closer attention to
the philosophical literature, did not settle for so bland a version of
the slave's claims to autonomy and did not loosely invoke
"deference" to parallel "labor." On the contrary, Hegel, who had
studied classical political economy with all the attention it continues to deserve, demonstrated that the deference, the degree of
autonomy, and most strikingly, the irresistible compulsion driving
the master to recognize the slave's existence as an independent
being, all had roots in the labor process. The master could not
avoid knowing that his existence depended upon the slave, that for
all his power and pretension he ultimately depended not only on the
labor but on the will controlling that labor of the despised slave.

Thus, we need not and can not accept Blassingame's alternatives:
(a) the slave may "truly believe the superordinate worthy of his
respect"; or (b) "he may feign respect through ritual deference."
Here again Blassingame suggests that "respect" equals moral admiration or affection, and he even adds an unconvincing discussion
of the slaves' response to "kind" masters. Specifically, slaves may,

as alleged, have produced better for "kind" masters, but an understanding of their action would require a close inquiry into their own definition of kindness and especially of their sense of its place in the larger social order. Enough evidence exists of slaves not only presuming on such kindness but treating it with contempt and hostility in certain cases. Such responses may have flowed from the sense of a threat to the slaves' own social order posed by "kind" masters whose inattention to duty risked the sale of members of the community or of the plantation itself; or from specifically psychological reactions to the discrete master-slave relationship; or, more likely, from some particular combination of both.

On this matter Freudian psychology, Hegelian dialectics, Machiavellian politics, and Sicilian folk-wisdom converge: "Respect" rests on fear, on the perception of superior power that, however good and benign, may just as readily be put to other uses. True, in its benign forms ("I respect Picasso's art") the superior power, being far removed, may appear wholly beneficial. After all, what harm can it do? But abstract exceptions aside and all liberal cant discounted, the power experienced by individuals, whether in the family or in the larger society, can deliver hard blows if it chooses to. And never mind that it does not choose to: There is a first time for everything.

In various ways, Blassingame, fully demonstrates that typically the slave was no fool. I should suggest, therefore, that the slave did indeed respect his master. That this respect concerned the master's power and not his person changes nothing. The Catholic Church wisely and properly has always demanded respect for the priest, who offers the body and blood of Christ; only scoundrels and imbeciles mutter about an occasional mistress or some illegitimate children. The office and its magic remain at issue; the person of the priest, like that of the layman, suffers the ravages of original sin and counts for nothing. The slave's respect for the master's power remained essential to the system; while not the only politically relevant kind of respect, it was the kind that mattered at the end. And indeed, as Blassingame well shows, this respect existed side by side with the slave's ability to detest his master's person, to judge him morally inferior, and even to hold him in contempt.

Was that respect, then, psychologically superficial, as Blass-

ingame would have it? Only in the most extreme cases. Its internalization existed on "a rather shallow level" only in those exceptional cases in which the individual slave had attained not only a
high level of personal self-esteem but also a high level of insight into the world around him. Short of that formidable achievement,
which appears sparingly among peoples throughout history, the
slave had to battle with contradictory impulses and readings of
reality. Thus, we should normally expect tremendous ambivalence
and a constant internal struggle, at a high level of tension, for
spiritual survival.

May I, then, press my disagreements with Blassingame in a series
of assertions that may contribute to further discussion even if they
cannot pretend to settle much?

The slave as a normal human being, as an infant hurled into a
dangerous and threatening world, immediately confronted the contradiction between the beneficent and hostile aspects of the external
power embodied in authority figures, first the mother, then—for
reasons too complex to review here but undoubtedly
familiar—more decisively, the father. All individuals from infancy
onward experience love and a derivative self-esteem in forms in-
separable from pain, frustration, and anger. To cope with this ambiguity, individuals normally try to separate the harsh, punishing,
evil father from the kind, loving, good father. When confronting a
real father, who is after all one person, this task proves, to say the
least, difficult. Projected outward to the larger society, it becomes
easier. Individuals seek surrogate fathers everywhere and can, up to
a point, compartmentalize their perceived contradictory features:
good master, bad master; good master, bad overseer; good
overseer, bad driver.

So far, however, despite the examples from a slave plantation,
the issue remains general. Consider some equivalents: good Tsar,
bad boyars; good general, bad platoon sergeant; good FDR, bad
southern Democrats; good Stalin, bad Yezhov. To this day Stalin's
blood purge of 1936-38, which claimed several million lives, 70 percent of the officer corps, and perhaps as large a percentage of the
party itself, is known in the USSR as the *Yezhovshchina*—the terrible years of Yezhov—after the demented chief of the secret police,
whom Stalin eventually shot. Stalin, whatever his faults, in his own

way well understood the ABC's of psychoanalysis—after all, he had been trained in the seminary—and besides, alone among the great tyrants of the modern world, he had a rich sense of humor.

The ubiquitous need to seek the protection of authority—of a power greater than oneself in a brutal and dangerous world—remains at issue, as does the no less ubiquitous need of the personality to rebel against domination and to assert itself. And at issue above all else remains the endless struggle to reconcile these tendencies, or rather to order them in such a way as to make submission palatable, rebellion legitimate, and the contradiction between the two bearable.

Thus, we may applaud Blassingame for writing, "It is obvious that the slave's personality was intimately bound up with the use of coercive power by the master" and yet not find useful his allusions to "total institutions," unless all life be judged both total and an institution. Contrary to Elkins and Blassingame, who follows him uncritically in these matters, the problem of the father constitutes the problem of freedom and order: the necessity both of individual assertion and of submission to authority if social life is to be rendered civilized or indeed even possible. "Total institutions," if such in fact exist, represent only a heightened form of commonplace psychological reality.

All individuals throughout history have had to struggle for a degree of autonomy (freedom) against the demands of social discipline (order) as embodied in authority. The transference of the individual's inherently ambivalent attitude toward authority, which reflects his struggle with his father as flesh-and-blood reality and as image and ghost, becomes projected onto others in society, for example, political leaders. This projection demonstrates much more than the inevitability of continuing to fight the old battles over and over again, as Freud taught. It also demonstrates that the conflict between individual needs and social demands requires the imposition of order and authority—of force. Hence, the recapitulation of the ambivalent attitude toward the real father on larger political terrain corresponds to the requisites of political and social reality. Great political leaders, whether revolutionaries like Toussaint L'Ouverture and Lenin, or counter-revolutionaries like Hitler and the conservative DeGaulle, or any outstanding liberals worth inserting in between, have always understood that they must master this deepest of human needs. And the polemical substitution of "the People," "the Nation," "the Party," or "the Movement" changes nothing. What did Antonio Gramsci call the "party of a new type"? He called it "the modern prince"—the collectivized, democratized, but nonetheless authoritarian father.

Did the slaves, then, perceive their masters as father figures? To an important if not readily measured extent, of course they did, much as people everywhere perceive those who hold power. And love, affection, kindness, or presumed heavenly days in Dixie have nothing to do with the issue. From this point of view, the whole range of behavior from slavishness to rebelliousness, a range mediated by "accommodation," which means what it says—not docility but a struggle to avoid the worst, so painstakingly sketched by Blassingame—becomes explicable. But also from this point of view we may avoid the trap, into which Blassingame seems to have fallen, in his quarrel with Elkins, of stark categorizations of complex emotions. We may avoid, that is, the attribution of shallowness to the tenacious and politically devastating internalization of, and identification with power.

Consider how far afield Blassingame's model can lead him. Notwithstanding his appreciation of human complexity .and the subleties of power relations, he finds it possible to write: "One of the most frequent reasons for the slave's industriousness was the feeling that he had a stake in the successful completion of his work. Many slaves developed this feeling because the planters promised them money, gifts, dinners and dances if they labored faithfully." (p. 192) The first sentence is on the mark; the second sells the slaves short. The primary reason that the slaves "developed this feeling"—one that does much credit to their intelligence and resourcefulness—must be located in their accurate perception of objective reality. They called the plantation their "home." That is, they described it as a place that housed their loved ones and friends and provided the staples of life. This judgment implied neither an acceptance of enslavement nor an indifference to exploitation and oppression. It did imply recognition of a life, however involuntarily, within a social system. The slaves, for reasons of their own as well as compulsion, had to produce, at least up to a point. What happened when they carried resistance to labor to the point of rendering the plantation unprofitable? It was sold, often at auction, with the result that slave families were split up and the community dismembered.

Thus, their attitude toward their master had to be ambivalent, and their internalization of respect for him, based on fear not only of his power but of the possible failure of his magic, could hardly have been shallow. In few other ways did the planter assert himself so authoritatively as "father." As the man who coordinated plantation affairs, assumed full responsibility for everything from production to marketing, and guaranteed the distribution, however inequitable, of the resultant income, everything depended upon him, or rather appeared to. His failure meant ruin for everyone. And again, love, kindness, affection, and generosity have nothing to do with the matter. The slaves might wish a cruel master dead, but only if they had reason to believe a more decent relative would take over the plantation intact or if the master was proving so utterly cruel that any change appeared preferable. The textural density of this violence-charged, master-slave relationship thus set, at the psychological as well as material level, firm limits to the degree of cultural autonomy the slaves could hammer out for themselves.

Blassingame's categories limp and, in particular, lead him into the serious error of asserting that the slaves might identify with a kind master but never with a harsh one. The problem of identification exists largely outside such categories. Rather, for reasons suggested by Blassingame himself, the slaves as a body struggled for manhood and achieved it to an impressive degree—to the extent that we know what it means. But for reasons Blassingame's model obscures, they faced an overwhelmingly difficult problem, which only small numbers of insurgents and runaways solved: transforming their manhood—their sense of personal selfhood and worth—into viable political forms with which to advance their collective interests as a people. The root of that difficulty lay in the sheer relationship of military and political forces, but the psychological dimension ("consciousness") played a part, as it always does.

Notwithstanding these quarrels, it should be clear that I share with many of my colleagues the opinion that Blassingame has significantly advanced the discussion of slave psychology and therefore of the inner politics of slavery. His attempt to turn Elkins against Elkins constitutes the strength and weakness of his effort. Earl Thorpe, whose work Blassingame recently saluted,* has been fighting a lonely battle for some time now to draw our attention to this terrain, and his particular use of Freudian theory deserves and will hopefully receive full and respectful criticism. However, as Blassingame has suggested and Earl Thorpe has been insisting, we are reaching the point at which much more attention must be paid to the psychology of the masters so that we may begin to do justice to the totality of the violence-charged intimacy of master and slave. *The Slave Community* marks important progress toward that end.

May I add, however, that we dare not lose sight of the larger problem, which Fogel and Engerman for all their sins saw clearly. The master-slave relationship, when all is said and done, rested on economic exploitation—on the expropriation of the fruits of some men's labor by others. However racial the modern form of slavery, it remained a class relationship—some people fed off others. Hegel's pioneering phenomenological analysis, as well as the work of historians on the slave's complicity in the system of production, demonstrates that the dialectics of master and slave return us to the labor process. Do we then allow ourselves to be buffeted from sociology to psychology to anthropology only to end back with economics? Or worse, do we forego the economics and settle for a depoliticized anthropology? That danger grows worse as social history itself plunges increasingly toward a vapid substitution of "culture" and other abstract anthropological categories for the politics that alone justifies historical inquiry. Blassingame's book, with its politically sensitive exploration of slave psychology, points in a much more rewarding direction and contributes toward the assimilation of the several perspectives to a unified interpretation capable of illuminating the larger political processes. I have expressed my deep disagreement with his psychological model; simply, I think it is wrong. But clearly, he has given us a book that transcends its own deficiencies. It is a book we can build on.

Editor's Note: Reference is made to Blassingame's "The Planter on the Couch: Earl Thorpe and the Psychodynamics of Slavery," *Journal of Negro History* 60 (April 1975), 320-331.

NOTES

1. Since I have been mistakenly associated with those who deny the relevance of psychology to history, perhaps I may be permitted a word. In an earlier work I suggested that the major historical problems could be addressed without plunging into the treacherous waters of formal psychology. Earl Thorpe, among others, properly took me to task for this illusion, although I might say, in my own defense, that I was protesting less against Freudian theory, which I have long admired, than against its many reductionist applications. In any case, my most recent book, *Roll, Jordan, Roll*, draws heavily on Freudian theory, although I saw no need to present an explicit "model."

2. At first glance it might seem odd to associate Fogel and Engerman with Elkins. Yet, both their major books take behaviorist ground, whatever their differences; indeed, the most vigorous critics of Fogel and Engerman—Paul David, Peter Temin, Herbert Gutman, et al.—also take this ground, although without seeming to be aware of it. Blassingame, like Elkins before him, differs from most of the others primarily in knowing precisely what he is doing. For a critique of the Behaviorist standpoint and a preliminary sketch of a psychoanalytic alternative, see Elizabeth Fox-Genovese, "Poor Richard at Work in the Cotton Fields: A Critique of the Psychological and Ideological Presuppositions of *Time on the Cross*," *Review of Radical Political Economics* 7 (Fall, 1975), 67-83.

EARL E. THORPE

The Slave Community:
Studies of Slavery Need
Freud and Marx

The truism, in scholarship as in other areas, that each generation has the advantage of being able to stand on the shoulders of their predecessors has relevance when an attempt is made to evaluate John Blassingame's book, *The Slave Community.* Such an attempt should be made from a perspective that considers the strengths and weaknesses of several other writers of general histories on the subject of slavery in America. These include Ulrich B. Phillips, Kenneth Stampp, Robert W. Fogel, Stanley L. Engerman, and others.

It is generally conceded that among the weaknesses in Phillips's writing on slavery are that he:

1. believed in the racial inferiority of blacks;
2. made too much of an effort to defend the pro-slavery propaganda of the Old South's ruling class;
3. used too exclusively records of the larger plantations;
4. made much too little use of the slave narratives;
5. failed to give a true picture of the cruel treatment of slaves; and
6. greatly underestimated the importance of slave resistance.

Phillips referred frequently to blacks as "niggers," "darkies," and "negroes" and generally depicted them as submissive, superstitious, chattering, light-hearted, nonchalant "Sambos." He wrote *American Negro Slavery* (New York, 1918) when Afro-Americans were at or near what Rayford W. Logan calls the nadir of their citizenship rights and opportunities and when racial segregation, lynching, and other expressions of white racism were most rampant. By the time that Kenneth Stampp wrote *The Peculiar Institution* (New York, 1956), the American military, major-league sports, and other segments of society were beginning to integrate racially, and the New Deal, World War II, and the birth of the age of the atom and the computer had been factors in the achievement of greater racial tolerance. Also, a number of popular writers, such as W. J. Cash, Clarence Cason, William Faulkner, and Erskine Caldwell, had written about the white South in a much more critical way than Phillips. Many persons had long called for a better general history of slavery in America.

When Phillips's *American Negro Slavery* appeared, *The Journal of Negro History* was only three years old. This journal, its parent organization, and their creator, Carter G. Woodson, contributed positively and mightily to the task of eliminating many of the anti-black, pro-slavery myths that were widely popularized by Phillips, other white historians, social scientists, politicians, and others. In part because of these positive contributions, Stampp declared in *The Peculiar Institution* that "innately Negroes are, after all, only white men with black skins, nothing more, nothing less."[1]

In contrast to Phillips, Stampp wrote from an anti-slavery black-sympathizer stance. He used a considerably wider range of sources than Phillips, on whose shoulders he may be said to stand. On this subject Stampp stated: "What I have written about slavery is built . . .upon what others have already written. . . . [of Phillips] I learned much from his methods, his sources, and his findings."[2]

Stampp's documentation is overwhelmingly from sources produced by Caucasians. His use of the slave narratives is largely restricted to two of his ten chapters, Chapters II and VIII, and to less than a dozen of the slave narratives. Although his bibliography lists the slave narratives collected by the Works Progress Administration, there is little evidence that they were used to any considerable extent. There is also little evidence that Stampp used *The Journal of Negro History, Negro History Bulletin, Phylon, The Quarterly Review of Higher Education Among Negroes, The Mid-West Journal,* and other important sources to anything like the extent that he should have.

John Blassingame's *The Slave Community* is the first distinguished general history of slavery in America by an Afro-American. Practically all previous histories had overwhelmingly relied on sources produced by Caucasians. He broke with this tradition. Also, practically all previous histories had been written by scholars who knew next to nothing about the black experience and black culture. Blacks, always in an oppressed-oppressor relationship with whites, have had different experiences and produced a different culture. Also of great importance are cultural origins: Europe for whites and Africa for blacks.

Compared with whites who have written on slavery, Blassingame had the advantage of far superior knowledge of the black experience and black culture, and he relied much more heavily than any of them on the slave narratives—black sources. He is the first distinguished general historian of slavery to have a proper appreciation for such very important sources as *The Journal of Negro History, Negro History Bulletin, Phylon, The Quarterly Review of Higher Education Among Negroes, The Negro Digest,* and the articles, chapters, and other writings on slavery by such scholars as William Wells Brown, George Washington Williams, Benjamin Brawley, W. E. B. Du Bois, Carter G. Woodson, J. A. Rogers, Lorenzo Greene, William Savage, Charles Wesley, James H. Brewer, and numerous other blacks. He is also the first writer of a distinguished general history of slavery in America to have a proper appreciation for the great significance of black folklore and the spirituals and other black music of the era of slavery.

In an interesting essay about writers on slavery in America that included Phillips, Stampp, Richard Hofstadter, and Stanley Elkins, Fogel and Engerman conclude: "The principal cause of the persistence of the myth of black incompetence in American Historiography is racism."[3] By implication, John Blassingame's *The Slave Community* became the first distinguished general history of slavery to make a complete break with this myth and this racism.

Although throughout *The Slave Community* Blassingame spends considerable time refuting the central thesis presented by Stanley Elkins in his book, *Slavery: A Problem in American Institutional and Intellectual Life* (Chicago, 1959), Herbert Gutman's statements that Blassingame's book is inappropriately titled and that the book is mainly the longest critique to date of the Elkins thesis is seriously in error.* Elkins's book has absolutely nothing at all to say on at least 80 percent of the topics treated in Blassingame's book and in other general histories of slavery. Elkins's book is *not*, by any stretch of the imagination, a general history of slavery. By any and all honest characterizations, Blassingame's book *is* a general history of slavery. Too much of Elkins's book has importance only as another item in a very long list of white-racist literature. Professor Gutman's refusal to categorize Blassingame's book as a distinguished general history of slavery raises some serious questions about how much Gutman may wear blinders similar to those worn by Elkins.

The Elkins thesis states that, like many inmates of Nazi concentration camps, slaves in North America were chronically regressed "Sambos"—infantile, silly, lying, lazy, thieving, irresponsible, and playful—due to the "infantilizing tendencies of power."[4] Blassingame joins the authors in *The Debate over Slavery* (Urbana, Ill., 1971), edited by Ann J. Lane, by showing that the black slaves had a great amount of real manhood, womanhood, creativity, and militancy.

Another very important factor about *The Slave Community* is its serious effort to connect the fields of history and psychology. Here Blassingame joins others not only in successful refutation of the Elkins thesis, but he helps to answer the call made by William Langer in his 1957 presidential address, "The Next Assignment," before the American Historical Association. Langer had as his central concern "the direction which historical study might profitably take in the years to come." He urged historians to cease to be "buried in their own conservatism" and to recognize "the urgently needed deepening of our historical understanding through exploitation of the concepts and findings of modern . . . psychoanalysis and its later developments and variations as included in the term 'dynamic' or 'depth psychology.' " Professor Langer's presiden-

---

Editor's Note: Gutman made this comment at the 1976 Chicago meeting of the Association for the Study of Afro-American Life and History in his paper on *The Slave Community* at the session, "Blassingame's *The Slave Community*: The Critics Respond."

tial address was an attack on what he called the "almost completely negative attitude toward the teachings of psychoanalysis" that historians have traditionally held. He also gave illustrations and suggestions on how historians can specifically apply this knowledge. Earlier calls had gone out for psychoanalytically oriented studies of the black experience.

After working for some time with emotionally disturbed black patients at a medical center for the emotionally disturbed, Philip S. Craven, a white American medical doctor, urged in 1930 that black studies of a psychological nature needed to be done. He wrote that "very little, if anything, has been attempted in the psychological study of the negro [*sic*] as is directly afforded, for example, by the employment of the psychoanalytic method." "A fertile field for future investigation is here awaiting development," he continued.[5] Between 1931 and 1943 there appeared in *The Psychoanalytic Review* a series of articles under the general heading, "Psychogenetic Studies in Race Psychology." These studies were arranged and edited by Dr. Ben Karpman, who was a member of the staff of the Department of Psychiatry, Howard University School of Medicine.

In 1954, three years before Langer's address, the black scholar W.E.B. Du Bois spoke significantly on this subject. In a new preface for his book, *Suppression of the African Slave Trade*, which was being reissued, Du Bois wrote:

As I read again this work of mine written over sixty years ago, I am on the one hand gratified to realize how hard and honestly I worked on my subject as a young man of twenty-four. As a piece of documented historical research, it was well done and has in the last half century received very little criticism as to accuracy and completeness. One area of criticism which I have not seen . . . but which disturbs me is my ignorance in the waning nineteenth century of the significance of the work of Freud and Marx. . . . the work of Freud and his companions and their epoch-making contribution to science were not generally known when I was writing this book, and consequently I did not realize the psychological reasons behind the trends of human action which the African slave-trade involved.[6]

When, in 1962, Winthrop D. Jordan reviewed the present writer's book, *The Mind of the Negro: An Intellectual History of*

Afro-Americans (Baton Rouge, La., 1962) for *The Journal of Southern History*, Jordan stated that he doubted that the Afro-American had an intellectual history. Jordan declared:

The use of the word 'mind' reveals an assumption . . . for which there is little justification . . . in the study of American Negroes, for the experience shared by most Negroes in the United States which has set them apart as a group has not been primarily intellectual but emotional. Most of the impact on the Negro of slavery and race prejudice has occurred at the irrational levels of personality. . . . What is lacking here, and badly needed in any attempt to discuss the Negro 'Mind,' is a firmly grounded conception of the psychological scars left by classic and newer forms of slavery, and the relation between the pressures on Negroes arising from assimilation to American culture and the rational pronouncements of articulate Negroes.[7]

On the subject of whether there is an intellectual history of Afro-Americans, Jordan was wrong. He was right to call for a psychoanalytic interpretation of the black experience, but he should have mentioned the equally great need for such a study of the white experience.

To these and other examples must be added works of such black psychiatrists as W. H. Grier, P. M. Cobbs, and Alvin Poussaint, and Abram Kardiner and Lionel Ovesey's *The Mark of Oppression* (New York, 1951). In his book *The Black Bourgeoisie* (New York, 1957), E. Franklin Frazier used some concepts that the student of psychohistory must deal with. In Frazier's picture of the black bourgeoisie, use by blacks of such mechanisms as repression, identification, sublimation, regression, and masochism is clear. The same is pictured to be true of this class in Nathan Hare's *The Black Anglo-Saxons* (New York, 1965) and in Harold Cruse's *The Crisis of the Negro Intellectual* (New York, 1967). The very recent *Journal of Black Psychology* is making a powerful contribution to the development of psychohistory.

Writing in 1962 in *The Nation* on the topic, "The Historian as Psychiatrist," one scholar posed the question: "What . . . has the study of history to gain from a greater psychoanalytical understanding of man?" "It would give rise to a new objectivity," was one of the answers that this scholar gave.[8] No scholar is being truly

objective when he gives no consideration to the repressed unconscious. For example, too much black history is written and
taught in an effort to use logic, reason, and historical evidence
alone in an "attack" on the negative image of blacks that is
presented by many whites. Since logic, reason, and evidence can
never satisfy a highly repressed mind, rather than attempt to get
such a mind to see the irrational elements in the fantasies it pro-
duces, it is more important first to get that person to see that his
mind is highly repressed. Psychohistory can help make this happen.

In his effort to connect seriously history and psychology, Blassingame is a pioneer. Although the present writer's books *Eros and
Freedom in Southern Life and Thought* (Durham, N.C., 1967) and
The Old South: A Psychohistory (Durham, N.C., 1972) also represent pioneering efforts in this area from Freudian perspectives,
Blassingame has chosen a different psychological orientation, that
of Interaction Psychology. Generally he does not use such Freudian
concepts as the repressed unconscious, preoedipal mother, primal
murder, sublimation, primal scene, reality principle, castration
anxiety, castration complex, libido; oral, anal, phallic, and genital
stages; phallic personality, genital organization, and repression. It
is highly significant, however, that a central thrust of Eugene
Genovese's critique of *The Slave Community* is recognition of the
importance of the effort to seriously connect history and psychology.

Although some Marxists are among those who lead the attack on
the Freudian approach, the present writer is firmly convinced that
those persons are in error who see no way to harmonize the essence
of the psychoanalytic and Marxian interpretations of history or
both of these with Christianity. Aspects of the former viewpoint
are included in *Radical Psychology* (New York, 1972), edited by
Phil Brown, while an indirect but eloquent commentary on the latter is in Teilhard Chardin's *The Phenomenon of Man* (New York,
1968).

Central to Marxism is production, while central to psychoanalytic theory is repression. George P. Rawick, in his essay on the
origins of European racism in his book, *From Sundown to Sunup:
The Making of the Black Community* (Westport, Conn., 1972),
points out that early modern capitalism needed, demanded, and

created workers or producers whose repression of bodily pleasure and spontaneity was extreme and unique. In his book *Eros and Civilization* (Boston, 1955), Herbert Marcuse points to subsequent increases of repression with increases of production. This is also a central theme of Sigmund Freud's *Civilization and Its Discontents* (New York, 1962), Norman O. Brown's *Life Against Death: The Psychoanalytical Meaning of History* (New York, 1959) and Joel Kovel's *White Racism: A Psychohistory* (New York, 1970). Advances in civilization are advances in production related to advances in repression. Jean Jacques Rousseau saw this before any of the above authors. There is no essential quarrel between Marx and Freud, and much of the call of Jesus was for that life of nonrepression that only a loving, forgiving, forgiven, humble, truthful, unfragmented, nonrepressed person can possess.

Blassingame's picture of the slave family generally is one of husbands who loved their wives and vice versa and of parents who dearly loved their children and vice versa. Although he usually presents the latest findings of facts and their interpretation, Blassingame generally breaks little new ground for those who already know black-oriented black history. This is true whether the topic is African background, African survivals, religion of the slaves, spirituals and other black music, folklore, slave work, beatings, miscegenation, abscondings, or plots and revolts. Here, as is often the case, the most recent findings and views by scholars have been published in such places as learned journals or as chapters in monographs before they appeared in general histories.

On some subjects, such as religion, spirituals, life in the slave quarters, runaways, and overseers, Blassingame is too brief and impressionistic. Approximately two hundred pages of text is too little space for such a broad and demanding subject as the slave community. For example, Chapter II, "Culture," is too brief to give an adequate coverage of the topics treated: slave recreation and social life, the conjurer, and secular songs and spirituals. Of approximately thirty-five pages in the chapter, about one-third comprise direct quotes, pictures, or footnotes.

In the following statement, as in numerous other places, Blassingame is at odds with Fogel and Engerman in their more recent book on slavery, *Time on the Cross.* "If he was lucky," Blassingame writes, "the slave belonged to a master who tried to foster the development of strong family ties in the quarters." (p. 80) Fogel and Engerman, who make the claim that their history of slavery is the most truthful of them all, state that this type of master was the rule rather than the exception.

On the question of the efficiency of slave labor, Blassingame is closer in some ways to most of his predecessors than to Fogel and Engerman. Where Blassingame is concerned, Fogel and Engerman's explanation that the depiction with which they disagree is due to "racism" raises some interesting questions. Here Fogel and Engerman do not directly mention Blassingame.[9]

While Blassingame depicts the fieldhand slaves as generally "sullenly obedient and hostilely submissive," and while planters and overseers frequently complained about indifferent labor from their slaves, Fogel and Engerman depict them as generally "diligent and efficient workers," "imbued like their masters with a Protestant Ethic."[10]

Although W. E. B. Du Bois pointed out in his *Suppression of the African Slave Trade* that slaves were illegally smuggled into the United States down to the eve of the Civil War, Fogel and Engerman contend that census reports that show that in 1860 less than 1 percent of the nation's slaves were born in Africa can be trusted. Fogel and Engerman appear to take no cognizance of the fact that even in the 1960s and 1970s the census reports on blacks are frequently as suspect as they were in 1860.

Fogel and Engerman state that only psychologically very healthy slaves could have been efficient workers, a theory opposite to that offered by George P. Rawick in his book, *From Sundown to Sunup*. Rawick's section on the origins of European racism points out that *in order to be very efficient* workers, whites in the most advanced capitalist nations during the early modern period of history turned themselves into what amounts to very repressed robotlike psychoneurotics, who virtually ruled play and spontaneity out of their lives and who radically redefined such things as childhood, insanity, and sin. In other words, under capitalism, psychologically sick workers are the best workers—a thesis also supported by Norman O. Brown and others.

Blassingame's picture of the domestic slave is considerably closer to the traditional white-minded "Uncle Tom" image than is Eugene Genovese's interpretation in his more recent book *Roll, Jordan, Roll* (New York, 1974). Blassingame says that these slaves "frequently internalized the submissive role" (p. 200), a statement probably beyond possibility of proof.

A number of the characterizations of slaves presented by Blassingame are similar to those depicted in *Roll, Jordan, Roll.* Rather than the David Brion Davis view that sees Genovese's "great gift" as being "his ability to penetrate the minds of both slaves and masters," the present commentator sees Genovese's chief contribution as the presentation of material and conclusion drawn from the comparative history approach. Although in *Roll, Jordan, Roll* Genovese tells us little about "The minds of . . . slaves and masters" that we have not received from other scholars, by use of the comparative history approach he does expand our view of the situation that victimized black slaves and white masters for generations.

Blassingame sometimes treats his topics too much in isolation. For example, after he discusses the religion of the slaves in Chapter II ("Culture"), he fails to sufficiently consider the role and significance of the secret black church and community life in the slave quarters in connection with other topics and chapters, such as "Rebels and Runaways." These connections are more clearly brought out by George P. Rawick in his book, *From Sundown to Sunup.* Blassingame also does not adequately show the depth, breadth, and significance of the militant side of the slave culture. Here again, Rawick has better success.

Blassingame says that on some plantations, where cruelty to slaves was most extreme, "many of the slaves became docile, submissive, and Sambo-like." (p. 193) "Many" is probably too strong a word here. Again he says that this type of treatment led to the result that "many of the slaves . . . soon lost all feeling of independence, self-respect, and sympathy for others." (p. 194) Again, "many" is probably too strong a word. At other points, Blassingame says:

Unremitting cruelty often subdued the slave and broke his will to resist. (p. 196)

The lash, frequently applied, often drained every
        ounce of manhood of resistance, self-respect,
        and of independence from the slave. (p. 196)

The cruel separations and constant floggings created a
        sense of despair among many slaves that was all con-
        suming. (p. 198)

There is too much of this picture of the slave stripped of "every ounce" of manhood and self-respect, especially when Blassingame so often uses words like "often" and "many" and "all." Frequently where Blassingame says"often," it is the present writer's belief that he should have said "sometimes," and where he says "many slaves," the statement should read "some slaves." As Blassingame and many others know, "manhood" and "self-respect" were shown in the thought and behavior of these slaves and ex-slaves during the Civil War, a story well-told in such works as George Washington Williams's *Negro Troops in the War of the Rebellion* (New York, 1880) and Benjamin Quarles's *The Negro in the Civil War* (Boston, 1953). When Blassingame says that "antebellum black slaves created several unique cultural forms" (p. 41), the present writer believes that the total nonmaterial culture of antebellum black slaves was unique. Again, Blassingame writes: "Much of the slave's culture . . . set him apart from his master." (p. 41)

Repeatedly Blassingame gives the truth that "the slaves's culture bolstered his self-esteem, courage, and confidence, and served as his defense against personal degradation." (p. 76) Blassingame generally does not show his readers enough of the remarkable creative genius of the black slaves. The most notable and praiseworthy fact about these slaves is not that they survived with a great amount of self-esteem, but that they were creative geniuses.

Blassingame states that there was "loose morality in the quarters" (p. 87) and that "the white man's lust for black women was one of the most serious impediments to the development of morality." (p. 82). As he did in his book, *Black New Orleans* (Chicago, 1975), Blassingame indicates in *The Slave Community* that he considers much of the sexual behavior of slaves to be immoral. In both books, when he writes about slave "immorality," he should put the word in quotation marks.

Although he is by no means alone here, Blassingame does not take sufficient account of the impact on slaves and masters of the dynamic quality of American history during the eighteenth and nineteenth centuries. General histories of slavery in North America usually give little or no indication that such events and movements as the struggle to write and establish the federal and state constitutions, Federalist and anti-Federalist tensions and struggles, the French Revolution and Napoleon, the War of 1812, Jacksonianism, the industrial revolution, and the European revolutions of 1830 and 1848 ever moved from the legislative, judicial, and other political centers to influence in numerous and very significant ways the thought and behavior of slaves, as well as their relations with the owning class. One checks in vain the indexes of general histories of slavery for references to these developments. The impact of the Haitian revolution led by Toussaint L'Ouverture is the only topic mentioned with any frequency.

For a slave to run away or to get a severe beating was not the same in 1800, 1832, and 1859. The act was the same, but it was significantly modified by the times and by the slaves' level of expectations. The slaves were changing with the times. Their minds were different—not necessarily in I.Q. or formal education—different because the national situation and mind were different in 1800, 1832, and 1859. The mind of the slave drew much from the national situation and mind, and vice versa.

Research and writing on the subject of slavery in America have changed profoundly since the days of U. B. Phillips. To write about the thought of blacks on such subjects as religion, overseers, white females, white males, or beatings is to write intellectual history. As W. E. B. Du Bois came to see, other aspects of this subject now require that a scholar be trained in dialectical and historical materialism and psychoanalytic theory. Now such specialties as those of the social historian, cliometrician, and others must be taken into account.

Because slavery is now such a broad and demanding subject, the definitive history of slavery written by one scholar is probably an impossibility. As the general histories of such nineteenth-century scholars as James Ford Rhodes, John Bach McMaster, Herman Von Holzst, and James Schouler gave way to such collective efforts as the "American Nation Series" or the "History of the South Series," such a development may now be necessary for the subject of slavery.

Afro-American history always has been cut more from the psychohistory mold than has modern white occidental history. This is because Afro-American history long has been concerned with such subjects as the sins and guilt of white men, God's or man's revenge against them, whether to hate, try to love, integrate with, or separate from whites, the extent to which the whites' myths about the character, personality, and destiny of each race are based on repression, guilt, and projection, obsession of many whites with the skin color and the genitals of blacks and with reality-principle activities, the negative impact of oppression on both whites and blacks, and too often the repression by whites of the blacks' best qualities to be more efficient as oppressors and exploiters of blacks. Although black historians seldom seem to have been well-acquainted with psychoanalytic terminology, their literature is replete with these concepts. For the black historian, then, a deliberate concern with psychohistory may involve little more than an expansion of vocabulary and sharpening of concepts.

Although the masses of Afro-Americans long have shown a bias in favor of the world of the repressed unconscious, with the Black Power movement there occurred a greater objective embrace of the world of the reality principle. In the interest of survival, the pre-1865 slaves were forced, to become "masters" when it came to the ability to deal effectively with the world of the reality principle.

Sigmund Freud often stated that there are two principles of mental functioning and that each corresponds to a specific set of culture and character and personality types. The reality principle is the world of labor, power, greed, oppression, linear time, dualisms, egotism, objectivity, postponements, fragmentation, stratification, "civilization," repression, sublimation, and the profane. The repressed unconscious is the world of spontaneity, nonrepression, symbolism, poetry, the magico-sacred, the "Now," the "Yes," and body-accepting. Compelled to be repressed around white people and "turned off" by the version of reality that oppression and exploitation molded for them, black slaves became unusually biased against the world of the reality principle. This bias also was characteristic of much of the original "posture" of blacks in Africa.

Some persons may not like the connection of black history to the thought of such European whites as Sigmund Freud and Karl Marx. Blacks who have written on the subject of theory and philosophy of Afro-American history, such as Carter G. Woodson, L. D. Reddick, Vincent Harding, John Hope Franklin, Charles H. Wesley, Harold Cruse, and Orlando Patterson, have provided both wide and narrow perspectives. Everything that can illuminate Afro-American history may be considered a proper part of this history.

Although a few blacks have made considerable use of the ideas of Karl Marx, there has been little direct connection of psychohistory to the black experience, in part because although blacks knew that Marx was a revolutionary thinker, they conceived of Freud as bourgeois and conservative. Yet, the revolutionary uses to which such thinkers as Herbert Marcuse, Norman O. Brown, T. J. Altizer, and some radical feminists have put the ideas of Freud indicate that in the future Afro-Americans may relate more psychohistory to the black experience. In addition, there is always the great need for blacks and whites to understand themselves and others at the levels to which Freud directed our attention.

For an Afro-American to associate black protest with the ideas of such white authors as Sigmund Freud, Karl Marx, Sören Kierkegaard, Friedrich Nietzsche, Norman O. Brown, Herbert Marcuse, Marshall McLuhan, Pitirim A. Sorokin, or T. J. Altizer would be indicative of an inferiority complex, if this is done because one felt that black protest does not have a sufficient base in the oppression, exploitation, and dehumanization of blacks. Just as Nat Turner did not need to be a religious fanatic to murder his oppressors, black protest can be based quite adequately on the black experience alone. But this protest needs to be critical of itself, although not overly so, and the interpretative emphases of blacks should be broad and sharp. For these tasks psychohistory has value.

Psychohistory of the type herein proposed may be defined as history that deals directly with such terms and concepts as id, ego, superego, repression, regression, projection, introjection, sublimation, anal or oral type, phallic personality, reality principle, and repressed unconscious. With psychohistory one must use the same terminology, such as repression, projection, identification, and oedipus complex, for blacks and whites. However, these words often have a different meaning and manifestation when the application is shifted from blacks to whites or vice versa. This is because race has been given such definition and importance in the modern occidental world and because the objective conditions of the races have been so different.

Psychohistory bases the historical process on the concept of repression and the eternally shifting relationship between id, ego, and superego as revealed inside individuals and among cultural institutions. It is an emerging new discipline. In his essay, "Cultural Psychology," Joel Kovel spells out some of the detail involved in this approach to history. At one point in the application of his theory to pre-1865 U.S. history, Kovel states: "Neither slavery in the South, nor its relative, capitalism in the North, were rational pursuits: both involved the headlong pursuit of impossible fantasies involving acceptance and rejection of feces so as, by magical action to restore union with the mother."[11]

Psychohistory is greatly concerned with fantasies. These have been defined as "remnants of infantile wishes" charged by aggression and sexual drives and culturally "nourished and perpetuated." Racist beliefs and practices rest on fantasies and greed as much as on anything else. For a scholar to dismiss the study of fantasies as "too Freudian" is for that scholar to be superficial. Fantasies are very important in the lives of individuals and societies, and the scholar should never accept the notion that classifies them as unimportant nonsense. The unconscious is powerful and rationality is always ambivalent; "sense" and "nonsense" are always paired or yoked together. Since the beginnings of civilization, the wisest of men have respected the significance and power of the irrational and the unconscious mind.

Joel Kovel's book is based largely on hang-ups and fantasies that are acquired during the anal stage of development. In contrast the present writer's book, *The Old South: A Psychohistory* (1900) is based largely, although by no means exclusively, on oral and genital hang-ups and fantasies.

Many whites, including Stanley Elkins, have viewed black slaves as chronically regressed. This is just one version of the view of blacks as mostly passion or id with practically no ego or reason and no superego or conscience. Other persons have depicted blacks with tails, horns, and elongated heels—all clearly phallic symbols. In more direct language, there is the view that black males characteristically have extra-large penises and that black males and females are super-lovers. There is also the view that a Black person who has seen a ghost or who has stolen a chicken can run as fast as the wind. In psychoanalytic terms, running and flying are often symbols for the sex act. In much of this there is imagery that is highly similar to that of the witch with her phallic symbols in the broom and long pointed nose and hat or of the devil with his phallic symbols in the long tail, pitchfork, and horns. The characterization of a witch or devil is strikingly similar to that which numerous whites have presented of black people. It is also strikingly similar to the image that psychoanalysis presents of the castrating-witch-devil-whore preoedipal mother and the rapist father.

Joel Kovel, Albert Memmi, and others have commented on the absence of feelings in many whites when blacks are hurt or killed. Perhaps whites generally associate blacks with what Freudians refer to as the castrating-witch-devil-harlot mother but usually not with the good mother. Tender feelings are reserved only for the good mother; sex and love must be kept apart. Near the end of Chapter III of her book *The Dialectic of Sex* (1970), Shulamith Firestone comments on the "sexual schizophrenia" in modern culture that makes it necessary for some men to degrade people in order to have sexual feeling for them—associating sex with the "good mother" violates the incest taboo. In this book Firestone has written of racism as "psychosexual degradation."

Along with other feminists, much of Firestone's optimism rests on the possibility of humankind soon achieving complete mastery of nature. Yet she, along with numerous other feminists, writes almost as if such words as "symbol," "fantasy," "anxiety," and "repression" do not exist. Fantasies also are part of human nature, and there is little or no evidence that the achievements of science are taming them. Many of these fear and hate-charged myths derive from the young infant's helpless condition and hence was not products of learning in a sex-schizophrenic culture. Firestone's stance is too much that of the rationalist.

In the critiques of the Freudians by the Women's Liberation Movement, there is considerable food for thought for those concerned with racism. Shulamith Firestone joins other feminists in the contention that the inability of some men to love adequately is due to alienation from their mothers, which begins when the oedipus complex is wiped out by the castration complex around the age of five or six years. The source of and pattern for society's paternalism and domination is the paternalistic nuclear family. To end the sickness, then, is to end the nuclear family. But Norman O. Brown has shown that the real alienation is from one's own body—in the form of repression or sublimation or making a god out of the function of such things as the genitals—which begins in the cradle during the earliest month of life. The first and most crucial alienations from the mother have nothing at all to do with the father but are based on the reality that the mother and child are two persons instead of one. The child develops hostility toward and fear of mother. The child who turns to the father already has been sick or alienated for several years. Firestone's choice of the onset of the sickness is only a convenience that suits the purposes of her argument. As with some other feminists, her solution to the sickness is to achieve real equality between the sexes by wiping out sexual distinction and privileges. Brown's solution is to develop a consciousness tough enough to accept death that can fully accept the human body with all its potentialities and limitations. Brown's argument must also be pitted against those who feel that only a direct conscious-level attack on racial or class distinctions and privileges can be successful and that to end the oppressed's landlessness and powerlessness will eliminate all of man's sickness. As with what Kate Millett calls sexual politics, racism is a secondary sickness. Although the practice of racism can intensify sickness, men are not racists first and then sick; they are racists *because* they are sick.

What Eldridge Cleaver would refer to as the journey from soul to ice, the culture of nonrepression to one of repression, is the fatal flaw that Sigmund Freud saw in civilization or in the fate of each maturing individual. It is what Arnold J. Toynbee says happens when civilizations proceed to the point where they commit the sin of pride or self-love; what Edith Hamilton saw when she said that wealth and power corrupted ancient Athens; what Marshall McLuhan sees as proceeding from Gutenberg's invention of printing by movable type that caused men to "change an ear for an eye"; What P. A. Sorokin sees in the shift from an Ideational or Idealistic culture to a Sensate one; and what Karl Marx saw as inevitable with the genesis of the class struggle. It is this journey that prompted the prophets and Goethe in Faust to ask: What does it profit a man to gain the whole world and lose his own soul?

Some persons have declared that the greatest gift of Afro-Americans to the United States is their labor. It is possible that their most important gifts are laughter, song, rhythm, dance, happiness, joy, and the health and dedication to life, justice, and freedom, which, are related to these. Eros and life and love are the voice of the untrammeled id and the body. So powerful has been this voice in black people that chains and oppression have not been able to mute it. Throughout the history of the United States, blacks have held a corner on the market of joy (and sadness) and on the fight for freedom and justice. Long before 1865, the entire nation was infected with the black man's fight for freedom and justice and his boundless capacity to laugh, joke, dance, sing, love, and live. Although the oppressors' icy death-oriented hands tried to crush happiness, joy, and life, even these oppressors may be saved by the health that is in the people whom they tried mightily to kill.

NOTES

1. Kenneth Stampp, *The Peculiar Institution* (New York: Knopf, 1956), pp. vii-viii.

2. Ibid., p. viii.

3. Robert Fogel and Stanley Engerman, *Time on the Cross* (Boston: Little, Brown, 1974), p. 223.

4. Stanley Elkins, *Slavery: A Problem in American Institutional and Intellectual Life* (Chicago: University of Chicago Press, 1959), p. 82.

5. W. L. Langer, "The Next Assignment," *American Historical Review* 62 (1958), p. 284.

6. W. E. B. Du Bois, *Suppression of the African Slave Trade to the United States of America, 1638-1870* (New York: Schocken Books, 1969), p. xxxi.

7. Winthrop D. Jordan, in *The Journal of Southern History* 28 (November 1962), pp. 496-97.

8. Theodore Roszak, "The Historian as Psychiatrist," *The Nation* (November 24, 1962), p. 348.

9. Fogel and Engerman, *Time on the Cross*, p. 223.

10. Ibid., pp. 231, 263-64.

11. Joel Kovel, "Cultural Psychology," *White Racism: A Psychohistory* (New York: Pantheon, 1970), pp. 205ff.

LESLIE HOWARD OWENS

Blacks in *The Slave Community*

Once again we turn our attention to a past that we must squarely face if we are to understand our heritage and the promise of our destiny. In this instance the past is slavery. Slavery has always brought us face to face with some of our most complex feelings and fears about ourselves, our futures, and our neighbors in white America. No wonder we have sometimes tried to repress, consciously *or* subconsciously, large elements of this past, to at least remove them to the level of lingering and bearable memory. But although some may find a fading memory satisfying, slavery's pains and lessons cannot be buried from sight. They haunt both our lives and scholarship like the skeleton in the closest. John Blassingame has shared with us some of his thoughts about this experience in his study, *The Slave Community*. His investigation gives us an opportunity to assess an important black interpreter's views about an experience central to an understanding of the developing Afro-American sunrise. Beyond this it also gives us a few moments to reflect together upon what we know, or perhaps more importantly, don't know, about the contours of our forefathers' lives.

The Slave Community presents for the serious student of bondage and repression some perplexing questions, as the investigation itself is unsettlingly contradictory in its basic assumption about slave life. *The Slave Community's* interpretations rest on the slave narratives written in the eighteenth and nineteenth centuries and on the insights of modern psychology. This is no idle claim, and all too often Blassingame does not seem clear about what he found in these rich resources. In fact many of his conclusions do not take us beyond what is obviously apparent in the narratives or the psychological insights said to clarify their meaning for us. The reasons for this lead us in many directions, but we need only point out at the beginning that slavery and slaves in the narratives possess fuller dimensions and wider complexities than emerge in Blassingame's study of physical and psychological bondage. Blassingame's historical vision and analysis of human behavior in fact misconnect many of the slave community's most arresting features, and at the same time his ambivalence about slave character distorts his discussion of slaves and their imaginative structuring of their surroundings.

This can be illustrated by a single but revealing example that has critical implications for the kind of community Blassingame tells us the slave community was. The narratives give many details about the interaction of slaves in America's earliest black social networks. In that setting the slavedriver (foreman) played many pivotal roles in his relations with other bondsmen and masters. Yet in Blassingame's study he appears in less than three full sentences. His omission is a major shortcoming not merely of fact but more importantly of the community that is set before us. If we are to believe that there is no effective place for the driver in this community, then it alters the nature of the community fabric Blassingame has woven. His community is unnecessarily incomplete, because the driver's insertion into the picture changes our perception of the relations between slaves and slavery at every level of behavior. With the driver out of the picture we cannot share in the slave's agonies and victories (at least on large plantations) in the manner we must to obtain a clearer viewing of the slave experience. In another time and place, although not exactly parallel, were we to remove street-corner speakers from their soap boxes and ladders on the streets of Harlem in the 1920s and 1930s, how would the black experience be shaped for those years? Marcus Garvey might not be too understanding, nor would W. E. B. Du Bois, although for different reasons. Blassingame, it seems, cannot be easily excused. But the narratives set us right in this area, for their authors realized that a discussion of slave communal life without temperamental drivers would be unthinkable. Frederick Douglass, Charles Ball, and Henry Bibb all might pause to reflect. Indeed, the nature of our insights into the slave community are only as good as our reflections about that community's intersection of human and natural forces. In a study whose psychological examinations depend heavily on identifying and examining "significant others" in the plantation environment, the driver was too *significant* an *other* to be brushed aside.

As we step away from drivers to areas of more generalized behavior among Afro-American slaves, we observe some interesting developments. In chapter 6, "Plantation Realities," and elsewhere Blassingame appears too eager to cast master and slave in the familiar garb of massa and Sambo when he makes the unwise statement: "Planters insisted that their slaves show no signs of dissatisfaction." (p. 161) A driver might convey dissatisfaction to a master for disgruntled workers, but inadequate food supplies and lack of decent health care, among other things, made slaves quite dissatisfied with their lot, and they showed it. Blassingame's claim can hardly pass us by when it is immediately followed by this sentence: ". . . they [slaves] were to demonstrate their humility by cheerful performance of their tasks." Clearly this was never a plantation reality. This cannot be supported in the narrative or wider evidence unless one believes that plantations ran according to ideal rules and that behavior among slaves can be so inflexibly delineated. Could a master expect cheerful behavior over a year, a life time? No way! Even masquerading slaves knew their acts would be difficult to keep up in the face of the ailments and pains of bondage.*

A slaveholder's reality taught him a great deal about the operation of his estate(s)—economically and otherwise—and the complexity of personality from his frequent and frustrating contacts with ego-conscious, nonsmiling Africans. Blassingame's psychological framework is the source of many of his interpretative prob-

---

Editor's Note: Owens develops this point further in Chapters 2 and 3 of his *This Species of Property: Slave Life and Culture in the Old South* (New York: Oxford University Press, 1976).

lems. Sullivan cannot help him. Freud cannot help him. But the slave narrators—excellent psychotherapists, and more, themselves—might wonder why as their own therapist Blassingame felt it best to keep confidential many of their most revealing sessions on the couch in the office of his mind. The slave's personality and culture were formed by a considerably wider array of motivations and influences than are mentioned in *The Slave Community*. We are instead supplied with some differently shaped stereotypes of blacks, slavery, and even of slavery's sources.

Our assessments of life involve us with difficult questions about human responses to life's situations, and these assessments are bound to be ambiguous at times. How could matters be different? Still, running throughout *The Slave Community* is a basic ambivalence about the nature of slavery and slave character. Bondage was harsh and destructive; imagine what it did to black men and women. But the psychology employed in *The Slave Community* is almost too easy and insufficiently shaped by realistic doses of joys and sorrows to adequately explain the impact of slavery on the slave. Nowhere is this perhaps more apparent than in the author's thoughts about a slave family in which he observes that much of the impetus for Afro-American kinship relations come from slaveholders rather than slaves: "A number of planters attempted to promote sexual morality in the quarters, punished slaves for licentiousness and adultery, and recognized the male as the head of the family." So much is true. Yet Africans hardly needed slaveholders who regularly split up their families by sale to preach to them about morality or to encourage "monogamy among them" for disciplinary reasons. Family was in their blood in forms Blassingame's psychological insights do not allow him to see. His emphasis is wrong, and time is wasted along this line of exploration. In places his wording may be questioned too, for although he shows that the lust of white men for black women was an ever-present threat to the sanctity of the slave family-unit, he notes that black men—seeing such predicaments—"pursued their black paramours with reckless abandon." (p. 85) How reckless can one be in slavery? Totally, perhaps, if survival and family were not so intertwined. "Sexual conquest," according to Blassingame, "became a highly respected avenue to status in the quarters." But what kind of status did it lead to after the bickering began? The portrayal of wise masters and "licentious" slaves is too unyielding, even when illuminated by later qualifications.

Let me suggest that most slaves were openly defiant to slaveholder intrusion in family affairs. Wives, husbands, and their children were too important to one another for things to have been different. It follows that personal sexual conquests by male slaves undermined their sense of community and sensitivity to their women's and children's sufferings. The slave was seldom so insensitive. He saw his situation for what it was, accepted what he had to of it—its pain and the need to redirect the pain for personal benefit—and showed his good sense by loving his black woman and child for their precious contributions to his own sanity and survival.

But whose authority was most important in shaping the slave family? "Old massa" could dictate certain standards of behavior beneficial to his interests, but he was not a real father figure à la Genovese, for the power he held over life and death stripped him of his paternal disguise. A problem with *The Slave Community*, then, is its author's packaged view of human behavior in the black community. He sees some of its variety but always in rigid patterns emanating primarily from masters. The family unit is given too little credit; its rhythm is lost as children were treated by "densely ignorant mothers" (p. 94), and although these same children "died in droves" from diseases and neglect, they also led an "idyllic existence." (p. 96) His mechanistic psychology traps him. The family was not simply "an important survival mechanism" with movable parts. It had historical soul, which it plucked from the past and projected into our day. For most slaves the family was their survival in ways masters seldom understood.

Blassingame's misdirection of the slave family and the origins of its strength derive from his larger ambivalence about slave character, which he links to the happy-go-lucky Sambo. Blassingame sees Sambo as one of the main personalities in his slave community. But how did Sambo function in a family? Did he marry another Sambo? Did his children shun him or become Sambo? Did he transmit his character to future generations? These are legitimate questions to raise about his slave community and the kinds of behavior his slaves exhibit. Blassingame's qualification seems a bit late. He adds, "it [Sambo] was not the dominant slave personality." But I am not consoled by realizing that, for him, Sambo exists in numbers beyond the level of current discussion. I cannot agree, therefore, with the repeated application of his psychologically inspired framework: "Some slaves were compelled to shape their behavior so completely to the white man's moods that they became Sambos. Nowhere was Sambo more ubiquitous than among house servants and slaves on small plantations who lived in almost constant contact with whites." (p. 200) This sounds just like Stanley Elkins, whose premises Blassingame set out to explore and expel from serious discussions of Afro-Americans. Nor can we be certain that domestics on small plantations were dominated by whites. On the contrary, they may in fact have had many opportunities to dominate the scene, serving even as a forceful "significant other" for a master. In a study based on some of the many revelations contained in the slave narratives, Blassingame should have been able to offer us a far more persuasive analysis of the slave experience. While the blacks in his account lead culturally significant lives, they still remain locked away in old categories of historical analysis and perception. They are limited more by their framework than their existence in historical time.

Of course this is not to say that Blassingame does not perceive variety and salvation in the slave's personality in the community he describes. He does; but it is the nature of that salvation that is so bothersome. He actually adopts only two personality-types other than Sambo to be substantiated by the narratives: Jacks (average slaves) and Nats (rebels). In his chapter "Plantation Stereotypes and Institutional Roles" he closes with the remark: "The predominance of the Jack and Nat stereotypes explains a great deal more about the white man's character than about the behavior of most slaves." But what are we to believe when he also writes that some slaves were authentic Sambos?

The slave's salvation remains bothersome. In his evaluation of slave resistance and revolts in the Old South, Blassingame offers us a definition with two parts. He defines a revolt as ". . . any concerted action by a group of slaves with the settled purpose of and the actual destruction of the lives and property of local whites" and: "In addition, the activities must have been recognized as an insurrection by public officials who called out the armed forces of the locale to destroy the rebels." Applying this far too unreasonable definition he says, "there were at least nine slave revolts in America between 1691 and 1865." (p. 125) But this definition has little applicability to the plantation South. Its formulation misleads us by suggesting an answer for a complex process that we have scarcely begun to investigate and conceptualize. The definition also reduces the action of the individual to insignificance. An individual must await his leaders to know that he has been resisting. Blassingame does not tell us all the revolts that fit his criteria, and by supplying his reader with such a narrow revolutionary mold, he does damage the intricate and subtle nature of black resistance in bondage and further demonstrates the nature of his self-fulfilling slave-community model.

In reference to Blassingame's assessment of slave resistance, some useful observations perhaps should be made about the dispersal of the evidence that he bases his arguments on. There is no citation to a narrative after footnote 17 in his chapter "Runaways and Rebels," the remaining forty-nine notes refer to three secondary sources. Frank Roy Johnson's *The Nat Turner Slave Insurrection* (Murfreesboro, N. C., 1966) is the only source he uses in his discussion of Turner found on pages 126 to 131. Johnson calls Turner's treatment of whites "barbaric" and accepts without question the notion: "To the blacks in most things the white man stood as a model to be emulated . . . from superstitions to straight hair." (p. 15)

One final reference to the evidence in *The Slave Community* may be helpful as a corrective measure. I can find in the footnotes to his study only two citations to the listing of a score of plantation manuscripts in the bibliography. But the problem does not lie here. In the preface to his book Blassingame writes that from these manuscripts an "all-powerful, monolithic view of the plantation" (p. vii) emerges. Other researchers should take care. I trust that he does not expect us to take him at his word on this matter, since the manuscripts listed in his bibliography alone quickly dispel this harmful judgment and reveal their value to the slave experience.

The interpretations set forth in *The Slave Community* are of disturbing value to thoughtful students of slavery and to the Afro-American experience, of which it forms a part. In terms of "the resources and choices theoretically open to Southern slaves" (p. 189), too many areas of motivation and evidence are felt unexplored: ". . . the master's kindness, confidence, and trust was repaid by faithful work on the part of the slave." (p. 191) How could they be unless we examine only a limited portion of the slave's humanity? The slave's motives appear as a reflex action with the psychologically complex ground swept clear: "Often the slaves were content with such [kind] masters" (p. 191) Blassingame may believe this, but we can hardly be expected to share his beliefs. His perception leads him to extremes: "Faced with unrelenting cruelty and depressed at every turn, many of the slaves despaired of resisting abuse, lived in deadly fear of all whites, and soon lost all feeling of independence, self-respect, and sympathy for others." (p. 194) Was slave behavior so plastic? Here the slave's loss of sympathy for others makes him sound more like his master. And finally it comes. Blassingame observes, "As a result [of punishment] some blacks wished passionately that they were white." (p. 199) But does he really want blacks to go this far; if we do, it means the total negation of our identities. The context of his discussion would have it no other way. Once again the psychological tools that Blassingame applies lead him off the track. The slave, fully unveiled, is not only a Sambo, a caricature; he is also a fool. Blassingame's statement is a far different charge from calling a black man an "Uncle Tom" or a black woman an "Aunt Minnie," terms that he says fall under the designation Sambo. The master triumphs, and in this extraordinarily controversial line Blassingame casts doubts about black identity for some time to come. In other phases of his study I have accepted his use of the word "some" without difficulty, but in this instance in seems that *some* refinement of his usage is in order.

I would expect that such an impactive statement would be explored in an ensuing discussion, yet no such discussion can be found, and the end of the book is drawing near. Two pages later Blassingame notes: "The docility of the slave was a sham, a mask to hide his true feelings and personality traits." (p. 201) Nonetheless, this remark cannot salvage his earlier statement. When he finally concludes that "the slave was no different in most ways from most men" (p. 213), I have to wonder why he thinks the slave experience meant so little to blacks. The observation bears some basic resemblace to Kenneth Stampp's 1956 notation that "innately Negroes are, after all, only white men with black skins, nothing more, nothing less." (pp. vii-viii)

In *The Slave Community* we are faced with a number of problems. A community is explored; but often the focus of the community is not clear, and sometimes the observations made about it alert us to it's abstract nature apart from the Old South. The picture presented, interesting or sympathetic as it may be, is not believable in many of its important particulars, because its insights appear hurriedly arrived at and marred by stereotypes that will serve us little better than the old stereotypes to which they are children if what we are after is a more accurate view of slave life.

Since Blassingame's study appeared in 1972, we have expanded our understanding of slavery both qualitatively and quantitatively with differing results, and most of these works have focused our attention on experiences we have grown intellectually complacent about. Future investigations will not be easy, as more and more methodologies must be mastered and explored. Many of us should begin our efforts if the Afro-American experience is to have a full and careful hearing.

RALPH D. CARTER

Slavery and the Climate of Opinion

A central element in the history of all Americans is the capture, forced emigration from an ancestral homeland, resettlement on foreign soil, and brutal enslavement of Americans of African descent. For more than three-and-one-half centuries these Americans have suffered racial oppression, discrimination, degradation, humiliation, and intense social rejection by white American society. Often there have been periods when white Americans have assaulted black Americans physically, with guns, ropes, and chains and psychologically with the instruments of pulpit and press and other forms of the media. Some black Americans reacted to these incidents with self-flagellating agony. Concurrently, some white Americans meted out punishment to another segment of black Americans who reacted aggressively by asserting their humanity. The retaliatory actions of whites has invariably been labeled justice. The causal factor in this vicious practice of physical subjugation and of maligning and distorting the images of black people, is the need on the part of some whites to achieve psychological, social, economic, and political security and stability for themselves. It further provides psycho-social control and hegemony over masses of blacks.

How does the historian deal with such a sad spectacle, a spectacle that is basic to understanding the character and culture of the American people and the society they have created? Leopold Von

Ranke, the nineteenth-century German historian, remarked that "the task of the historian was simply to show how it really was."[1] This is not what American historians have done. The demands of the present and the longstanding racist philosophy in America have hindered American historians from coming to grips with black Americans, their African heritage, the institution of slavery, and the impact that these tremendous elements have had on influencing the shape and structure of the American Republic as a whole.

The late British philosopher, R. G. Collingwood, defined the tasks of the historian:

It is thus the historian's picture of the past, the product of his own a priori imagination, that has to justify the sources used in its construction. . . . - The a priori imagination which does the work of historical construction supplies the means of historical criticism as well. . . . Freed from its dependence on fixed points supplied from without, the historian's picture of the past is thus in every detail an imaginary picture, and its necessity is at every point the necessity of the a priori imagination . . .[2]

This is the problem of slave historiography: The a priori imagination of the historian, which theoretically can only be known through deductive reasoning and not through experience, has been used as the presumptive reason that certain empiricist slave historians developed their revisionist historical theories on the slave South. The current social scene supposedly has had nothing to do with the new scholarship that strangely influences and often answers problems that occur during social, political, racial, and economic crises. The fact that historians can be shown to be influenced by the current social scene is demonstrated by the literature on slavery in which new theories display a strange proclivity to the racial and social mood of the country at the time of their publication. However, there are constant denials that such is the case.

The American historian, Robert Skotheim, speaking about the influence of public opinion on historical writing, stated:

The problem lies precisely in the fact that, despite the impossibility of recapturing the past in totality, the historian and his readers expect something more than a history based upon a complete capitulation to the interests of the present. The historian and his readers demand obedience to the integrity of the past, even though they recognize the necessity of viewing the past through the lens of the present.[3]

Public opinion is influenced by the prevailing philosophy of the society. The prevailing racial philosophy in America continues to be the assumption that a correlation exists between physical characteristics and moral qualities and that mankind is divisible into superior and inferior stocks. Black Americans are still believed to be inferior, thus justifying their oppression and necessary separation. Consequently, the exploitation and brutalization of black Americans is used to socially control masses of whites who might otherwise challenge the status quo. Many whites psychologically clutch at the myth of black racial inferiority for their own psychosocial and economic stability. This belief pervades all aspects of American life, including the historical profession and historical writing.[4]

White American historians have defined slave historiography. They have set the limits and parameters within which inquiry and research takes place. They have established which issues are relevant and which are not. Finally, white scholars have audaciously and arrogantly made erroneous statements about the personal lives and intimate histories of black Americans, the knowledge of which would require the acquisition of citizenship papers in the black community, to even venture into such vast unchartered seas.[5] The crowning insult is that they have several of their colleagues, who usually know even less about blacks, review their books and articles in prestigious journals and other media, thus establishing themselves as the white experts of the "black problem."[6]

Black scholars need to do more than react to what these white historians have established. It is imperative that they take part in defining the relevant issues in slave historiography and their importance to American society.

Precedence for this oppressive psychological deception, which is utilized by the dominant class to maintain a system of power and stratification, is older than the American historical profession itself. However, the immediate problem in racist scholarship can be traced to the time of World War I, when lynchings, racist literature, and movies were prevalent and when institutionalized segregation had been completed.

It seemed inevitable that some scholarly book would appear to justify these racial persecutions. Such a book was Ulrich Bonnell Phillips's *American Negro Slavery* (1918). Phillips set white Americans' guilt-ridden consciences at ease. He widened the gap between black Americans and the rest of society by depicting the slaves as a separate and inferior people. Phillips portrayed them as uncivilized, possessing no heritage or culture of their own, and merely imitating the dominant culture, a culture that was not influenced in any positive way by blacks except through the necessary utilization of their labor.[7]

During World War II, American propaganda's major focus was the Nazi brand of racism and its incompatibility with the American creed. In order to avoid direct comparison with the Nazis, many Americans felt the need to temper the most overt and violent aspects of their own racism. Actually, the war propaganda supplied anti-racists, both white and black, with weapons to attack the racists.

A brief period of intellectual liberalism occurred at the end of the war that was concurrent with the civil rights campaign led by blacks. The scholarly community supplied ammunition for those seeking a more equitable distribution of institutional rights and power.

In slave historiography a number of writers tempered the Phillips myth of slavery as a benign institution. Abbott E. Smith's *Colonists in Bondage* (1947) indicated that all white Americans could not trace their ancestry to the English nobility and landed gentry. Many had lowly class origins and did labor equivalent to and alongside of black slaves. Frank Tannenbaum's *Slave and Citizen* (1949) implied that the English and American forms of slavery were the most brutal in the history of mankind. Kenneth M. Stampp's *Peculiar Institution* (1956) attacked Phillips directly and portrayed slavery as brutal. This created a rational belief in the vicious exploitation of black Americans and the necessity for change in contemporary society. Finally, Stanley M. Elkins's *Slavery* (1959) extended the thesis of the brutalization of black Americans to an apparently logical conclusion. Accepting the Tannenbaum thesis and extending Stampp's thesis through a cross-disciplinary approach, Elkins compared Southern slave plantations to Nazi concentration camps and discovered tremendous similarities. He claimed that the shock and trauma of the slave trade and the closed system of the Southern plantation severed the African from his world, leaving him to be molded into Sambo, the predominant plantation type. Although attacking Phillips's notion of slavery as a benevolent institution, the above writers continued to view the slave community and slave culture as separate from the dominant society and culture.

The Elkins thesis stirred such a controversy that much of the recent material written on slavery can be viewed as a response to Elkins. This is particularly true of John W. Blassingame's, *The Slave Community,* which has done an admirable job of demolishing the thesis. However, there are now post-Blassingame works that are creating new uproars and controversies in the scholarly community, of which more will be said later.

In practically every thesis on the institution of slavery, blacks have been treated as denizens of the institution, and of course many of them were. However, the focus of this writing has been on the institution itself, rather than on the occupants.[8] John W. Blassingame's book focuses attention on the slaves as human beings caught in the pathos, circumstance, and agony of historical change. It is a direct frontal assault on the Elkins thesis of the Sambo personality. Blassingame uses a cross-disciplinary approach to arrive at his thesis. He even employs some of the same psychological methods that Elkins used to arrive at different conclusions. Blassingame's emphasis is different. Instead of just using the traditional sources—that is, plantation records, diaries, and journals—he focuses on the personal records left by the slave, especially autobiographies. However, attention is also given to traditional white sources and to travel accounts of northerners and European travelers.

Blassingame's thesis is that there were many different slave personality-types. The Sambo-type was just one of them. In replying to Elkins's closed-plantation theory, Blassingame retorts that because masters varied so much in character, the system was open at certain points, and that the slave's quarters, religion, and family helped to shape behavior.[9] Consequently, he claims that the slaves had varied responses to their varied conditions, and he records them as such.

Blassingame's discussion on the enslavement of Africans, focusing attention not only on those ethnic groups who were enslaved but also on those who escaped and why, is not novel but an excellent introduction to this short concise volume on slavery. His use of the slave narratives of Venture Smith and Gustavus Vassa (or Olaudah Equiano) in discussing some aspects of African culture is excellent. The use of slave narratives by Africans, which are of a different perspective than the indigenous Afro-American slave narratives, is invaluable in attempting to give the reader some understanding of the horrors of slavery.[10] Nevertheless, Blassingame narrows his ability to communicate to the reader the importance of slavery to all Americans when he succumbs to definitions set by earlier scholars in his discussion of acculturation:

The significance of the continuing debate over African survivals in black music is not whether African or European patterns predominate or whether the environment of the plantation was the primary determinant of its character. The very existence of the debate is important in any discussion of acculturation for it proves that there is at least a reasonable possibility that there were some survivals of African forms in slave culture. The sophisticated research of ethno-musicologists, anthropologists, and folklorists, coupled with the evidence in a large number of primary sources, suggests that African culture was much more resistant to the bludgeon that was slavery than historians have hitherto suspected.[11]

However, on an earlier page he had written that "acculturation in the United States involved the mutual interaction between two cultures, with Europeans and Africans borrowing from each other."[12]

This latter statement is the essence of the debate. The issue is not that there were African survivals in the slave culture but that there are large amounts of Africanisms in the entire society. It should not surprise anyone familiar with American history to find more Africanisms ("soul") in the whites of the solid South than one finds in the so-called black Brahmins of Boston, New York, or Philadelphia, who trace their ancestry through several centuries of residency in those respective cities. Peter Wood, Roger Bastide, Melville Herskovits, Edmund Morgan, James H. Johnston, and Blassingame himself have shown that mutual borrowing and mixing existed not only in music but also in work tools (hoes, boats, etc.), religion, language, agriculture, cooking, clothing, and sexual relations as well.[13] The reason credit is not given to the African for his cultural contribution to American society is deeper than just applying the term racism to this peculiar phenomenon.

In Latin American history there is an attitude that general degeneration of whites took place when Europeans were exposed to the warmer climate and exotic peoples of the western hemisphere. Thus, whites born in Latin America—Creoles—were lower in rank than whites born in Spain or Portugal. Therefore, the Creoles did everything they could to improve their standing, including developing habits of dress, adornment, house styles, liveries, and other living practices that seemed exaggerated, ostentatious, or excessive to the eyes of those in Spain.[14]

Dunn reports similar reactions of the English to the fear of degeneracy in the West Indies:

The English were a narrowly ethnocentric people, exceedingly reluctant to live among foreigners of any sort, even Scots, or Irish or Dutchmen, let alone really alien peoples such as Jews or Indians or Negroes.[15]

This xenophobic fear led these Englishmen to do everything they could to hang on to their Europeaness. Thus, planters' wives wished to keep their complexions as white as possible in contrast to their black-skinned slaves and red-necked servants. In what must have been very uncomfortable for anyone living in a tropical climate, these ladies shaded their faces from the sun with hoods and covered their hands with gloves. The planters did the same, wearing broad-brimmed hats, neckcloths, stockings, and gloves.[16]

Americans, likewise, feared a loss of their Europeaness and did everything they could to prove their purity of blood. Their paranoid fears of losing esteem in the eyesight of those in the motherland, coupled with the lowly class origins of many of their citizens, moved them to take measures in many ways more extreme than their Latin American or West Indian counterparts. For example, the progeny between black and white relations—the mulattoes —were not given a special category, as they were in the West Indies and Latin America. Rather, they were grouped with other blacks. Everything was either black or white with no in-between.

Therefore, anything of value that developed or occurred in the society and was adopted by the entire society had to be interpreted as being of white origin, thus denying Amer-Indian and African origin to much of what is commonly referred to as white American culture, but is more accurately called American culture. Since no one denies that black music came from the experience of black slaves, the only point of contention is whether, as Blassingame says, African or European music predominates. Those who stress the latter echo Ulrich Phillips' claim of the imitative genius of the black American, which in essence is a paranoid fear that to credit anything of value to black Americans is to detract from and discredit white Americans in the eyesight of their European brethren. Consequently, one can clearly understand the reason why white Americans renamed race music, calling it "jazz," and then gave the title "king of jazz" to one of their own instead of to King Oliver, Jelly Roll Morton, or any number of other jazz greats of the era. This is also why jazz is not considered by many as serious music and why the genius of black musicians is only now beginning to be belatedly honored. It should be noted that whites sought to claim jazz only after Europeans declared it a valuable art form.

Blassingame is at his best in the discussion of slave culture. Here he discusses the recreational activities of the slaves, their folktales, dances, slave music, and musicians. Blassingame claims that the folktales, although primarily used as a means of entertainment, were also a distillation of folk wisdom used as an instructional device to teach young slaves how to survive.[17] The effects of these tales, particularly the Brer Rabbit tales, were so important to black survival that Joel Chandler Harris, who made a fortune from commercializing them, interjected the Uncle Remus character to subvert the actual intentions of the final moral of the tales. Uncle Remus continually spoke of good masters and the "good ole days" that were slavery.

In his discussion of religion, Blassingame introduces Henry Clay Bruce, a former slave. Bruce recalls an old slave preacher, who forgot about the white man who was present at a religious meeting that he presided over and in his enthusiasm prayed: "Free indeed, free from death, free from hell, free from work, free from white folks, free from everything."[18]

This old slave preacher expressed not only the sentiments of most of his fellow contemporaries but also those of a great many blacks today who desire to escape the crushing burdens of racial oppression. In a similar vein, the narrative of the fugitive slave Lunsford Lane highlights one of the central ambiguities of black-white relations. Lane recalled white ministers telling blacks how good God was in bringing blacks over to this country from dark and benighted Africa and allowing them to hear the gospel.[19] Many of the slaves, and contemporary blacks as well, believed this, but for different reasons than whites preached. Whites are too often ignorant of the fact that frequently what they taught or preached was not necessarily what slaves heard or interpreted. Many religious or educational lessons were and are interpreted to fit the needs and experiences of slaves or contemporary blacks.

In many black sermons today, as in the past, one can hear the preaching of a belief that God has a special design for black Americans. The trials and tribulations experienced at the hands of violent and oppressive white Americans are only momentary sufferings in the grand design, in which black Americans will someday in the near future reemerge, as world leaders. This belief is the reason for the suffering at the hands of evil whites. Black Americans have a mission to save the world from a holocaust through the example and wisdom of their suffering, which is similar to their savior—Christ. Thus, black Americans, like white Americans, manifest a belief in a sense of mission.

In initiating his discussion of the slave family, Blassingame states that the Southern plantation was unique in the New World because it permitted the development of a monogamous slave family. He believes that a basic reason for this was an equitable sex ratio among the slave population. In contrast, among Latin American slaves, the great disparity in the sex ratio restricted the development of monogamous family patterns. Blassingame shows that the sex ratio of slaves in the United States from 1820 to 1860 was far more equitable in most Southern states than it was among whites of the

South. There was an over-balance of white males in this region, suggesting that both white and black males competed for the numerically superior black females. Although he alludes to the greater problem of the sex ratio among whites in the South, he discusses it only in passing, instead of elaborating on it.[28] Yet, this is extremely significant when one realizes that the Latin American racial atmosphere developed in a climate that was a direct result of the sex ratio of the entire populace.

During the colonial period of development in Latin America, there were few Spanish women in the colonies because Spain's early intentions were not to settle the region but to exploit it and expropriate its wealth. Coupled with the type of labor needed in particular areas of Latin America, this discouraged the significant or equal importation of black females and created a similar imbalance of the sex ratio among the slave population. Thus in the mining areas of Columbia, Mexico, Venezuela, and Chile and on the sugar plantations of the Caribbean and Brazil, where the conditions demanded large numbers of male slaves, both master and slave competed for the Indian females that were available. The Iberian experience with the custom of mistresses, in addition to the imbalanced sex ratio and greed for quick profits (debating that it was cheaper to buy new slaves than to cultivate a slave population), discouraged the importation of African females and the development of a monogamous slave family.

The situation was much different in the English continental colonies. England began dumping large numbers of her excessive and unwanted population into her colonies in the early and middle decades of the seventeenth century. Of importance was the introduction of a significant number of white women. They were introduced into the colonies with the understanding that permanent settlement would take place. Their position in the English colonies was different and superior to what their experience had been in England. In England there was a greater proportion of women to men. Therefore, women such as widows, divorcees, and unmarrieds with no dowry were not sought after with any enthusiasm, if at all. In the colonies, such was not the case. The numerically superior white males valued all white women, including those with tainted reputations, as good marriage partners. The custom of hypergamy—the proscription of women to marry below their class —played an important role in race relations in the English colonies. Moreover, through their enhanced influence on family and community life, women unintentionally became the foremost agents in the establishment of racial barriers. Thus, the development of public aversion to racial miscegenation in the thirteen colonies can be traced to the invasion of feminine sentiments into colonial society, sentiments that were controlled and manipulated by white men who had a monopoly on white women.

This situation, combined with the absence of the Iberian custom of mistresses, produced a covert rather than an overt propinquity toward race mixing. Despite the fact that the English colonies had more white women than the Latin America colonies, white women were still a minority, and therefore, as previously stated, white men also sought out non-white women as sexual partners. All of these factors influenced the relationship between the masterclass and the slaves and were significant ingredients in the formation of the slave family.[21]

Another aspect in the development of the slave family was the development of the master's family. Blassingame has an interesting discussion on certain peculiarities characteristic of many Southern-plantation families that he believes influenced the planters' treatment of the slaves. However, this discussion does not appear in the chapter on the slave family.[22] This is an important shortcoming of an otherwise very impressive presentation. In this chapter Blassingame exclaims:

The white man's lust for black women was one of the most serious impediments to the development of morality. The white man's pursuit of black women frequently destroyed any possibility that comely black girls could remain chaste for long. Few slave parents could protect their pretty daughters from the sexual advances of white men. This was particularly true when the slaves belonged to a white bachelor or lived near white bachelors.[23]

Blassingame's theoretical model of the characteristics of a white family, which appear in a later chapter, would be better placed in the chapter on the slave family for comparative analysis. For example, he believes the white child grew up in a society that "stress-ed formalized courtship, romanticized women as angelic, made a fetish of the family, frowned on public displays of affection, en-couraged prolific childbearing, and promoted early marriages." He says that "the planter's family was patriarchal, deeply religious, and filio-pietistic." He claims that white male planters were given "religious and moral lessons as well as being taught to be ag-gressive, proud, independent, courteous, courageous, chivalrous, honorable, and intelligent."[24] He might have added the char-acteristics of assertion and ambition.

The characteristics that were taught to white males of the planter class were real, but they were what white males aspired to, not what they became. The power the planters held over their black slaves was unnatural. The slaves were constantly watched and frequently coerced or punished to get the desired labor and behavior from them. This exacted a heavy toll on the white male masterclass. For while the basic desire of the masterclass was to obtain psychological and economic security through domination and control, realistical-ly their position was insecure. No man could escape the frightening pressure of holding masses of people against their will to labor for values from which they received no benefit. Blassingame says that "the white man's fear and his anxiety about the slave was so deep and pervasive that it was sometimes pathological."[25]

This covert fear created mass irrational behavior patterns. First, there were continuous preparations for slave revolts. Second, elaborate methods were used to prevent slave revolts. Finally, the anxiety and apprehension of anticipated rebellions created an anomalous militant society that manifested an air of violence and barbarity mixed with gentility and culture. This suggests that white men measured their true manhood by their ability to control and direct black men rather than by the ideal characteristics to which they were aspiring. The defense of slavery as a positive good, with black men and women treated as childlike, semi-human beings, was concurrent with his love-hate image of the black mammy and his sexual lust for black women in general. These schizoid tendencies, emanating from the white males, could not help but affect the other members of the plantation community.

The Southern white planterwoman was reared in the same environment as the white planterman. Because she was the symbol of purity and placed on a pedestal above all other women, her father and husband did not openly display overt affection toward her. She observed their circumspection toward other white women and their frequent and supposedly clandestine sexual visits to the slave quarters.[26] These covert visits became public when she and others could easily observe mulatto children running around the plantation, often bearing a striking resemblance to her husband or father. For her to have imitated the white males' actions would have been too risky. William Taylor, in *Cavalier and Yankee* (1961), claims that this was the reason for placing the white woman in a lofty position—to control her.

What were her alternatives and how did this affect the black family? One might suggest that the Southern white woman was not only frustrated sexually but also with the role that had been defined for her. She was probably deeply jealous not only of the sexual freedom of white men and black women but also of the latter's ability to give affection to and receive affection from both the white and black man. Black women displayed emotions that white women were taught to suppress. As a result, there were surely some animosities directed at black women and their mulatto children as well as resulting abnormalities that manifested themselves within the white family. The supposed natural state of things in the plantation society, coupled with the white woman's publicly defined unnatural role that conflicted with her natural desires, created tensions and anxieties in her that further intensified and twisted the race relations of the plantation community.

The master's debasement of the slave male, his sexual abuse of the slave's "wife" and daughter, and the concomitant abuse of slave women and their mulatto children by the white female could only have wreaked havoc within the slave family. However, there are some distinct differences between living together as slaves and the institutions of marriage and family.

First, the plantation South had a monied economy. Free and slave families were diametrically opposed to each other. Free families could acquire material objects through purchase, and these became their permanent property. A free family could save money or accumulate wealth, including slaves, for the future. Slaves, on the other hand, were part of the monied economy: They were property and also a medium of exchange, thereby becoming accumulated wealth for slaveholders. Slaves had no future other than as units of labor. It was a rare slave that acquired material goods or provided for his family, and yet those that he did accumulate were not permanently his. They could be commandeered by the master. Consequently, there could be no Horatio Algers among the slaves. The slave did not have the financial responsibility for his family that the free man had. The master had this duty. In fact, the planterclass only permitted families to exist when it was profitable. If it became unprofitable for a slave family to exist, the planter eliminated the family structure with impunity.

Most experts on the family agree that the cultural and separable functions of the family must always, in some form or another, subsume the necessary functions of reproduction, child protection and enculturation, economic cooperation, kinship structure, and the patterning and control of affectionate and sexual relations.[27] Traditional patterns and institutions such as the church are also strongly influential in the institutionalization of sex. However, in the plantation society it was the masterclass who controlled and determined family functions and who institutionalized sexual relations. Since the slave family had no legal existence, each individual slavemaster institutionalized the affectionate, marital, sexual, and reproductive patterns of the slave family according to his own personal and economic needs. The slave family was only partially responsible for the enculturation of slave children. The greater portion of this burden fell on the masterclass, who wrote numerous articles on the different methods developed to assist slaves in achieving competence in the slave culture. Consequently, the values, sentiments, and living habits that slaves acquired were forced upon them through their enslavement and not as a natural consequence of their experience in a new environment. The ambivalences and ambiguities of slave life and culture militated against slaves achieving the emotional and psychological stability that is an important function of family life. Blassingame discusses much of this throughout his chapter on the slave family.[28]

However, other valid statements by Blassingame seem to be contradictory to this:

In spite of the loose morality in the quarters, in spite of the fact that some men had two wives simultaneously, there was a great deal of respect for the monogamous family. . . . Affection, not morality, was apparently the most important factor which kept partners together. . . . Because they were denied all the protection which the law afforded, slaves had an almost mythological respect for legal marriage. . . . In no class of American auto-biographies is more stress laid upon the importance of stable family life than in the autobiographies of former slaves.[29]

This does not contradict but actually highlights a central factor in slave life—the gap between the hopes and aspirations of the slaves and the realities of the plantation South.

Kinship, identity, and the acquisition of one's surname were other aspects of the problem confronting the slave family. We live in a patrilineal society. In such a society the children acquire their father's surname. This helps the child identify and distinguish himself from his peers and others in society. For blacks, the patrilineal system was destroyed when Africans disembarked from the slave-ships. The slave did not have his own surname. He was given his master's surname. As a result, he could not readily identify himself with his father, grandfather, and great-grandfather, but rather, he acquired the identity of his white master (who in some cases was his biological father).

If he changed masters, he changed his surname and therefore his identity. Since the patrilineal system was denied to the slave, his actual ability to gain complete identity was deliberately denied him. This is still a very real problem in contemporary society. For although the patrilineal system reemerged immediately after emancipation, one still finds significant numbers of black Americans desiring to change their surnames, usually to Arabic or African names, that are not historically accurate with the realities of their heritage. The reasons for changing one's surname are complex. First, it is professed to be a rejection of the slave heritage and especially a rejection of the master's name. Black nationalists argue that European names were given to the slaves by their masters and are thus badges of slavery.

However, in reality, due to race mixing, the Americanization of the African, and Western dominance, it was inevitable that European names would predominate in the United States as well as in the rest of the new world. Consequently, this surname syndrome is the acceptance of the master's successful attempt to convince blacks that one's surname, or more importantly one's own pater-familias, is unnecessary for one's identity. This psychological rejec-tion of one's own father is also due to a rejection of the abject con-ditions he has been forced to accept since emancipation and is, con-sequently, a publicly voiced attempt to avoid having those same hu-miliating experiences. The struggle of the black male for manhood recognition, no matter how noble, has been erroneously interpreted by some as failure. It is this interpreted sense of failure, with all the accompanying images of ghetto life, child desertion, crime, etc., from which many individuals wish to escape.

Blassingame claims that slaves could rarely escape frequent dem-onstrations of their powerlessness,[30] a problem of black males in contemporary society as well. The frequent demonstrations of powerlessness in American society affect the evaluations given them by young black males who are determined not to succumb to the crushing fist of white authority, a fist that is continually demonstrating its power over black men and women.

It is interesting that the vast majority of surname changes occurs among black males. Denying that the patrimony received from one's father is necessary for the individual to achieve identity, respect, and equality in contemporary American society can be traced directly to the slave heritage:

Sexual morality, often imperfectly taught (or violated by whites with im-punity) drifted down through a heavy veil of ignorance to the quarters. Consequently, for a majority of slaves, sex was a natural urge frequently fulfilled in casual liaisons. William Wells Brown's mother, for example, had seven children fathered by seven different men, black and white.[31]

In another statement Blassingame claims:

Many slaves vowed early in life never to marry and face separation from loved ones. If they had to marry, the slave men were practically unanimous in their desire to marry women from another plantation. They did not want to marry women from their own and be forced to watch as she was beaten, insulted, raped, overworked, or starved, without being able to protect her.[32]

This distressing series of circumstances was underscored by the slave's inability to protect his wife and children from the overt actions and reactions of the masterclass. Recognizing the vicious realities of these hard facts and realizing that certain group dynamics, such as the relationship between husband and wife, father, mother, and children, are extremely difficult to quantify, some social scientists are led to question methods that attempt to quantify these relationships.

Anticipating recent works on the slave family and the methods used, Blassingame observed:

The best objective evidence available concerning the separation of mates by planters appears in the marriage certificates of former slaves preserved by the Union army and the Freedmen's Bureau in Tennessee (Dyer, Gibson, Wilson, and Shelby counties), Louisiana (Concordia Parish), and Mississippi (Adams County) from 1864 to 1866. Although these records contain the best material available on the actions of masters in regard to the slave family, they must be used with caution. In the first place, the number of unbroken unions may be exaggerated: Those blacks who had retained the strongest sense of family would be most likely to come to the posts to be married. Second, multiple separations by masters were apparently understated (often old slaves simply noted how they were separated from their first mate). Third, it was sometimes impossible to determine from the army record whether a childless couple had been united in slavery.[33]

The horrors and debilitating effects of slave family and communal life invariably created tensions and anxieties that inevitably led to desperate acts of violence and rebellion. Hence, the planter-class was compelled to devise methods that would prevent, minimize, or discourage such acts.

The spectacle of a public hanging was, in itself, supposed to provide a deterrent. Plantation owners hoped that dramatic public punishments had a repressive impact, forcing slaves into patterns of docility. In large measure the effect could hardly have been otherwise. Such regular displays and the network of arbitrary controls they reinforced inevitably drew forth from many blacks a submissiveness which, no matter how unnatural, could be outwardly affected. However, Blassingame indicates that the docility displayed by many slaves was multifaceted and often contradictory. He supplies sundry examples of slaves who acted contrary to the

Sambo image of docility. He highlights this discussion with the example of one slave who was so trusted that he was sent out to look for a runaway and then became a fugitive himself. This indicates that this slave, while giving the impression of submissiveness, was actually very rebellious and desirous of freedom. Blassingame quotes Orville W. Taylor, author of *Negro Slavry in Arkansas* (1958), who after systematically examining notices of fugitives in Arkansas newspapers concluded that they illustrated "among other things, that slaves were as individualistic as white people, despite the regimentation of slavery.' "[34]

It is not Blassingame's intention to deny that an air of submissiveness was not present in the slave society. Rather, he makes the argument that Sambo, the extreme example of submissiveness, was not the prevalent character on most plantations. While one may agree with this thesis, there is still the lingering question of how deep the submissive attitude of slaves went. To further complicate this question, we can examine the freedmen in the first few years after slavery. Were the freedmen seething with hatred for the former system, aware of what freedom meant, and eager to move into the mainstream of American life with assertiveness, aggressiveness, ambition, and courage? In reality, it appears that the freedmen displayed a variety of their slave characteristics but basically many ex-slaves continued to lack confidence in their ability to carry on successfully under freedom. Given the conditions that they faced under freedom and the determination of whites to maintain the status quo, what other characteristics could we expect from these forlorn, neglected, and racially abused human beings?

The black scholar, Henderson H. Donald, discusses the tendency of some freedmen to behave as though they were still slaves in *The Negro Freedmen* (1952). Donald believes that a general characteristic of freedmen was the continued docility of their former slave days. He claimed that throughout their lives they had been under the guidance and control of masters, who made all the decisions relative to their life activities. As a result, they neither learned nor had the opportunity to take the initiative in regard to their affairs. Thus, when set free, many did not feel that they would be able to succeed under their own direction. In short, slavery and the plantation system had not prepared them for life under freedom.[35]

Donald quotes several northern travelers who sojourned in various areas of the South after the Civil War. They recorded similar impressions on the submissiveness of the freedmen. One traveler observed life on a large plantation in Louisiana:

Late in the evening of a certain day, a delegation of black field hands would come to see the planter, whom they called 'de Cunnel.' Their object was to ask favors of him, such as writing a few letters, or bringing small parcels from town on his next visit to the plantation. The men would come huddling in, bowing awkwardly, and with caps in their hands stand as near the door as possible as if ready to run on the slightest provocation. If he looked at them steadily they would burst into uneasy laughter and move away.[36]

After painfully reading such a moving description of freedmen struggling to survive in the aftermath of slavery, one is moved to ask: What happened during slavery to create such a pathetic spectacle? Blassingame has already supplied the answer to this appalling aspect of the slave experience in various chapters of his book and particularly in "Plantation Realities." No one can read this essay without realizing the pathological condition of the plantation community that Blassingame and other slave historians have reported to develop out of the psychological necessity of masters augmenting their image and power at the expense of the humanity of their slaves.

However, is it historically accurate to view the master as a power and authority unto himself? Who were the people or institutions responsible for his wielding power? The answer goes beyond the enculturative process of the plantation South. It involves not only Southern institutions, business, commercial interests, and government, but Northern institutions, commerce, business, and the national government as well.

Perhaps the best answer was supplied during the slave period. In May 1835, Reverend Samuel J. May, a well-known leading abolitionist, was given the reason perhaps not only for the existence of slavery, but of racism as well. A wealthy merchant attending the annual meeting of the American Antislavery Society in New York City, at which Mr. May was speaking, asked Mr. May to step outside for a moment and said:

"Mr. May we are not such fools as not to know that slavery is a great evil, a great wrong. But it was consented to by the founders of our Republic. It was provided for in the Constitution of our Republic. It was provided for in the Constitution of our Union. A great portion of the property of the Southerners is invested under its sanction; and the business of the North, as well as the South, has become adjusted to it. There are millions upon millions of dollars due from Southerners to the merchants and mechanics of this city alone, the payment of which would be jeopardized by any rupture between the North and South. We cannot afford, sir, to let you and your associates succeed in your endeavor to overthrow slavery. It is not a matter of principle with us. It is a matter of business necessity. We cannot let you succeed. And I have called you out to let you know, and to let your fellow laborers know, that we do not mean to allow you to succeed. We mean, sir," said he with increased emphasis—"we mean, sir, to put you abolitionists down—by fair means if we can, by foul means if we must."[37]

Thus, in a microcosm, the reason for the submissiveness of slaves and freedmen is found in the very core and fiber of our total society and involves the basic tenets of our culture. Of course, there were powerful economic motivations to destroy slavery and the slaveholders' power. They finally prevailed. However, the enculturative process that was actually developed and controlled in the Southern plantation community is responsible for the actions of masters and slaves alike. The personal and individual interactions that developed between these two groups have been ably described by Blassingame in his extensive discussion of the relationship between superordinate and subordinate individuals.

However, Hegel supplied other dimensions of this phenomenon in his discussion of the self in his chapter "Lordship and Bondage." Hegel believed that both bond servant and master develop an understanding of self through dynamic interaction with each other. Thus, both master and slave are governed by the give-and-take of the human and environmental situations in which they are involved. The master is enculturated into the plantation community to limit his ability to move beyond the prescribed sanctions of his master role. Consequently, when Blassingame discusses kind masters, he is, as they were, caught in a bind.[38] For a truly kind and humane person would of necessity emancipate his slaves and not be a master over anyone. Masters were proscripted from this action not only by state laws but by the enculturative process that created them, whether they aspired to be good, kind, and humane men or not. Their material needs and the threat of socio-political retaliation by other masters also tempered their acts of benevolent manumission. This is likewise true of Blassingame's statement that religion was one of the strongest forces operating against cruel treatment.[39] Frederick Douglass's experience was that some of the cruelest masters were also some of the most religious. In addition, the record demonstrates that Southern churches and some Northern churches sanctioned slavery. Similarly, religion does not appear to have had much effect on the elimination of racial prejudice in contemporary America. This evidence is in contradistinction to Blassingame's statement concerning religion.

When we understand this dynamic interaction between master and slave, we can see why some freedmen acted in the aforementioned fashion. We must realize that just because people are told that they are no longer slaves or masters does not immediately erase decades or centuries of extensive enculturation that prepared the entire society for such roles. These roles were determined by a schizophrenic and decadent society. There is some concern as to whether contemporary society is ready to accept the elimination of such roles. Although the old master-slave characters have faded into the background, they have been replaced by master-servant behavior patterns that are incompatible with current international trends toward the oneness and commonality of mankind. These trends are due to the emergence of third-world nations and their wars of liberation against colonialism and imperialism.

If the intellectual community is to be part of the vanguard of this humane and necessarily changing movement within American society, then it must begin by ceasing to compromise with the demands of the racist public or political and economic interest groups, who feel a necessity to influence what is taught to the masses. Historians must attempt to better "tell it like it was." At present, it is debatable as to whether we're writing history or supplying tract material for public consumption.

The challenge for black historians is to write bold new definitions of the way it was for whites as well as blacks in the America of yesterday. If not, the black historian will continue to react to

ephemeral theories on the nature and existence of blacks in yester-
year's America that have been dictated by the present climate of
opinion. An excellent example of this is Blassingame's *The Slave
Community*. For no sooner had his book been digested and accepted as the final nail in the coffin of Elkins's thesis than new controversies surfaced with the appearance of Robert W. Fogel and
Stanley L. Engerman's *Time on the Cross* (1974), Eugene D.
Genovese's *Roll, Jordan, Roll,* (1974), Ira Berlin's *Slaves Without
Masters* (1974), and Herbert G. Gutman's *The Black Family in
Slavery and Freedom* (1976).[40] It is not the controversies that are
unhealthy but the themes themselves. Taken as a whole, none of
these books have deviated from the Phillips model of separation of
the two racial communities. In each book, slaves are separated
from masters as though what happened to slaves and their actions
and reactions to slavery did not influence the rest of the society.

Concomitantly, these theses have sought to diminish the perceived corrosive and poisonous effects to race relations created by the
Stampp and Elkins books. It was deemed particularly important to
soften the stark image of the concentration camp that Elkins so
subtly superimposed over the plantation.[41] The obvious reason for
this new direction in slave historiography (besides as supplication
of the society's trend towards ''benign neglect'' of black people)
was stated by the eighteenth-century French philosopher Montesquieu, who demonstrated that slavery destroyed the humanity of
both slave and master and thus violated natural law.[42] Consequently, any interpretation of the peculiar institution has the ultimate effect of equally judging master and slave. It appears to be extremely
difficult for white Americans, both lay and professional, to come
to grips with what Montesquieu and Hegel wrote in the eighteenth
and nineteenth centuries, that is, that slavery brutalized both master and slave. This brutality cannot be singularly focused on one
group but must be studied for the debilitating results it exacted
from the total society.

Since black Americans are still brutalized, it is therefore inconse-
quential whether one recently arrived on an immigrant ship or
traces his/her heritage into the colonial era. The acculturative-
enculturative processes and the realities of present-day America
pass the guilt on to all white Americans.

We have written volumes of essays on the problems of blacks in
American society, avoiding their actual problem: the twisted, tor-
mented fear that whites are too apprehensive and insecure to face
the beast within themselves. They thus project their anxieties and
problems on those whom they oppress.[43] It is as though we had
written volumes on child abuse, focusing on the problems of the
child, while completely disregarding the actual cause of the child's
problem, which is the parent. Any study that does not examine the
problems of the parent and the factors that motivate the parent to
abuse the child is doing a disservice to both parent and child—the
real problem can never be solved. This is likewise true of slavery
and racism, of blacks and whites in American society, and consequently of slave historiography.

Happily, however, while this game continues, new positive
trends have appeared on the horizon with Peter H. Wood's *Black
Majority* (1974), Edmund S. Morgan's *American Slavery, American Freedom* (1976), and the black historian Earl E. Thorpe's *The
Old South; A Psycho-History* (1972), and his earlier work, *Eros
and Freedom in Southern Life and Thought* (1967). Each of these
books presents the problems of American society with a more inte-
grative intention in mind. Blacks are pictured as major elements in
the growth of the entire society, not as separate nonentities to be
considered only as social pariahs. Yet, one cannot overlook the reality of the existing situation and the need for black historians to
answer the deceptions and distortion that continue to develop in
historical writing concerning blacks. For this reason, Blassingame's
The Slave Community was not only badly needed but is an excellent
contribution and valuable model for young black historians and
future aspiring scholars of all races.

NOTES

1. Edward H. Carr, *What Is History?* (New York, 1962), 5.
2. R. G. Collingwood, *The Idea of History* (New York, 1966), 245.
3. Robert A. Skotheim, *The Historian and the Climate of Opinion*
(Reading, Mass., 1969), 4-5.

4. Edmund S. Morgan, *American Slavery, American Freedom: The Ordeal of Colonial Virginia* (New York, 1976), 316-315; Gwendolyn M. Hall, *Social Control in Slave Plantation Societies: A Comparison of St. Dominque and Cuba* (Baltimore, 1971), 136-151; Dante Puzzo, "Racism and the Western Tradition," *Journal of the History of Ideas* 25 (October-December 1964), 481-487.

5. Carter G. Woodson, *The Mis-Education of the Negro* (Washington, D. C., 1933), 129-130.

6. Peter Passell, "An Economic Analysis of the Peculiar Economic Institution," *The New York Times Book Review* (April 28, 1974); C. Vann Woodward, "The Jolly Institution," *New York Review of Books* (May 2, 1974), 3. Woodward stated that many of the findings of the controversial book *Time on the Cross* would serve as documentation of the pro-slavery argument and are the best defense of the peculiar institution since the days of George Fitzhugh.

7. Ulrich Bonnell Phillips, *American Negro Slavery* (New York, 1918), 1-5, 290-291; Richard Hofstadter, "U. B. Phillips and the Plantation Legend," *Journal of Negro History* 29 (April 1944), 109-124.

8. Winthrop D. Jordan, "Review Article of *Black Majority,*" *New York Times Book Review* (December 22, 1974), 12.

9. John W. Blassingame, *The Slave Community: Plantation Life in the Ante-Bellum South* (New York, 1972), viii.

10. Ibid., 10-17.

11. Ibid., 28.

12. Ibid., 17.

13. Ibid., 165-169; Peter H. Wood, *Black Majority: Negroes in Colonial South Carolina From 1670 Through the Stono Rebellion* (New York, 1974), 95-191; Roger Bastide, *African Civilizations in the New World* (New York, 1971), 70-87, 89-169; Melville J. Herskovits, *The Myth of the Negro Past* (Boston, 1941), 14, 292-299; James H. Johnston, *Race Relations in Virginia and Miscegenation in the South, 1776-1860* (Amherst, Mass., 1970); Edmund Morgan, *American Slavery, American Freedom* (New York, 1975), 333-336; Edward B. Reuter, *The Mulatto in the United States* (New York, 1918), 299-314.

14. Charles Gibson, *Spain in America* (New York, 1966), 130-131.

15. Richard S. Dunn, *Sugar and Slaves: The Rise of the Planter Class in the English West Indies, 1624-1713* (New York, 1972), 258; Winthrop Jordan, *White Over Black: American Attitudes Toward the Negro, 1550-1812* (Chapel Hill, 1968), chap. 1

16. Dunn, *Sugar and Slaves,* 285-286.

17. Blassingame, *Slave Community,* 57.

18. Ibid., 66.
19. Ibid., 63.
20. Ibid., 77-78.
21. Herbert Moller, "Sex Composition and Correlated Patterns of Colonial America," *William and Mary Quarterly* (April 1945), 136-139; C. R. Boxer, *Women in Iberian Expansion Overseas, 1415-1815* (New York, 1975) 35-62; Verena Martinez-Alier, *Marriage, Class and Colour in Nineteenth Century Cuba: A Study of Racial Attitudes and Sexual Values in a Slave Society* (London, 1974), 1-7, 11-19, 57-63, 120-139; Fernando Henriques, *Children of Conflict: A Study of Interracial Sex and Marriage* (New York, 1975) 7-115
22. Blassingame, *Slave Community*, 166-167.
23. Ibid., 82.
24. Ibid., 166.
25. Ibid., 140.
26. Ibid., 167; Julia C. Spruil, *Women's Life and Work in the Southern Colonies* (Chapel Hill, 1938; reprinted New York, 1975), 3-11, 39-56.
27. Arthur W. Calhoun, *A Social History of the American Family* (New York, 1960 reprint); Edward B. Reuter and J. R. Runner, *The Family* (New York, 1931); E. W. Burgess and H. J. Locke, *The Family* (New York, 1953, 2nd ed.), passim.
28. Blassingame, *Slave Community*, 82-89.
29. Ibid., 87.
30. Ibid., 88.
31. Ibid., 82.
32. Ibid., 85.
33. Ibid., 89-90.
34. Ibid., 114.
35. Henderson H. Donald, *The Negro Freedman: Life Conditions of the American Negro in the Early Years After Emancipation* (New York, 1952), 10.
36. Ibid., 8.
37. Samuel J. May, *Some Recollections of Our Antislavery Conflict* (Boston, 1869), 127-128, in William Loren Katz, *Eyewitness: The Negro in American History* (New York, 1968), 173; Philip Foner, *Business and Slavery: The New York Merchants and the Slavery Controversy* (New York, 1942), 3-7.
38. Blassingame, *Slave Community*, 165; G. W. F. Hegel, *The Phenomenology of Mind* (New York, 1967), 228-240.
39. Blassingame, *Slave Community*, 169.
40. L. D. Reddick, "Black History as a Corporate Colony", *Social*

Policy (May-June 1976), 4.

41. Thomas L. Haskell, "The True and Tragical History of *Time on the Cross,"* *The New York Review of Books* (October 2, 1975), 33.

42. F. T. H. Fletcher, "Montesquieu's Influence on Anti-Slavery Opinion in England," *Journal of Negro History* (October 1933), 414-416; David Brion Davis, *The Problem of Slavery in Western Culture* (Ithaca, 1966), 394-396.

43. Jordan, *White Over Black,* 578-582; Joel Kovel, *White Racism: A Psycho-History* (New York, 1970), 191-230.

STANLEY ENGERMAN

Reconsidering
The Slave Community

The past five years have seen a vast outpouring of work on all aspects of American Negro slavery, representing a quantity of publications on one subject within a limited time-span that has occurred for no other subject and at no other time in American history.* So extensive have been the sweeping revisions and reinterpretations of all aspects of the slave experience and their effects on blacks and whites, North and South, that it is often quite difficult to remember the basic interpretations of the slave system that existed in the preceding years, particularly in that decade and a half that was heavily influenced by the work and interpretations of Kenneth Stampp and the questions of Stanley Elkins. To attempt to describe a or one basic view of slavery that is held by a majority of historians is, of course, a major oversimplification and does an injustice both to practicing historians and, more particularly, to those scholars whose major contributions have shaped the views of that "peculiar institution." Yet there are important differences in shading of presentation. And there are subtle distinctions between attention paid to what was regarded as "typical" of a distribution

---

*This outpouring makes it difficult to look at any one work, such as Blassingame's, in isolation, since to discuss specific points in his work leads, either implicitly or expicitly, to comparisons and contrasts with the works of others. To expand on these points, however, would mean going beyond the specific purpose of this essay. I should like to acknowledge the helpful comments of Robert Fogel, Eugene Genovese, and Bertram Wyatt-Brown on an earlier draft.

of events and what were seen as crucial differences between that distribution and others. All scholars seem, at critical moments, to find usable and acceptable some basic generalization to apply to the past and thus put aside their comprehension of the richness and variety of responses that actually did occur. In no area of history has such a shift been more pronounced than in the study of slavery in the past several years. For, however consistent all the new writings may ultimately appear to be with the writings of Stampp, Elkins, and Phillips, it clearly seems that we now are looking at slavery quite differently than we were when this decade started.

For these reasons it is difficult to recapture fully the views of slavery held at the time Blassingame's book was first published and to understand the questions he was responding to and using to frame his analysis of what he called the slave community. To step back, and to try to regain some perspective, let us look at a review of *The Slave Community* that I published in the *Journal of Political Economy* in 1973. The review was written for an audience of economists and was originally part of a joint review with Alan Adamson's *Sugar Without Slaves* (New Haven, Conn., 1972). Adamson's book concerned the attempts of the British Guyanese planters to obtain a plantation labor-force after slave emancipation in 1838, and thus, in comparison with Blassingame's book, provided a counterpoint between the nature of slavery and of (post-slavery) freedom.

These two books raise several important questions concerning the role of institutions and their economic and social effects. Blassingame's reinterpretation of the cultural and personal development of the American slave on antebellum plantations serves as a corrective to those who might regard the plantation as comparable with a concentration camp or a jail. He points out that the plantation was an establishment in which the objectives of the owner included making money, and that the master's implicit negotiations with his chattel required some compromise and accommodation. To a great extent this implied restraints upon the owner's ability to interfere with many aspects of slave life, and Blassingame argues that the slave "gained a sense of worth in the quarters, spent most of his time free from surveillance by whites, controlled important aspects of his life, and did some personally meaningful things on his own volition." The slaves were not systematically starved or overworked, nor did they generally become passive and docile creatures lacking drive and responsibility. What constrained the master's power? One force was economic interest—the planter was "dependent on the slave's labor for his economic survival"; another was the infeasibility of very restrictive and close supervision at all times. Thus a major thrust of Blassingame's book, in regard to master-slave relationships, is that of a certain flexibility, mutual accommodation, and economic reasonableness, existing within the almost absolute power permitted the master by legislation. . . .

Blassingame, as well as a number of other scholars working on American slavery, has shown the constraints upon the master's power due to his desire to obtain output from the slave. . . .

Neither of these books is written by or for economists, and they make only limited use of economic analysis. Blassingame and Adamson are historians, and they utilize more traditional historical sources and methods. Blassingame's major sources were the autobiographies of former slaves written in the nineteenth century, though he also draws upon planter autobiographies and traveler reports. (Surprisingly he makes no mention of the more than 2,000 WPA interviews of former slaves recently published by Greenwood Press, Inc., in a nineteen-volume set edited by George Rawick.) Given the concern with the "personal autonomy" and culture of the slave, much of the book is devoted to the African heritage; to slave music, religion, and folklore; and to the discussion of the slave family and other personal relationships. It is a book written at a time of transition in the interpretation of slavery and black culture, and the author at times seems unsure of the direction in which he is pointing. Blassingame does effectively show the difficulties of the concentration-camp image and the Sambo myth, but too often the analysis is incomplete in its presentation of a different and more complex scene. . . . [Stanley Engerman in *Journal of Political Economy* 81 (November-December, 1973), pp. 1476-77.]

It is important, therefore, in rereading *The Slave Community* that these earlier views be remembered; otherwise it may seem too easy to be critical of his work and of his arguments as being somewhat incomplete and not as fully developed as some subsequent work in the area.

Whatever one might feel about the limitations of more recent works, Genovese's *Roll, Jordan, Roll* (New York, 1974) presented a richer discussion of the master-slave relationship and of slave life, and Gutman's narrower *The Black Family in Slavery and Freedom,*

1750-1925 (New York, 1976) more detail on the nature of the black family, and both drew upon a greater number of sources in describing slave society than did *The Slave Community*. Blassingame's major sources were the autobiographies of ex-slaves, and these account for most of his primary references, although there is some interesting use of traveler reports, agricultural journals, and other familiar secondary sources. The omission of the WPA narratives, despite the arguments that Blassingame subsequently presented in a journal article and in this collection of essays on p. 169, remains surprising, and in general a narrower range of sources were used than have been employed by, for example, Genovese and Gutman. On specific topics their works, as well as those of Rawick, Owens, and others, often provided us with more information and detail than did Blassingame, and indeed for many of the topics he covered there are now discussions available that are necessary complements to, supplements of, or replacements for his chapters. Given that his basic text is only 216 pages, this should not be surprising, nor should it be disturbing to Blassingame.

The basic problem for Blassingame, and for most writers on slavery in the 1960s, was how to deal with the interesting and powerful arguments of Stanley Elkins. In many ways, of course, all subsequent work on slavery has been heavily influenced by Elkins—the highest tribute to be accorded a scholar—even when most of it has shown that Elkins had tried to explain the wrong thing and thus had not provided an adequate answer to an important historical problem. While just about all post-Elkins works have indicated that the plantation did not resemble the concentration camp in most particulars and that Sambo was not the most typical resident on the plantation nor was his manner of behavior the dominant slave characteristic, the attempt to answer Elkins by delimiting the entire range of slave personalities has meant a complete shift in the focus of the study of slavery. Most importantly, Elkins emphasized the interaction of slave and master, although given his interpretation of that interaction, this might be more accurately described as the effect of master on slave. Whatever the limitations with their implications on the autonomy of the slave, it did recognize one fundamental aspect of the way the slave system operated:

Legally the masters had "absolute" control, or at least considerably more control over slave lives than they seemed to utilize, if
they wished to exercise it. Thus an extension of Elkins's argument
need not deny slave autonomy in certain areas, but, following his
logic, the ability for autonomy to exist tells us some very important
things about the masters. The challenge he presented to the next
generation of historians, especially those interested in describing
the full range of slave culture, was to provide a portrayal that yielded consistent patterns of behavior for masters and for slaves. While
the specific consistency of pattern Elkins suggested now seems
doubtful, he did indicate that to understand the behavior of
masters, one had to study the effects that slaves had upon them,
and that to understand the behavior of slaves one also had to study
their masters. The latter point does not, of course, mean that the
slaves merely responded to and had their behavior fully, or even
principally, formed by masters. It means, rather, that we must look
at the difference in what the masters had legal authority to do and
what they actually could do, and at how this discrepancy permitted
the slaves to make their own choices in certain important areas of
life. Further, it means that we must study how the nature of slavery
and the psychological and social impact resulting from this master-
slave relationship affected the manner in which such choices were
made and the specific form they took.

The issue of master-slave interaction remains one of the most difficult problems for historical analysis. While Elkins may be seen as
representative of one extreme position—that masters fully imposed
their wills upon slaves—and Gutman of another—that slave patterns of behavior were apparently little influenced by masters—it
would seem that the actual outcomes would represent more interaction between slave and master than either extreme would indicate. In certain areas the masters would permit "space" and thus
some slave autonomy to exist, a point demonstrated in Blassingame's discussion on the importance of African carryovers. To attempt to impose their wills upon slaves in all areas of life would not
only have been too expensive, and given human values, impossible,
but, for the Hegelians among us, ultimately self-defeating. At issue
is not whether any autonomy of slave personality and culture existed, nor whether slaves had any behavior patterns not shaped by

masters. Since the answers to these questions are now clear, the critical questions are the extent to which masters were forced to recognize their limits within a slave system, the full extent to which the slaves were able to draw upon their own independent, individual, and cultural resources and the actual outcomes resulting from these master-slave interactions. Thus, as Blassingame indicates, to argue that the legal system led to an unequal power relationship is not to accept Elkins's argument that everything the slaves did was completely shaped and molded by their masters.

In responding to Elkins, Blassingame has presented a basically plausible and consistent interpretation of this interrelationship of slave and master. He points to the diversity of slave personalities, suggests reasons why masters would allow "space" to the slave population, and discusses the various sources that would influence slave patterns of belief and behavior. He presents one basic statement of some determinants of this interaction of master and slaves and why the master's motives, which included obtaining output from his slave labor, and his inability to exercise complete and continuous control permitted "space," particularly to field hands. In this sense, therefore, Blassingame does explain those aspects of master behavior that permitted the "space" on the plantation to exist. He develops the theme that the master's economic survival imposed certain important constraints upon the master's behavior and notes in somewhat less than delicate phrasing that "the slave's life was worth considerably more than a bullet." (p. 193) Of course, he also comments that planters did not always live up to this standard and points out: "However kind his master, the slave had no guarantee of benevolent treatment," (p. 165) depending in part on the psychological state of the master. Blassingame notes several fundamental problems of master-slave contact and power relations (though without the broad philosophical view presented by Genovese), and he also provides a judicious summary statement regarding one set of issues: "Most masters were neither pitiless fiends nor saints in their relationships with slaves." (p. 165) And while Blassingame argues: "Within these limits, however, on many plantations abuse, constant floggings, cruelty, overwork, and short rations were part of the slave's daily life," (p. 193) he does point out the role of more positive incentives in producing the "slave's

industriousness.'' Nevertheless more still remains to be determined
about the mix of these various incentives as well as the markedly
different psychological impacts these could have upon the slaves.

At times, Blassingame seems to run together two different
themes—the "openness" in various areas that all but the most brutal (and ultimately financially suicidal) masters would allow and the
diversity of character in the many masters. Both, however, represent important points at which to begin a study of the slave system.
The first of these, as Blassingame argues, did not mean that if the
masters allowed space the slaves merely reflected white beliefs, and
he devotes much of one chapter to the question of African survivals, noting their possibility in several other areas of behavior.
Yet the role of African carryovers, however important they might
be for certain issues, is, of course, not the only way to argue for
some autonomy of individual slaves and in slave society and culture. Some modified forms of acculturation in earlier generations
need not mean that later generations do not choose their own patterns, even if these cannot finally be traced backward to Africa.
There are several suggestive discussions on the importance of the
different size of farms on the degree of black-white contact and of
the impact of different occupations (for example, house vs. field,
the slave driver) upon this contact as well as on patterns of behavior, all of which remain to be pursued. There were obvious differences in size of farms and black-white contact between the
American South and the West Indies, as well as over time within
the South, which point to questions about the extent to which patterns of behavior varied both over time and over place. Similarly,
the importance of analyzing the impact of different masters upon
slave behavior is amply demonstrated by any reading in the autobiographies and slave narratives, and represents, it would seem, only
the statement that many aspects of behavior are affected by the
day-to-day conditions of life that people find themselves in.

Thus, while the occasional contradictions Blassingame presents
only pages apart are disconcerting, they perhaps can be justified as
indicating the variety of patterns to be found among millions of enslaved and thousands of masters. He makes the strong point that
tidy generalizations and attempts to depict uniformities may not be
possible. Nevertheless, Blassingame's failure to place several of

these variations and apparent contradictions in a fuller context means that a number of opportunities to more fully develop this theme—for example, the importance of the fact that there were many masters—are ignored.

There are, of course, some points on which the treatment of slave personality could have gone further. The showing of a wide variety of slave personalities is useful, and, in retrospect, not at all surprising, but too little is said about one of the central concerns of the southern master in regard to his slaves, a point of some psychological subtlety. This was the extent to which the same slave might contain several of these so-called different personalities, with the specific patterns of behavior being dependent upon both the inner psychological forces of the slave as well as the specifics of external circumstances that might exist at any one time. Blassingame's attempt to show diversity on this subject is successful but leads to a certain lack of richness in presentation. Similarly, as with many post-Elkins writers, there is often so much emphasis on demonstrating the relative absence of Sambo, or at least the relative infrequency of an internalized deferential attitude among most slaves, that little is said about the complete impact of enslavement upon the slave personality and the extent to which slavery imposed psychological costs. For example, as a response to Elkins, the following statement seems highly doubtful:

Most slaves lived on such large plantations, had such little contact with their masters and overseers, or went through the ritual of deference so infrequently, that no master made an important impression on their personalities. (p. 214)

Perhaps the problem here reflects several distinctions made elsewhere and should not be read out of a fuller context. Blassingame does provide a useful correction in noting that, contrary to some earlier writers, submission need not mean "infantile dependency" and "abject docility," a point that he presents as following from the many obvious distinctions between the concentration camp and the plantation (and presumably the less than plantation-sized units on which many slaves lived). However, there is some lack of clarity on the full meaning of submissiveness, since Blassingame seems at times to suggest that it was all ritual with no internalization, and thus, he argues, would have been of limited importance to the overall personality development of the slave. Granted that Sambo may have been overdone and that, as Blassingame shows, there were "rebels and runaways" and also that the responses of slaves would vary with the size of units, the frequency of contracts with whites, and the attitudes of whites. But the statement seems to overlook one of the questions raised by Elkins: What were the costs of slavery to the slaves and to the development of black culture? To argue that the effects of slavery upon black culture were not as dramatic as Elkins had first agrued is not to say that they were nonexistent or that slavery had only a minimal impact on the enslaved. The issues that remain are how extensive were these impacts of slavery, the distribution of experiences and responses under slavery, and what these meant for the distribution of behavioral patterns after emancipation.

Nevertheless, this basic framework for studying master-slave interaction remains useful and relevant today. Blassingame's work is perhaps best put in context by comparing it with subsequent workers in the field. Whatever specific difficulties arise, it remains that he was one of the first of the "revisionists" to present in book form a consistent, coherent framework for understanding the patterns of behavior of masters and slaves.

As already noted, Blassingame's principal sources were the autobiographies of ex-slaves, although a large gamut of primary and secondary sources were also drawn upon. These autobiographies had, of course, been used before, most extensively in Charles Nichols's *Many Thousand Gone* (Leiden, E. J. Brill, 1963) as well as in several unpublished dissertations. However, Blassingame's concentration on their use in answering the set of questions posed by Elkins provides a systematic framework for their examination. In the preface he argues convincingly for the use of these sources to study the "personality development of slaves" and indicates what was generally correct at the time of writing, that many historians had not fully utilized these sources (although his "deliberately ignored" has a rather invidious tone). Yet many interesting historiographic issues are swept aside by his linking together of what he calls the planter "good press" and the view of the plantation as an "all-powerful, monolithic institution," with the Sambo stereotype the inevitable outcome. The causes of this stereotype and of this view of the plantation are more complex. That Blassingame was able to imaginatively use southern agricultural journals to understand how planters regarded slaves when they discussed personnel problems in production indicates that such stereotypes were not usually instrumental in their daily business decisions.

More importantly, to attribute the view of the plantation as an all-powerful institution to the planter's "good press" overlooks the acceptance of this image that had been central for most antislavery critics. It is also useful to note that in earlier debates the anti-slavery critics often accepted the Sambo image while rejecting its racial implications and argued in Elkins-like writings that this was the necessary result of slavery. One of the more recent themes in the post-Elkins debate has been not whether Sambo existed but rather whether Sambo fit his stereotype or whether he was mainly feigning an attitude for white consumption. Thus while it is true that some historical views of the plantation as ongoing institutions were distorted, as Blassingame argues, the interesting point is that it came from a different strand than that which provided the planter a "good press." Indeed the Elkins-like description of the plantation as a total institution is one that the leading historical writers, such as U. B. Phillips, often took to be presenting the planter-class views, would find difficult to accept. Yet this issue does pose the fundamental dilemma for those writing on slavery, today as well as in the past.

If one does accept, on one hand, the monolithic image of the planter and his power, and clearly this does reflect the actual legal and official political-power relationship, then many of the recent discussions of slave culture, family, etc. might seem awkward to deal with. For if this monolithic power was not exercised, and the slaves were permitted some autonomy in family and sexual mores, in work rhythms, etc., we must again ask what this is telling us about the masters and their behavior. There is an awkward implication that the more sanguine the assessment of slave culture, and the greater the cultural achievements of slaves under slavery, the more "reasonable" the masters may seem to look. This is, of-course, an unnecessary dilemma for a moral judgment of slavery, since we all know slavery was an evil system. Nevertheless the issues posed by a felt need for moral judgment on all aspects of slave life do raise fundamental questions concerning the description and analysis of day-to-day arrangements and living conditions and the examination of southern society. To his credit, Blassingame does not avoid these questions of trying to understand what life under an immoral system meant. In part, this reflects his use of the ex-slave autobiographies, since these often provide rather subtle descriptions of the complexities of slave life and the details of what it actually meant to a slave.

Blassingame defends his use of these autobiographies in a "critical essay," which presents a reasonable case, although it seems overly optimistic on several counts. Nevertheless, to the extent that he draws upon them mainly to describe some of the aspects of slave life, their use is generally quite acceptable. He is aware of some of the difficulties in accepting everything at face value, but that is only one of the problems involved in an analysis of slavery based upon these sources. There remains the customary historian's problem of generalizing from sources, some questionable, and in this Blassingame is perhaps less sensitive both to problems of the existence of biases and to the possible uses of data biased from some view than might be anticipated. In several places he does note a pattern in the background of the writers of these autobiographies, or at least the slave with whom the volume was concerned (he does, of course, discuss the issue of who did the actual writing and what problems of unreliability this might result in), but in general the text presentation does not fully deal with the difficulties this gives rise to. On page 112, for example, he gives a residential breakdown of eighteen fugitive autobiographers (seven urban, eleven from plantations) and an occupational breakdown for an uncertain number of them. In the latter it seems clear that house servants and craftsmen were over-presented compared to field hands, while the former indicates a disproportionate number of urban slaves. Further, one would anticipate an overrepresentation of slaves from the Upper South. Later, on page 235, he summarizes the background of seventy-six black autobiographies—twenty of them by slaves who were manumitted or purchased their freedom and twenty-six by fugitive slaves (and thus presumably thirty by slaves freed by the

Civil War and emancipation). This again suggests the rather atypical nature of this sample for which such observations are available relative to the overall slave population. To the extent these autobiographies are reliable, they can provide an accurate portrayal of the specific population sampled, and since they are not used for quantitative purposes, these biases might not be a cause of deep concern; yet such a basic discrepancy between sample and population could distort the overall view of the slave system.

Further, the differences between ex-slaves in size of farms lived on, location, skill, and means of obtaining freedom are not fully exploited in the text in a manner that might be expected, given a listing of the conditions making for diverse slave personalities. An important opportunity to explore differences in experience is suggested on page 190 but then not pursued. Blassingame notes that eight writers of autobiographies had one master, two had eight, and one, fourteen. This would seem to suggest a detailed examination of the differences that arose due to the variations in the pattern of sales, but the author rather disappointingly notes that: "As a consequence of having an average of three masters, the slaves were extremely conscious of the differences in human character and contended that there was great variety among slaveholders." (pp. 190-91). Thus not only has Blassingame confounded the issue, since by his count the "modal" slave had only one master, but he has not explored the differences in behavior between slaves who had been sold frequently and those who, during their slave experience, had not been sold once.

The use of quantitative methods is clearly not of central concern to Blassingame, although two short tables are presented. One is from Marion Russell's 1946 *Journal of Negro History* article describing "slave discontent" as seen in "Records of the High Courts." This shows 1,094 cases of runaway, violence, and discontent and insubordination in 226 years. An average of less than five per year indicates something, but hardly that "the slave's desire for freedom was eventually translated into action," (p. 108) or at least not for the greater majority of them. The other table, drawn from the Freedmen's Bureau marriage certificates, provides totals that remain mysteriously different from the totals and breakdowns of the same data presented by Gutman and by Ripley. Nevertheless Blassingame's conclusion that "in spite of their callous attitudes, masters did not separate a majority of the slave couples," (p. 92) seems correct, even if his estimates of the number of marriages broken by masters seems too high.

But more important than the specifics of the particular tables presented is the extent to which, after reading Blassingame and other writers on slavery, many of the problems always discussed are, in a sense, basically quantitative issues. As in all studies there is frequent use of the words "many," "most," "often," and related phrases to describe patterns, where, if it were possible, one would like to obtain a better order of magnitude. It is not that counting can provide a full answer to the questions, but at least it could help give the reader some appreciation of the relative frequency of particular patterns of behavior and thus provide the basis for a better understanding of human behavior. For example, we should like to know much more about the frequencies of different forms of household and family organization, of the probabilities of sale and of family separation, of the numbers of believers in different forms of religions, of the magnitudes of different forms of punishments, and of the frequencies of many other things before we can be comfortable with the understanding we derive from that sample of information that survives.

All students of slavery face a basic quantitative question, suggested in this case by Blassingame's description of what he calls the three major slave characters—Sambo, Jack, and Nat. While it obviously will be impossible to try to estimate the relative numbers in each category, clearly the importance and usefulness of such a count seems implicit in the presentation. Blassingame himself, after describing the wide range of behavior he believes to have existed, does conclude (on page 216) by describing "the typical slave," but without providing any feeling for either the quantitative magnitude or the relevant distribution. More directly, one can describe many of the past debates on slavery as the outcome of some implicit quantification, and Blassingame's work is no exception.

The problem is that the wide range of observations makes any attempt to generalize, or to describe certain of them as typical, rather complex. Such a problem is true of many other historical issues, and the question here is not whether a quantitative approach is different from other approaches, but whether in trying to understand what happened to large groups in the past we can get information on the frequency of various nonquantitative attributes. This difficulty is more acute in the debate on slavery since often the specific points at issue are not fully clear. Not only is it difficult to establish what is typical and what unique, but in the past it has often been that attention has been placed upon what was thought unique to the slave system and unusual in the world at that time (questions often of particular importance to the condemnation of the system), rather than what had been most typical and thus experienced by most individuals who lived under the system. It is, in large measure, in this shift of question that Blassingame's book came at a transitional stage in the study of slavery. Most debates in interpreting slavery have not been upon what did or did not happen, but rather, given that certain events occurred, how frequent these were, which happened most often, and how they affected the slaves and their masters.

It is in the failure to accept the fundamental difference between these two questions—what could happen and what did happen most frequently—that much controversy in studying slavery has always existed and still remains. While frequency of occurrence may be only an imperfect guide to understanding impact upon individuals, it is an obvious starting point. And, since for enough of the possible happenings under slavery, threat or infrequent occurrence would be sufficient for any moral condemnation, the distinction between these two questions need not detract from the moral issue. On these points, which are quantitative in spirit, Blassingame does rather well. He recognizes the diversity of experience, attempts to provide an understanding of how such variation arose, and attempts to place these variations in some perspective.

In looking at Blassingame's work as transitional we can better see the questions that should be most prominent in writings on slavery over the next decade. There has already been a shift away from a rather mechanical discussion of the physical treatment of the slaves that has been used as a basis for making moral judgments about the masters. More attention is being given to the reactions of the slaves within the conditions arising out of enslavement, and we have become much more sensitive to the psychological costs of slavery and are in the process of studying such costs without resorting to the extremes posed by Elkins, Aptheker, or Phillips. While some critics have argued that the first presentations from this perspective have led to an overly sanguine view of slave culture and slave personality, they do provide a more realistic starting point for the study of the psychology of the slave (and of the master) than do earlier views. Once we accept that not all slaves were Sambos and not all slaves were rebels and that the worldview of the enslaved and their expectations were not necessarily the same as those who were raised in freedom, we should be able to more fully probe the tragedy of slavery and its aftermath.

The Slave Community remains an important reexamination of the impact of slavery on the enslaved and helps to explain both why "space" was permitted the slaves and what they did with it. If five years later reservations remain about some answers, the questions and the framework will still remain of central concern to scholars, and the problems Blassingame grappled with will still confound the study of slavery today, and, no doubt, will continue to do so in the future.

JOHN HENRIK CLARKE

The Slave Community and the World Community: Some Notes Toward a New Inquiry into the Historiography of the Atlantic Slave Trade

The writing of African history—the history of slavery in particular—is a flourishing industry for the white academic community. In most of their new books on slavery and the slave trade, the trend is toward transfering the guilt for the slave trade from the beneficiaries of slavery to the victims. Because John W. Blassingame's *The Slave Community* goes against this trend, it is to some extent a pioneering work. His work was published seventy-four years after W.E.B. Du Bois's classic study *The Suppression of the Slave Trade in the United States.*[1] In the intervening years between the publication of these two books—nearly three quarters of a century—no extensive study of slavery by a black writer appeared in print. Did black writers abdicate their role in this field to white writers? The answer is no. Proposals and outlines for books on the subject of slavery were not seriously considered by white publishers. Black writers continued to write monographs, conference papers, masters theses, and Ph.D. dissertations on the subject to a limited audience.

In March 1976, Oxford University Press published Professor Leslie Howard Owens's book, *This Species of Property: Slave Life and Culture of the Old South.*[2] Dr. Owens is an associate professor at the University of Michigan, Ann Arbor. In his book he used some of the same slave narrative material that John W. Blassingame drew on so heavily with good insight and creativity for his book, *The Slave Community.*

Slavery in Africa, especially the Atlantic slave trade that started in the fifteenth and sixteenth centuries, is the most written about and the least understood of all the events in African history. There is a need to understand what happened in Africa "before this agony." There is also a need to understand the interplay of events and powerful forces in the world that set the slave trade in motion.

The Europeans have always been geniuses in their ability to channel the diseased pus of their political sores to the soil of other peoples and nations. Had there been no market for the slaves, there would have been no slave trade. The market was created by the opening up of the so-called New World and the plantation system that followed. The insensitive and systematic destruction of the Indians coupled with their retreat to the frontier made the early European explorers search for another labor supply. They turned their attention to West Africa at a time when these nations were least able to defend themselves.

This is part of the background and the missing preface to John W. Blassingame's *The Slave Community*. In examining his book, there is a need to look both at Africa and at Europe on the eve of the slave trade.

A crisis in the African family of nations began to develop early in the fifteenth century. Like most tragedies, it began slowly, almost accidentally. The European awakening that had started with the Crusades was by this time a movement to explore and exploit large areas of the world outside of Europe. For the great states in West Africa this was a time of tragedy and decline. Europe's era of exploration and internal strife in Africa was a contributing factor to the development of the philosophy of mercantilism that would dominate political and economic thought for the next three hundred years.

The story of the African slave trade is essentially the story of the consequences of the second rise of Europe. In the years between the passing of the Roman Empire in the eighth century and the partial unification of Europe through the framework of the Catholic Church in the fifteenth century, Europeans were engaged mainly in internal matters. With the opening of the New World and the expulsion of the Moors from Spain during the latter part of the fifteenth century, the Europeans proceeded to expand beyond their homeland into the broader world. They were searching for new markets, new materials, new manpower, and new land to exploit. The African slave trade was created to accommodate this expansion.

The slave trade prospered, and Africans continued to be poured into the New World. Figures on the subject vary, but it can be conservatively estimated that during the years of the African slave trade, Africa lost from 60 to 100 million people. *This was the greatest single crime ever committed against a people in world history.* It was also the most tragic act of protracted genocide.

The great destroyer of African culture and the greatest exploiter of the African was the plantation system of the New World. The African was transformed into something called a "Negro." He was demeaned. This is what is uniquely tragic about the African slave system. Of all the slave systems in the world, no other dehumanized the slave more than that initiated by the Europeans in the fifteenth century. Using the church as a rationale, they began to set up myths that nearly always omitted the African from human history, starting with the classification of the African as a lesser being. The Catholic Church's justification for slavery was that the African was being brought under the guidance of Christianity and that he would eventually receive its blessings.

In the English colonies that became the United States, slaves were bought in small lots and often resold within weeks after purchase. This cruel custom broke up the African families and shattered their cultural continuity without completely destroying it.

The Afro-American connection with Africa is not new. In fact, this connection was never completely broken. "African consciousness," in varying degrees, whether good or bad, has always been a part of the psyche of the African people in forced exile in South America, the Caribbean islands, and the United States. There has always been a conflict within the black American's Africa consciousness. This conflict was created early and extended beyond the limitations created by the mass media of the twentieth century; jungle movies, elementary textbooks on geography and history, travel books written to glorify all people of European extraction; in essence—white people. These distorted images have created both a

rejection of Africa and a deep longing for the Africa of our imagination that was our home and the first home of what man has
referred to as "a civilization."[3]

In *Black Nationalism: A Search for an Identity in America*, Professor E. U. Essien-Udom wrote: "The tragedy of the Negro in
America is that he has rejected his origins—the essentially human
meaning implicit in the heritage of slavery, prolonged suffering,
and social rejection. By rejecting this unique group experience and
favoring assimilation and even biological amalgamation, he thus
denies himself the creative possiblities inherent in it and in his folk
culture. This 'dilemma' is fundamental; it severely limits his ability
to evolve a new identity or a meaningful synthesis, capable of en-
dowing his life with meaning and purpose."[4]

This most revealing statement is only true in parts. In specific
cases the charge is true. Generally, the charge is neither true nor
fair. There is more diversity in the lives of black Americans than
among other Africans in exile. The cruel nature of our experience
and survival has dictated this. What Professor Essien-Udom has
noted is basically true about some aspects of Afro-American life.
Contrary to what he said, most of the literate Africans in exile have
always had a positive view about Africa. They have rejected the image of Africa as a backward and barbarous land. To the extent that
the information was available, the early black writers and thinkers
made every attempt to locate Africa on the map of human
geography.

They soon discovered that Africa and her people had a history
older than the history of their oppressors. They also learned how
and why the Europeans came to Africa in the first place and the circumstances in Africa and Europe that set the slave trade in motion.
They learned why the "christian" church had to read the Africans
out of the respectful commentary of human history. While the
pretense was that Africans were being civilized and christianized,
this was really the beginning of what Walter Rodney has called
"The Under-development of Africa." In his book on this subject,
Professor Rodney analyzes the first European impressions of the
people and cultures from the west coast of Africa: "Several historians of Africa," he pointed out, "after surveying the developed
areas of the continent in the 15th century, and those within Europe

at the same time, find the difference between the two in no way to Africa's discredit.''[5]

He quoted a Dutch account of the city of Benin in West Africa to prove that, at first, the Europeans compared African cities and cultures favorably to their own.

The town seems to be very great. When you enter into it, you go into a great broad street, not paved, which seems to be seven or eight times broad-er than the Warmoes Street in Amsterdam. . . .

The King's palace is a collection of buildings which occupy as much space as the two of Harlem, and which is enclosed with walls. There are numerous apartments for the Prince's ministers and fine galleries, most of which are as big as those of the Exchange at Amsterdam. They are sup-ported by wooden pillars encased with copper, where their victories are depicted, and which are carefully kept very clean.

The Town is composed of 30 main streets, very straight and two hundred and twenty feet wide, apart from an infinity of small intersecting streets. The houses are close to one another, arranged in good order. These people are in no way inferior to the Dutch as regards cleanliness; they wash and scrub their houses so well that they are polished and shining like a looking glass.[6]

Professor Rodney further documented how a highly developed Africa became underdeveloped and how the Europeans changed the image of Africa in order to justify the slave trade that followed. He called attention to the economic, religious, social, and political strucures in Africa as the Europeans found them and showed that these purely African institutions began to decline with the increase of the European presence and the spread of the slave trade.

Contrary to the massive European propaganda-literature on this subject, Europeans brought nothing constructive to the countries of Africa. They played one nation off another to gain slaves and brought chaos to the African political and economic structures. The Africans' image of themselves began to decline. Africa was made into a market for cheap European goods, much of which was inferior to crafts previously produced in Africa. This was especially true of the cloth made in Manchester, England, that was sold almost exclusively in Africa. The Africans' skill in manufacturing and marketing their own goods declined. Some African heads of state requested aid in the fields of technology and medicine, in which the Europeans were more advanced at the time. These requests were refused, for fear the Africans might develop to a position where they could commercially compete with the Europeans. And thus began the scheme of African underdevelopment that continues to this very day. The commercial underdevelopment helped to accommodate other distortions such as the image of Africans as people without a history and a culture.

When the people of Europe reemerged on the world scene in the fifteenth and sixteenth centuries, they started the Atlantic slave trade and systematically began to colonize most of the world. They reversed the trend of history in order to give the impression that the world waited in darkness for Europeans to bring the light. Quite the contrary, the Europeans destroyed more civilizations than they built. Many of these civilizations were already old when Europe was born. Academically, European "scholars" and others of European extraction began to dominate the interpretation of history, especially the history of slavery and colonialism. This is why books on slavery by white writers such as[7]: *The Atlantic Slave Trade: A Census,* by Philip D. Curtin;[8] *The Political Economy of Slavery*[9] and *Roll, Jordan, Roll,*[10] both by Eugene D. Genovese; and *Time on the Cross,* by Robert Fogel and Stanley L. Engerman[11] were critically acclaimed while the same critics, in most cases, neglected John W. Blassingame's book, *The Slave Community.*

This colonialization of information about history and its interpretation continues into the present. A case in point: Near the end of May 1976, the New York Academy of Sciences convened a unique conference on slavery, "Comparative Perspectives on Slavery in New World Plantation Societies." It was called a bicentennial conference, and it was supported by grants from the Ford Foundation, National Science Foundation, The Research Institute for the Study of Man, and The Wenner-Gren Foundation. Most of the participants were white. There were no African or Afro-American participants; the big question: *why*? About five Caribbean "scholars" attended who either read papers or were discussants. They were tokens, and only two of them, Edward Braithwaite of the University of the West Indies, Kingston, Jamaica, and Dr. Oruno D. Lara of the Caribbean Institute of Historical Research, Guadeloupe-Antilles, seemed to have realized this. One of the black participants, Franklin W. Knight of John Hopkins University, defended the composition of the conference and rationalized the exclusion of African and Afro-Americans.

In April 1975 another conference on this subject was held at Queens College in Flushing, New York. The participants were mostly black because most of the white scholars who were invited refused the invitation. The following is a summary of my opening remarks:

It is no accident that we have gathered here this evening to begin a dialogue on an old subject and an old institution with new dimensions. Figuratively, we stand at the crossroads of history, watching the changing of the guards in front of the palace of power. The tenants in the palace are ill at ease. There is a revolt in the servants' quarters. This revolt will change the world and also change the tenants in the palace of power.

The new tenants, from the servants' quarters, will take on new names and demand a new interpretation of their lives. They will no longer answer to the name "slave." They will ask how and why did the slave trade come about, and they will find the answers.

Out of these answers a new interpretation of slavery in the slave trade will emerge. This interpretation, coming from the victims of slavery, will ultimately prevail.

We have gathered here to begin an examination of a rash of new books on the subject of slavery. Our examination will go far beyond the books being examined and questioned. This is an academic battlefield, and the stakes are high. There have been a number of good and bad books published on slavery in the last ten years. The bad books seem to get the most attention. Why was no conference called to examine John W. Blassingame's good and useful book on the subject, *The Slave Community* (1972)? This book, in my opinion, is the best new interpretation of slavery in the United States. It is all the more important because its author is a young and able black historian who will go far beyond this impressive beginning.

Before the publication of Professor Blassingame's book, all we had of recent insight into the subject was what the Nigerian historian, Dr. Okon E. Uya, called "The Culture of Slavery: Black Experience Through a White Filter" *(Black Lines Magazine*, Winter 1970). Mainly, that is what we still have, and that may be what this conference is really about.[12]

In his article, Professor Uya wrote:

A common feature of many studies dealing with slavery has been the attempt to capture the Black experience through analysis of the white experience. This methodology assumes that the general limits of fhe Black slave's experience are rather clearly defined by certain impulses and institutional mechanisms and that the scholar, by being able to identify the impulses and institutional mechanisms operative at a given time, can deduce their consequences for the lifestyle and culture of the Black community. The general assumption here is that the Black experience can be understood by analysis of white-oriented external determinants of which the black is deemed a function. An examination of some of the most important works on slavery reveals the limitations of this posture.[13]

There is a need to broaden our approach to the subject of the European slave trade and to view it and its aftermath as an event in history that affected most of mankind. In "The Destiny of the Negro in the Western Hemisphere" (1947), the scholar Frank Tannenbaum wrote

The settling of the western hemisphere by people coming from Europe and Africa was an adventure on a grand scale, involving diverse people, varying cultures, millions of human beings, and hundreds of years. The common element was the New World. Its physical features and cultural types were strangely dissimilar, but the student discerns many an analogous design patterned by the newcomers as they established themselves in the strange and unexplored regions.[14]

Writing further on this subject, Dr. Okon E. Uya has noted: "No period of the Black experience in the United States has received greater scholarly attention than the two and a half centuries during which most Afro-Americans were slaves. . . .Despite the profuseness of the literature on slavery, however, we still know very little about the lifestyles of the Black slave."[15]

This is why *The Slave Community* by John Blassingame is so important at this juncture in the debate over how the slaves lived and how they reacted to their servitude. In his inquiry, Blassingame ventured inside the slave quarters for first-hand knowledge of the slave's family life, music, religion, and folklore through his use of the slave narratives. He showed how the slave was able to control parts of his own life while wearing whatever masks needed to face the harsh realities of plantation life.

There is more dishonesty related to the interpretation of this subject than any other subject known to man. If we concentrate only on the issue of slavery and the new books about this subject, our time will be poorly spent.

If we are to talk honestly about slavery, we will have to enter into its broader aspects—the crisis in western historiography. This will lead us to an examination of still another area of history—the consequences of the second rise of Europe in the fifteenth and sixteenth centuries.

In spite of the many years of trying to be Americans and of literally begging white America to accept us as such, we may still be more African than anything else. My distinguished colleague, Lerone Bennett, has observed in his book, *The Challenge of Blackness*:

> . . . if Black people are not what white people said they were, then white America is not what it claims to be. What we have to deal with here therefore is a contestation at the level of reality. We are engaged in a struggle over meaning, in a struggle over the truth. And it is my argument here that Blacks and not whites embody the common interest and the truth of American society.[16]

What Bennett has said about American society may well be true, at least in part, of human societies in general. Slavery, the slave trade, and its after-effects will never be honestly defined by the people who are beneficiaries of this cruel system. They will, of course, with their great research facilities have many interesting things to say; but the final word about this system will rest with the victims.

This is where Blassingame's book starts, and this is the essence of its true value. To the extent that information is available, he tells the story of "The Slave Community" through the lives of the slaves. Here again, there is a need to extend his preface and deal with the interplay of events and powerful forces that established the slave community in the English colony that became the United States.

In another book on this subject, *The Shaping of Black America* the social historian, Lerone Bennett, Jr., has called attention to the need to deal at length with the forgotten pages of white and Indian history in order to deal more correctly with black history. He reminds us that the Dutch ship that landed at Jamestown, Virginia, in 1619 changed what was to become the United States in a way that, henceforth, would never again be the same. The seeds of the only original culture that America can show to the world arrived on this Dutch ship, together with a conflict that after more than three hundred years is still unresolved. Lerone Bennett refers to this cargo as "Black Gold" that made capitalism in America."[17] In this reference he is completely on the case. This cargo of "Black Gold," and other cargoes that were to follow, made many other things possible. Nationally, it gave America the means to become a world power. Internationally, it created the basis for the industrisl revolution and the modern world of science and technology.

The drama that is known as the African slave trade had been acting itself out for more than one hundred years when the colony of Virginia was founded in 1607. The Africans who arrived in 1619 were not chattel slaves. They were indentured servants. This is a major point that is often missed. After their period of indenture, this first generation of blacks became early Americans in many ways. Some of them became the owners of land and slaves. Others became part of the craft and technology class that helped to tame a young and raw America. Labor was needed, and this is what these first Blacks meant to the colonies.

The indentured servant system was not created for the blacks who landed in Jamestown, Virginia, in 1619. The system was intact long before they arrived. There were a large number of white indentured servants already in the system. The legal status of the early black forced immigrants was higher than the first white indentured servants. Of course, this status did not last very long.

For the first one hundred years during the period of European exploration into the broader world, Europe as well as Africa was the hunting ground for slaves. Sometime during the second century of the settlement of America, the white slaves began to shake off their bondage. They rapidly became racists in order to identify themselves with the rest of white America. They measured their identification and their status as furtherest from the red man and black man in appearance and in human consideration. It was only then that the color factor became prevalent in black and white relationships.

It is only against this background that there can be a full and meaningful appreciation of John W. Blassingame's book, *The Slave Community*.

NOTES

1. *The Suppression of the Slave Trade in the United States*, by W. E. B. Du Bois. Russell and Russell, Inc., New York, 1965. This is the first book in the Harvard Historical Series written by W.E.B Du Bois in the closing years of the nineteenth century. Dr. Du Bois's treatment of the subject is still relevant and is a better example of good scholarship than most of its previous books on the subject of slavery in the Americas and in the Caribbean islands.

2. *This Species of Property: Slave Life and Culture in the Old South*, by Leslie Howard Owens. Oxford University Press, New York, 1976.

3. "The Afro-American Image of Africa," by John Henrik Clarke, in *Black World Magazine*, Chicago, Ill., February 1974, pp. 4-21.

4. *Black Nationalism: A Search for an Identity in America*, by E.U. Essien-Udom. Laurel Edition: Dell Publishing Co., New York, 1964, p. 9. *See also Early Negro Writing 1760-1837*, by Dorothy Porter. Beacon Press, Boston, Mass., 1971, pp. 1-86.

5. *How Europe Underdeveloped Africa*, by Walter Rodney. Howard University Press, Washington, D.C., 1974, p. 69.

6. Ibid, p. 69.

7. "The African Roots of War (1915)," by W.E.B. Du Bois, in *W.E.B. Du Bois A Reader*, edited by Meyer Weinberg. Harper and Row, New York, 1970, pp. 360-371.

8. *The Atlantic Slave Trade: A Census*, by Philip D. Curtin. The University of Wisconsin Press, Madison, Wisconsin, 1969.

9. *The Political Economy of Slavery*, by Eugene D. Genovese. Pantheon Books, New York, 1965.

10. *Roll, Jordan, Roll, The World the Slaves Made*, by Eugene D. Genovese. Vantage Books, New York, 1976.

11. *Time on the Cross*, Vols. 1 and 2, by Robert Fogel and Stanley L. Engerman. Little, Brown and Co., Boston, Mass., 1974.

12. Queens College Conference on "The Slavery Debate: What Does It Mean?" April 11-12, 1975. Convener: John Henrik Clarke.

13. "The Culture of Slavery: Black Experience Through a White Filter," by Okon E. Uya, in *Black Lines Magazine*, Winter 1970, p. 27.

14. *The Destiny of the Negro in the Western Hemisphere,* by Frank Tannenbaum. *The Political Science Quarterly,* New York, March 1946, p. 1.

15. "The Culture of Slavery: Black Experience Through a White Filter," by Okon E. Uya, p. 27.

16. *The Challenge of Blackness,* by Lerone Bennett, Jr. Johnson Publishing Co., Inc., Chicago, Ill., 1972, p. 1.

17. *The Shaping of Black America*, by Lerone Bennett, Jr. Johnson Publishing Co., Inc., Chicago, Ill., 1975, p. 5. *See* Preface and Chapters 1 and 2: "The First Generation" and "White Servitude," pp. 5-60.

JAMES D. ANDERSON

Political and Scholarly Interests in the "Negro Personality": A Review of *The Slave Community*

A significant change in historical interpretation of American slavery has taken place in the last decade. A new body of historiography has emerged, and it appears formidable enough to shatter the traditional story of black slavery. According to the traditional story, the shock of initial capture, the blunting of slaves' emotions and feelings during the Middle Passage, the annihilation of their African heritage, and the forced adjustments to American plantation routines all conspired to make Afro-Americans largely a society of helpless dependents. Hence, slavery emasculated the blacks, made them shiftless, irresponsible, and promiscuous, prevented the development of strong family ties, and stripped them of any sense of self-esteem. As late as the mid-1960s, historians and social scientists believed that the Sambo portrait—blacks were submissive, indolent, faithful, superstitious, improvident, and musical—was a sound description of the dominant black personality. Within the last few years, however, scholars have restudied American slavery and subjected old interpretations to critical scrutiny. The new scholarship has already succeeded in demolishing the most cherished pillars of the traditional story. This new literature, which includes the works of Leslie Howard Owens, George P. Rawick, Peter H. Wood, P. Sterling Stuckey, Herbert G. Gutman, John W. Blassingame, Eugene D. Genovese, and Vincent Harding, stresses the hard fight for survival, human development, and liberty, which raged in the slave quarters. These historians emphasize the

richness, complexity, and creativity of black culture, the maintenance of strong family ties, the moral and responsible character
of the slave community, and the variety of ways in which Afro-
Americans rendered tolerable the most difficult aspects of slavery.
Certainly, these scholars document the external forces that conspired to dehumanize the slaves, but they are convinced that in spite
of the physical and mental oppression, the slaves utilized their own
resources and creativity to minimize the damage to their inner
selves.[1]

These studies are far superior to the traditional story of slavery
and will undoubtedly become the new orthodoxy. Rarely will present-day historians defend the Sambo image as the dominant slave
personality, deny the significance of slave culture, doubt that slaves
had strong family ties, or question the unrelenting struggle of many
slaves for freedom. Indeed, Blassingame's *The Slave Community*,
which helped pave the way for the new orthodoxy, now seems more
conservative than when it was published in 1972. To be sure, he
broke sharply with the traditional historians, but on certain points
he conceded too much to them. That we realize such, however,
largely indicates how much has been accomplished since his book
was published six years ago. But *The Slave Community* was written
against the backdrop of a very different historical and social-
science portrait of the Afro-American past. Prior to the mid-1960s
many of the leading books on black life and culture presented the
Sambo image with scarcely a reservation. Blassingame's book
(along with Rawick's *From Sundown to Sunup*, also published in
1972) represented the first substantial break from the traditional
story. This was no easy task because of the crucial role the Sambo
image played in American intellectual and political life. A review of
the Sambo personality thesis and its connections to American social
policies and entrenched intellectual attitudes may be helpful before
reviewing Blassingame's contributions to this subject.

In a collection of essays on black subjective culture, the authors
discuss certain political implications of "Negro personality" and
cultural theory that have characterized the thinking of the
moderate segment of America's academic community in the post-
World War II period. They explain that if the Negro personality is
pathological, the solution to the "Negro problem" is to assimilate

blacks into white middle-class or working-class culture. They contend: "This can be accomplished through social work, psychiatry,
and education." This idea of social reform underlay the war-on-
poverty programs developed during the 1960s and it remains the
orthodox view of the progressive center in both governmental and
academic circles. A second viewpoint holds that the "Negro problem" stems from legitimate cultural differences and that its remedy
requires minor institutional modifications in order to achieve interracial cooperation and uniform adjustment to the rules set by
dominant organizations. The advocates of this view emphasize the
integrity of subcultures and tend to think that cross-cultural understanding will resolve much of America's racial conflict. In addition
to advocating bicultural training programs, they also recommend a
minor shift of resources from the majority society to the institutions serving minority groups. The third viewpoint argues that the
Negro problem emerges from fundamental class and racial oppression. The proposed solution, of course, is "to come after a revolution, which must destroy the total structure." In short, Negro personality theory has been basic to certain ideas of American social
reform.[2]

Significantly, Negro personality theory gained ascendancy
among American historians and social scientists after the downfall
of pre-World War II scientific racism. In the late nineteenth and
early twentieth centuries, biological and eugenic theories were embraced to explain and justify the subordinate status of racial and
ethnic minorities. These theories were also used to interpret the
Afro-American past, especially in U. B. Phillips's history of
American slavery. At the same time, however, qualified in-
vestigators in clinical, biological, and behavioral sciences, like
Franz Boas and W. I. Thomas, were already destroying some of the
most cherished pillars of scientific racism. But it was the fervent
support that the world's eugenicists gave to Mussolini, Hitler, and
fascism that caused many intellectuals to question the wisdom and
morality of using biological and eugenic theories to develop social
policies. In 1939 the Seventh International Genetics Congress at
Edinburgh officially condemned eugenics, racism, and Nazi doc-
trines. In the wake of the temporary downfall of scientific racism,
certain cultural and personality theories emerged as convenient

doctrine to explain the socioeconomic position of the underclasses. The moderate segment of the American academic community embraced the Sambo or Negro personality theory to argue that blacks' socioeconomic position was basically commensurate with their character and intellectual achievement.[3]

Interestingly, both eugenicists and Negro personality theorists shared a common concern for maintaining the existing social economy, which they viewed to be favorable and essentially just. Both groups resisted fundamental social reform and used their respective theories to justify the status quo. First, both camps located the principal cause of socioeconomic disadvantages in alleged defects within the Afro-American population. The eugenicists attributed the Negro's lack of social progress to inherited racial genes, and the personality theorists located the problem in the Negro personality. Secondly, with almost the same fervor that eugenicists attempted to influence American social policies in the pre-World War II era, personality theorists drew out the implications of their research for public policy in the postwar period. Since both groups located the Negro problem in either the Negro's personality or genetic structure, their proposed reforms were designed primarily to manipulate the black race and to leave the social system intact. The eugenicists proposed compulsory sterilization and immigration restriction laws to block the spread of "inferior genes," and the personality theorists proposed social work, psychiatry, and education to rehabilitate the Negro's personality. Thus, despite their cry for detachment and objectivity and their expressed disgust for ideologically motivated scholarship, both groups established firm connections between their research and its appropriate application to social policy. Consequently, the postwar Negro personality theorists, like the prewar eugenicists, stood to lose more than an academic viewpoint. Underneath their scholarship lay a social reform ideology that rested heavily on a certain definition of Afro-American personality.

Gunnar Myrdal's *An American Dilemma* (1944) was one of the first distinguished studies to stress the alleged pathological nature of the Afro-American personality.[4] A basic theme of Myrdal's book was that slavery and its aftermath stripped blacks of their African heritage and left them with a distorted and pathological form of general American culture. It was Abram Kardiner and Lionel Oversey, however, who elaborated the relationship between the Negro personality and Afro-American social and historical development. In 1951 they asserted that slavery destroyed black culture, prevented blacks from forming permanent familial ties, and altered significantly the "internal organization" of the Negro personality. In their view, the Negro personality formed under slavery was characterized mainly by self-hatred and the lack of self-initiative to improve the race's lot.[5] Using their theory of Negro personality to interpret the black past and to evaluate the Afro-American's socioeconomic advancement, Kardiner and Ovesey argued that Negro personality organization was the greatest drawback to Negro progress. They argued, for example, that between 1865 and 1915 blacks were unable to migrate to the North, where chances for socioeconomic advancement "were undoubtedly better," because nominal political freedom could not alter habits of adaptation overnight. "The internal organization of the personality of the average freed slave was not yet capable of exploiting the minor opportunities in the North that were available prior to World War I." And when blacks migrated to the North in 1915, Kardiner and Ovesey attributed the change to a powerful stimulus (World War I), "external to the personality."[6] As of 1951, they maintained that Afro-Americans had not freed themselves from the "mark of oppression" and concluded that blacks had not materially improved their position primarily because their personality organization made them unable and unwilling to compete in mainstream America. This cultural and personality theory of black subordination would be repeated by liberal social scientists until well into the 1960s.

In 1930 historians Samuel Eliot Morison and Henry Steele Commager had provided historical justification for this sociological view of the Negro personality with their description of the typical slave as "Sambo," a "childlike, improvident, humorous, prevaricating, and superstitious" being. Yet, it was Stanley Elkins' work in 1959 that combined historical research and psychological theory to develop the classic Sambo image of the black past.[8] Prominent social scientists of the 1960s, like Nathan Glazer, Charles Silberman, and Daniel Moynihan, embraced the Sambo thesis to define and recommend social policy for the Afro-American population. In an introduction to the 1963 edition of Elkins's book, Glazer stressed the political implications of the Sambo theory: "The political repercussions of objective studies of the personality of the Negro, and the damage it suffered under slavery and the conditions that succeeded it, are potentially enormous." Glazer contended that to deal with such Negro problems as earning capacity, self-confidence, and motivation and to devise effective forms of Negro education, it was necessary to "know more about the Negro personality."[9]

In 1964 Charles E. Silberman published his book, *Crisis in Black and White,* and used Elkins's "most brilliant and probing study of slavery in the United States" to conclude that "the 'nigger' with which Baldwin is obsessed, the 'Sambo' of Southern folklore, was a reality and to a considerable extent still is." "If all discrimination were to end immediately," argued Silberman, "that alone would not materially improve the Negro's position." Racial oppression was basic to the Negro problem, but it was not the most important factor. "In short," said Silberman, "apathy appears to be the crux of the Negro's 'Negro problem.' " Apathy itself, however, was "just a cover for a more basic problem: self-hatred." Silberman concluded that Afro-American social progress depended more on personality rehabilitation in the Afro-American community than on fundamental social reform in the larger society.[10] This view was carried to its scholarly and political extreme when, in 1965, Daniel Moynihan recommended that the federal government take hold of the Afro-American family and rid it of the "tangle of pathology." Like Glazer and Silberman, he used the Elkins thesis to explain the primary cause of Afro-American socioeconomic disadvantages.[11]

Certainly, we need not probe the motives of these liberal scholars as they probed the intricacies of the Negro personality. After all, they began with an outcry against scientific racism, but unfortunately they ended by creating their own environmental mythology of black subjugation. At critical points they did almost as much damage as the eugenicists. Silberman, for example, contended that the Negro was afflicted by such an identity crisis that "he begins to wonder if he really exists at all." Indeed, such a being belongs in a mental institution, and most persons would probably prefer to have a low I.Q. score than be afflicted by the Negro personality. In fact, many whites with low I.Q. scores hold good blue- and white-collar jobs, which is more than we expect from a worker who "wonders if he really exists at all." At any rate, Negro personality theorists strongly defended their Sambo version of the Afro-American experience. They viewed white historians who constructed a different black experience as well-meaning, misguided liberals and radicals who were vainly trying to exorcise the legacy of Sambo. Silberman insisted that historians Kenneth Stampp and Herbert Aptheker, who stressed the slaves' courage and rebelliousness, were attempting to counter racism by calling the Sambo portrait a stereotype without realizing that it was the dominant black personality. Many black scholars who often differed with intellectuals like Elkins, Silberman, and Moynihan were told that their responses were too racial and emotional and that they were guilty of myth-making and historical fabrication to serve political ends. The revisionists had to wage a difficult struggle to shatter the Sambo mythology in much the same manner that early twentieth-century biological and behavioral scientists fought to destroy the pillars of scientific racism. Hence, no matter how absurd the discussions of Sambo appear today, a few years ago it was necessary to take the Sambo thesis with alarmed seriousness.[12]

The traditional Sambo story held that blacks had little to aspire to except the sanctions of the slave system that required and sustained infantilism as a normal feature of behavior. In breaking with this interpretation, Blassingame contends that Africans created a subterranean life in the slave quarters that was far more powerful in the personality development of generations of slaves than the masters' authority. The slaves, bringing in their minds a wealth of cultural resources from Africa, "made European forms serve African functions." (p. 17) The slaves skillfully used their own songs, folktales, religion, customs, beliefs, and ceremonies to set themselves apart from their masters' cultural frames of reference. In contrast to the masters' ideals and values, the slaves' culture uttered their longing for freedom and desire for revenge and expressed their awareness of themselves as a cohesive human community with common experiences and common interests. "Since the slave viewed all whites as enemies, his master as a tyrant, and himself as being without protection before the law, he generally developed a strong sense of loyalty to other blacks." (p. 210) This solidarity enabled them to unite in their struggles against their masters. In short: "The slave's culture bolstered his self-esteem, courage, and confidence, and served as his defense against personal degradations." (p. 210)

Using a rich variety of sources, particularly the autobiographies of fugitive slaves and survivors of slavery, Blassingame demonstrates convincingly that most slaves were not childlike and docile. The slaves found a purpose in life through kinship, religion, cultural creations, and in their struggle against their oppressors. This contribution is the book's major strength. Its major weakness is that Blassingame's important interpretation is muted by an unnecessary acceptance of traditional viewpoints. This weakness is most noticeable in his discussion of the black family. His analysis of slaves' sexual and marital relationships absorbs basic aspects of the Elkins-Moynihan conception. Blassingame argues that "for a majority of slaves, sex was a natural urge frequently fulfilled in casual liaisons." (p. 82) To him, "the casual sexual contacts among slaves" (p. 168) represented a spirit of "loose morality" in the quarters. Hence: "Affection not morality, was apparently the most important factor which kept partners together." (p. 87) Herbert Gutman's *The Black Family in Slavery and Freedom* demonstrates convincingly that slaves were far more moral in their sexual behavior than as they are depicted in *The Slave Community*. More importantly, however, Blassingame's conception of morality embraces too much of the traditional story that designates sexual behavior as the cornerstone of family morality.

The focus on sexual behavior causes Blassingame to downplay the significance of his own findings. He informs us that slave parents "lavished love on their children." "Fathers regaled their children with fascinating stories and songs and won their affections with little gifts." (p. 94) The mothers were "held in even greater esteem." Moreover, "Grandmothers frequently prepared little tidbits for the children, and grandfathers often told them stories about their lives in Africa." (p. 102) Yet, Blassingame failed to emphasize the moral achievement of enslaved parents who "lavished love" on their children and regaled them with fascinating stories. Our modern society, with an alarming rate of child abuse and neglect, could learn much from the moral performance of slave families. The slaves successfully fought off the apathy, the blunting of emotions, and the feeling that one could not care any more, all of which often characterize the psychological reactions of the oppressed. It seems, therefore, that the quarters were filled with the highest form of morality. Thus, it is difficult to believe that such men and women could only establish "casual liaisons" among themselves.

It is also difficult to reconcile Blassingame's view of the church with his beliefs about sexual morality in the slave quarters. We are told that "the church served as the major social center in the quarters." (p. 74) If, as he contends, "religion was more powerful than the master," (p. 75) we have to wonder about the black church's code of sexual behavior. Unless the church sanctioned "loose morality," it is not clear why such a powerful social center could not establish a different code of conduct. It appears that something has to give; the church either sanctioned "loose morality" or was unable to significantly shape sexual beliefs. If the latter is true, we might question whether religion was indeed more powerful than the master.

Blassingame's treatment of the slaves' compliance to plantation routine is much less ambivalent and breaks sharply from the traditional story. "The slaves," he admits, "were generally submissive and obedient in most of their relations with whites." But he rejects the notion that slaves were obedient because of fundamental alterations in their personality structure. "Southern planters were able to crush every slave rebellion with relative ease, and more importantly to prevent the development of a tradition of successful revolt in the quarters. Unless he were totally blind, a slave could not fail to perceive how hopeless revolt was, given the size and undeniably superior fire-power of the whites." (p. 125) Thus, "the penalities for non-conformity were severe." Most slaves, therefore, resorted to customary obedience and ritual deference to avoid punishment. Even so, the master's "primary guarantee of obedience was the lash," (p. 150) which was "the linchpin of his regime." (p. 160) Plantation rules "could only be enforced by most planters by constant floggin's," (p. 162) and "rarely did the slave

identify with a master who frequently flogged and abused him."
(p. 193) Moreover, even the kindest master could not disguise the
oppressive nature of the slave system. "Characteristically, stocks
closed on hapless women and children, mothers cried for the in-
fants torn cruelly from their arms, and whimpering black women
fought vainly to preserve their virtue in the face of the lash or
pleaded for mercy while blood flowed from their buttocks." (p.
163) And it was not the floggings that hurt the most—it was the
mental agony caused by the injustice, the irrationality of it all.

Blassingame's major contention is that Sambo was not the dominant slave personality. "The typical slave simulated deference, was
hostilely submissive and occasionally ungovernable, and rebellious." (p. 216) Some readers might get sidetracked by Blassingame's careful and judicious attention to other aspects of slave
personality. He writes that "some blacks wished passionately that
they were white" (p. 199) and that "some slaves were always
docile." (p. 213) We might ask for a more precise definition of
"some," but we will do better to remember his essential argument,
that "most slaves hated and were suspicious" of their oppressors.
(p. 209)

The Sambo or Negro personality mythology was used to shape
social policy "in the Negro's behalf" during the early and mid-
1960s. This policy, based on a largely fictional history of Afro-
America, aimed to correct problems that existed mainly in the
minds of America's moderate academic community. The Sambo
myth fitted well the ideological interests of this group even if it was
not entirely developed. It was used to promote many misguided
educational and social welfare programs and to argue against the
need for fundamental social change. To be sure, Blassingame's
book does not point toward any social policy. That is not his concern. His book, a sensitive and balanced analysis of slave culture
and personality, simply demolishes an old environmentalist sanction of black subordination. It marked a new direction in the study
of Afro-American history, and it remains a valuable part of the
new literature that will surely remove the Sambo preface from liberal social-reform programs.

NOTES

1. John W. Blassingame, *The Slave Community: Plantation Life in the Antebellum South* (New York: Oxford University Press, 1972); George P. Rawick, *From Sundown to Sunup: The Making of the Black Community* (Westport: Greenwood Publishing Co., 1972); Herbert G. Gutman, *The Black Family in Slavery and Freedom, 1750-1925* (New York: Pantheon Books, 1976); Peter H. Wood, *Black Majority: Negroes in Colonial South Carolina From 1670 Through the Stono Rebellion* (New York: Alfred A. Knopf, 1974); Eugene D. Genovese, *Roll, Jordan, Roll: The World the Slaves Made* (New York: Pantheon Books, 1974); Leslie Howard Owens, *This Species of Property: Slave Life and Culture in the Old South* (New York: Oxford University Press, 1976); P. Sterling Stuckey, "The Black Ethos in Slavery," *Massachusetts Review* IX (Summer 1968), pp. 417-37; Vincent Harding, "Religion and Resistance Among Antebellum Negroes, 1800-1860," in August Meier and Elliot Rudwick, *The Making of Black America* (New York: Atheneum, 1969), pp. 179-197.

2. Harry C. Triandis (editor), *Variations in Black and White Perceptions of the Social Environment* (Urbana: University of Illinois Press, 1976). For an excellent treatment of political interests in Afro-American culture, see Charles A. Valentine, *Black Studies and Anthropology: Scholarly and Political Interests in Afro-American Culture,* Module 15 (Reading, Massachusetts: Addison-Wesley Publishing Company, 1972).

3. Kenneth M. Ludmerer, "American Genetics and the Eugenics Movement: 1905-1935," *Journal of the History of Biology II,* No. 2 (1969), p. 358; Clarence J. Karier, *Shaping the American Educational State: 1900 to the Present* (New York: The Free Press, 1975), Chapters 6 and 9; Ulrich B. Phillips, *American Negro Slavery* (New York: D. Appleton and Company, 1918).

4. Gunnar Myrdal, *An American Dilemma* (New York: Harper and Row Publishers, Inc., 1944), 1964 edition by McGraw-Hill.

5. Abram Kardiner and Lionel Ovesey, *The Mark of Oppression: Explorations in the Personality of the American Negro* (New York: The World Publishing Company, 1951), 1972 edition, pp. 360-361.

6. Ibid, p. 363.

7. Samuel Eliot Morison and Henry Steele Commager, *The Growth of the American Republic,* Vol. I (New York: Oxford University Press, 1936), p. 145.

8. Stanley M. Elkins, *Slavery: A Problem in American Institutional and Intellectual Life* (Chicago: University of Chicago, 1959).

9. Nathan Glazer, "Introduction," in Stanley M. Elkins, *Slavery: A Problem in American Institutional and Intellectual Life* (New York: Grosset and Dunlap, 1963), p. xv.

10. Charles E. Silberman, *Crisis in Black and White* (New York: Random House, Inc., 1964), pp. 70-71, 77.

11. Lee Rainwater and William L. Yancey, *The Moynihan Report and the Politics of Controversy* (Boston: MIT Press, 1967), p. 62.

12. Silberman, *Crisis in Black and White,* pp. 79, 109; Eugene D. Genovese, "The Nat Turner Case," *New York Review of Books* (Sept. 12, 1968), pp. 34-37; Jack Richardson, "The Black Arts," *New York Review of Books* (Dec. 19, 1968), pp. 10-11; J. H. Plumb, "Slavery, Race, and the Poor," *New York Review of Books* (March 13, 1969), p. 3.

JOHN W. BLASSINGAME

Redefining *The Slave Community*: A Response to the Critics

Forcing an author to confront a book six years after its publication is cruel and unusual punishment. In the interval, passionate beliefs often change and memory fades. Contemplating *The Slave Community* today, I am like the black poet Robert Hayden, who wrote in "Traveling Through Fog":

> Looking back, we cannot see,
> except for its blurring lights
> like underwater stars and moons,
> our starting-place.
>
> Behind us, beyond us now
> is phantom territory, a world
> abstract as memories of earth
> the traveling dead take home.[1]

The Slave Community was an attempt to explore a complex institution with a limited vocabulary; sometimes the words were burdened with meanings they may not have clearly conveyed. The book began as a comparative study of slavery in Latin America and the South, then detoured to urban slavery and black autobiographies, and ended by attempting to explore the psychological dimensions of bondage. I am extremely grateful for the opportunity to discuss with my critics any false trails I may have pursued or any problematic aspects that the book may have presented. In many ways their own work has served as a corrective for any errors of omission or commission. Acknowledging my debt to all of them, I will begin by answering some of the specific questions raised by the critics and then present some general reflections on the study of slavery.

I have no argument with what Genovese sees as the "vast psychological ravages" of fear; *The Slave Community*, it seems to me, demonstrated many of them. In a sense, the conditions facing the slave were similar to those described by Hobbes for man in a state of nature in which there existed "No arts; no letters; no society; and which is worst of all, continual fear, and danger of violent death."[2] But the slave's fear was almost always an outgrowth of harsh treatment. In 1855 a former Maryland slave recalled her cruel master and asserted: "We were all afraid of master: when I saw him coming, my heart would jump up into my mouth, as if I had seen a serpent."[3]

The shock of floggings caused slaves to faint, to become incoherent, and to have nightmares years after their bondage ended. But, contrary to Genovese's claims, the fear induced sullen obedience more often than identification with the master. The pain led to acquiescence, not acceptance; desires for revenge, not consistent internalization of the behavior planters demanded. The most apt characterization of the slave's behavior is that Lucy Dawidowicz used to describe the ghettoized German Jews in her magnificent book, *The War Against the Jews:* "They learned not only to invent, but to cirumvent; not only to obey, but to evade; not only to submit, but to outwit. Their tradition of defiance was devious rather than direct, employing nerve instead of force."[4]

We know that the planters both lived with and transcended their fear of the slave. Genovese should at least consider the possibility that the bondsman was similarly capable of transcending his fear of the master. In this regard, we are reminded of the words of America's most perceptive writer on slave life and culture, Elma Stuckey. In the poem "Rebuked" one slave says:

> Y'all talkin' crazy when yer ask
> A man like me that's black
> Why I let Marsa beat me
> And put marks on my back.

> I was not scared, the point I make,
> You see, I was not free,
> No more than one o' Marsa's mules,
> Don't be so hard on me.[5]

Genovese strongly objects to two other points I made. First was my assertion: "The subordinate may give deference at no emotional cost. He may, for instance, truly believe the superordinate worthy of his respect. If not, he may feign respect through the ritual of deference in spite of his low opinion of the superordinate." (p. 188) Second was my declaration in the course of explaining interpersonal theory that "a person may identify with the dominant person either because of affection or fear. In the latter case the identification or internalization of the ideals of the dominant person is directed toward avoiding punishment and is on a rather shallow level." (p. 186) Somehow, Genovese misread these statements and concluded that I was suggesting that "respect equals moral admiration or affection." Then Genovese asserted: "On this matter Freudian psychology, Hegelian dialectics, Machiavellian politics, and the Sicilian folk-wisdom on which I grew up converge: 'Respect' rests on fear, on the perception of superior power. . . ."

Reliance on Hegel's musings on the development of self-consciousness has led to some intellectual mischief in writings on slavery. When considering the Hegelian dialectic, we must remember the philosopher presented no systematic exposition of the relationship between the master and the slave. Moreover, his reflections in *Philosophy of Right* raise some questions about his understanding of the social reality of bondage. According to Hegel, "if a man is a slave, his own will is responsible for his slavery, just as it is its will which is responsible if a people is subjugated. Hence the wrong of slavery lies at the door not simply of enslavers or conquerors but of the slaves and the conquered themselves."[6]

In his famous essay, "Lordship and Bondage," Hegel explored the evolution of consciousness of self and the condition of subordination evident in social interaction. For the slave, Hegel argued that work was essential in the formation of consciousness. Fear, while an element of the slave's consciousness of self, is also func-

tional—"the fear of the lord is the beginning of wisdom."
Misreading Hegel, Genovese posits the theory that fear is absolute.
He has apparently forgotten those passages in *The Phenomenology
of Mind* where Hegel comes close to claiming that fear can produce
identification on a shallow level. "Without the discipline of service
and obedience, fear remains formal and does not spread over the
whole known reality of existence. Without the formative activity
shaping the thing, fear remains inward and mute, and consciousness does not become objective for itself."[7]

As Genovese surmises, I do not deny the existence of the Omnipresent Father. Whatever the rantings of detractors, he will not go
away whether we are discussing New England factories or Southern
plantations. But as long as the patriarch continues to appear in the
guise of the kindly old man, I will approach him with caution. The
slaves gave us the analytical tools for viewing the Father. In their
minds he appeared malevolent when his identity and self-esteem
depended on their remaining perpetual *children*. Then, too, there is
something incongruous about the Father. Frederick Douglass described the incongruity clearly in *My Bondage and My Freedom:*

> The relation of master and slave has been called patriarchal, and only
> second in benignty and tenderness to that of parent and child. . . . I admit
> that there are individual slave-holders less cruel and barbarous than is
> allowed by law; but these form the exception. . . . To talk of *kindness*
> entering into a relation in which one party is robbed of his wife, of
> children, of his hard earnings, of home, of friends, of society, of
> knowledge, and of all that makes life desirable, is most absurd, wicked,
> and preposterous.[8]

The Father and paternalism have been raised to a new level by
Genovese; the complexity of his formulation in *Roll, Jordan, Roll,*
absolved him from Douglass's charge. We both, however, take
Douglass's admonition seriously. So did the slave. It was exactly at
the point when a master relieved the slaves of that litany of wrongs
that Douglass depicted that they described him as "kind."

With all due respect to Sicilian folk-wisdom, it seems to me that
slave behavior was sometimes based on respect and that blacks
were sometimes loyal to kind masters. This is not to argue, of
course, that kind treatment always produced loyalty and submis-

sion. The fact that many "faithful" slaves followed the North Star and that Nat Turner rebelled against his kind owner shows that kindness often produced just the opposite behavior in slaves. But again, characterization of these responses does not depend on psychological theory, as Genovese implied; it is evident in the sources—it is what the slaves themselves said.

I agree, however, with Genovese that an overwhelming majority of slaves were not deferential out of love and respect for their masters. I noted this on several occasions. At one point I wrote that "ritual deference and obedience to plantation rules could only be enforced by most planters by constant floggings." (p. 162) And I also held that "while a planter could demand obedience, he could not always obtain the slave's respect." (p. 183) Slaves who were contemptuous of their masters "gave deference only as a result of fear." (p. 183) Basically, coercion was the major reason for slave compliance to the master. To admit that some blacks had genuine respect for some masters is not, of course, to say that personal relations on the plantation were not strained.

Professor Rawick has presented the outlines of the new historical portrait of slavery. In brief, I do accept the general features of the consensus on slavery he describes, although I may have been conservative in my approach. My conservative framework is most evident in the underlying caution in using sources. I know of no writer on slavery who felt compelled to use as much space defending his sources as I did. But it is a testament to the changing times that my framework can be described as conservative in 1978 in contrast to the reviewer who argued in 1972 that my approach was neo-abolitionist. I will accept Rawick's characterization as long as he concedes that the frameworks used by many of my predecessors were reactionary.

Although historians have not systematically analyzed slave social structure, I do not see how focusing on the occupations of slaves, as Rawick suggested, will advance our understanding. The complexity of slave social structure is astonishing. Perhaps for this reason its essential character has eluded most scholars. Traditionally the focus has been on the occupational divisions in the quarters. Viewed through the eyes of the planters, this made sense; the status of a black was inextricably tied to his contribution to the plantation economy and his physical proximity to the master. Historians using this planter-centered view have described slave society in simplistic terms: At the apex was the house servant; then followed drivers, artisans, and field hands.

A slave-centered view of the quarters yields a diametrically opposed pattern of social structure, one oriented toward service to the black community and distance from the master. In terms of service, preachers and elders gave most to the community, providing encouragement, hope, and counsel. Conjurers and midwives helped to conquer sickness or played a key role in the ritual of birth. Creative blacks, such as musicians and storytellers, transmitted group values and provided entertainment.

The Slave Community was written by a man using language replete with male images and was based on sources written largely by males. Given these limitations, it contains no long discussions of woman's role as mother, lover, wife, and worker. But it may be overstating the case to describe it as a representation of male chauvinism. Women do appear in the book as both parents and rebels. I agree, however, that this subject must be explored more.

There are, as Rawick suggests, some limitations in my treatment of the spirituals. The appearance of John Lovell's *Black Song* led me to modify somewhat my characterization of these songs. In contrast to what I wrote in 1972, I would now argue that the spirituals were not only songs of sorrow and hope, but they were also songs of resignation and rebellion. Nevertheless, the secular songs contained more explicit protest than the spirituals.

In contrast to Rawick's reading of the book, there was an explicit emphasis on communal struggle for survival. At one juncture, for instance, I observed that their distinctive culture "helped the slaves to develop a strong sense of group solidarity. They united to protect themselves from the most oppressive features of slavery and to preserve their self-esteem. Despite their weakness as isolated individuals, they found some protection in the group from their masters." (pp. 75-76) From folklore to religion, from the help runaways found in the quarters to maroon activity, my discussion centered on those bonds uniting blacks in the struggle for freedom. The "community" was a state of mind—"we" against "they."

In response to Earl Thorpe, I should begin by declaring that I consider brevity a virtue. I also believe that it is literally true that a picture is worth a thousand words. Throughout *The Slave Community* the illustrations constituted a vital part of the evidence. And while the entire book was a testament to the creative genius of the slave, I do not think we denigrate that genius by admitting that some of the slaves' nonmaterial culture was similar to that of their masters.

While I discussed the many slaves who became submissive as a result of unrelenting cruelty, Thorpe probably recalls that I also said: "Strong-willed blacks were restrained, but were not broken by the lash." (p. 211) In terms of relative emphasis, it is significant that all of Thorpe's quotations were drawn from eight pages devoted to the impact of cruelty on slaves. The following ten pages focused on how the slaves resisted oppression. Then, too, one whole chapter was devoted to resistance as symbolic of the assertion of manhood *and* womanhood in the quarters. I admit, however, that the exploration of slave resistance could have been more systematic. A portrait of the leaders of slave revolts would have given us more insights into resistance. Delineation of the differences between runaway slaves during the colonial period and the nineteenth century would have helped to illuminate the preconditions for resistance.

I believe, unlike Thorpe, that too much of slavery scholarship has tried to relate events in the quarters to the national and international arenas. Developments in Europe did not cause the slaves to resist bondage, and the fulminations of presidential candidates and white abolitionists did not contribute greatly to the bondsman's self-esteem. One learns of these developments only by examining the internal dynamics of the quarters.

Leslie H. Owens raises significant questions about the methodology of *The Slave Community*. He charges, for example, that the slave narratives "possess fuller dimensions and wider complexities than emerge in Blassingame's study of physical and psychological bondage." It is, I believe, impossible to convey the "full dimension" of sources as rich and complex as black autobiographies. Writing about a similar phenomenon, Camus observed: "To be really realistic a description would have to be endless. . . . To write is already to choose.''[9] The historian's task is to focus on those salient features in the documents most revelatory of the group he is describing. Unless he is writing biography, the historian is forced to discard some of the excess baggage of human particularity. I might suggest in this regard that what Owens sees as "obviously apparent" in the narratives in 1978 may have been clouded by some obscurity before 1972. Still, I share his frustration over not being able to reveal more of the complexities of slave life contained in black autobiographies and other sources.

Despite myths to the contrary, planter records are not the sole embodiment of truth. Even so, Owens chides me for citing so few planter records, which he contends I mistakenly characterized as monolithic in their portrait of the slaves. On the other hand, he feels that such manuscripts are "valuable resources" for examining the slave experience. Among serious scholars, that is not a debatable issue. What is debatable is whether the planter's or the slave's records rank higher as sources for examining slave life.

Planter observations of slave thought and behavior must be used with extreme caution. They do not, by and large, deal with the interior life of the bondsman. Planter records are crucial indices of agricultural operations, managerial opinion, and planter life and culture. But they leave much to be desired as records of slave life. Robert Starobin noted this in *Blacks in Bondage*:

Plantation journals deal mainly with the master's farming operations and only rarely with the motivations of the slaves. . . . The basic problem with these traditional sources, however, is that they present slavery entirely from the white man's point of view. Such evidence generally depicts black people more as whites (even sympathetic whites) wanted or imagined them to be than as they actually were. The standard sources tell more about the mentality of masters than about the character of their chattels. Indeed, by their very nature they depict slavery from the top down than from the bottom up.[10]

Other scholars familiar with planter records found they were unreliable when describing slave thought. Clement Eaton, in *The Mind of the South,* observed:

White Southerners maintained that, having lived intimately with Negroes for generations, they knew the Negro mind. Yet their views of the Negro were distorted by powerful stereotypes, especially concerning a belief in the inherent inferiority of the Negro. The slave studied closely the white man, and seems to have been far more astute in reading the mind of the master than was the latter in penetrating the psychology of the black man. . . . Even highly intelligent masters and mistresses whose interest it was to understand the subject race found the inner thoughts of slaves veiled and inscrutable, for they were noncommittal and evasive in conversation with the white man.[11]

When writing about the thoughts and behavior of slaveholders, planter records must be the main source utilized by the scholar. By the same token, scholars writing about bondsmen must recall the 1855 assertion by the former slave, John Little: "T'isn't he who has stood and looked on, that can tell you what slavery is—'tis he who has endured."[12] Planter records are good sources for determining many of the contours of plantation life; but in the minuteness of detail about the life of the bondsman, they fall far short of those left by the slaves; and in matters of feeling—joy, grief, pain, and pleasure—immeasurably short.

Ironically, contemporary scholars have more faith in the reliability of white observations of slaves than the planters themselves had. Kenneth Stampp, for example, asserted in 1976 that while slave letters, interviews, and narratives had some value, he thought "the diaries, letters, and other contemporary writings of slaveholders are plentiful and vastly superior as sources."[13] Many of Stampp's "superior" observers disagreed. In 1842 the Georgia rice planter Charles C. Jones observed that whites "live and die in the midst of Negroes and know comparatively little of their real character."[14] Similarly, Edward A. Pollard, the author of *Black Diamonds* (1859), wrote in 1871:

It is astonishing how little the slaveholders of the South, despite their supposed knowledge of the Negro, really knew of what was in him; . . . The difficulty was that slavery was a perpetual barrier to an intimate acquaintance with the negro; it regarded him as a *thing,* and was never concerned to know what was in the sodden and concealed mind of a creature that represented only so much of productive force, and was estimated, body and soul, in dollars and cents.[15]

While we should follow Owens's suggestion to mine the slave-holders' records more intensively for information on slave be-havior, we should remember the disclaimers of the planters them-selves.

Owens's penetrating critique indicates that even when the scholar is most careful, he or she is likely to reveal the slave's character through a dark veil. I may have, as he argues, contributed more confusion than light to the debate over the slave's personality. It should be noted, however, that I began my study of slavery with a great deal more appreciation for the complexity of the institution than Owens suggests. Contrary to Owens's assertions, a clear dis-tinction is made in *The Slave Community* between planter ideals and expectations (pp. 144-53) and actual slave behavior (pp. 184-216). Indeed, Owens's declarations that plantations did not run "according to ideal rules" and that the planter's contacts with ego-conscious slaves taught him about "the complexity of personality" types in the quarters read like paraphrases of the following sentences in *The Slave Community:* "the slaves did not internalize the roles and automatically submit unconditionally to their mas-ters. . . . How, exactly, did the planters characterize slaves? For the most part, they felt there was great variability among them. . . .The first premise of the planter was that there were so many different kinds of slaves that he had to combine several techniques in order to manage them." (pp. 150-53)

Owens apparently misunderstood my discussion of Sambo. How could he seriously ask did Sambo "transmit his character to future generations?" After all, I said repeatedly that personality traits were neither immutable nor heritable. Here, Owens's desire to view most slaves as "openly defiant" misleads him: he rejected the possibilities for self-hatred as well as "authentic Sambos." Surely scholars can no longer follow Owens's lead and make the slaves one-dimensional heroes. Instead, we should heed the advice of a character in Martin Delany's classic novel *Blake* who declared: "We must take the slaves, not as we wish them to be, but as we really find them to be." Similarly, Owens should not view my dis-cussion of a few blacks who wanted to be white as an indication of my pathological bent. Rather, we should conclude as Delany did when writing about a similar group in 1859: "Oppression is the author of all this. . . ."[16]

Quite frankly, I must treat one of Owens's observations as a humorous jest. Commenting on the variety of personalities I found in the quarters, Owens writes: "When he finally concludes that 'the slave was no different in most ways from most men' I have to wonder why the slave experience meant so little to blacks after all." Since the phrase has been wrenched out of context, it might be best to quote the paragraph in which it appears:

It is obvious from the discussion above that there was great variety in slave behavior. Some slaves were always docile; others were docile most of the time and rebellious at other times. Likewise, some resisted bondage throughout their lives in various ways, while others, generally docile, might be rebellious only once. In other words, the slave was no different in most ways from most men. The same range of personality types existed in the quarters as in the mansion. The slaves, it is true, were generally submissive and obedient in most of their relations with whites. Obviously, slavery could not have survived had it been otherwise. (pp. 213-14)

Occurring in a chapter titled "Slave *Personality* Types," appearing after 213 pages describing the slave condition, written in English, and in the context of the paragraph, the phrase means one thing and one thing only: The personality of black slaves was similar to that of any other people under similar oppressive conditions.

Since Owens concedes that I saw "variety and salvation for the slave's personality," he realizes, without saying so, that each of the personalities and stereotypes he rejects should be read in tandem with the others to obtain the full picture. One example of Owens's misperception is his statement that I suggested that "an individual must await his leaders to know that he has been resisting." Fifteen pages (pp. 104-16, 211-13) were devoted to *individual* resistance by slaves.

In the conventional analysis stressed by Owens, the driver was a significant personage in the slave community. An agent in the coercive machinery of the plantation and an inhabitant of the quarters, the driver was, as Genovese argues, a marginal man. But as I have contended elsewhere, the driver may not have been as significant in the slave's social structure as Owens implies. To date, the image we have of the driver is a blurred one. I certainly did not help in 1972 to sharpen it.

One of the many sins of our graduate schools is that they chain us to footnotes containing every source at which we glanced. They also often leave us in some confusion about the distinction between primary and secondary sources. It is important, therefore, to clarify some of Owens' observations of my use of evidence. Fifteen narratives are cited in the chapter, "Runaways and Rebels," and fourteen appear in chapter six, describing resistance. There was no reference anywhere to the declarations by F. Roy Johnson that Owens cites. All of my citations to Johnson refer to the *appendix,* containing a reprint of what is usually accepted as a *primary* source: *The Confessions of Nat Turner.* While thirty-six of the footnotes in chapter four contain primary sources, I did, like most historians, acknowledge my debt to my predecessors in twenty-three notes containing references to nineteen secondary works.

I tried to treat the testimony of slaves as central to the documentation of their resistance. My concern was the same as that expressed by Paulo Freire in his *Pedagogy of the Oppressed:* "Who are better prepared than the oppressed to understand the terrible significance of an oppressive society? Who suffer the effects of oppression more than the oppressed? Who can better understand the necessity of liberation?"[17]

Although I find statistical analyses of footnotes somewhat less than exciting, they are necessary in order to clarify some of Owens's comments. Owens says he found only "two citations" of the plantation manuscripts listed in the bibliography; actually, there were six. But, as Owens declares, "the problem does not lie here." If there were no *published* planter records, questions about the citations of manuscript records would appear less anachronistic. A count of the published and manuscript planter records cited in the footnotes might relieve some of Owens's anxiety on this point. At any rate, his criticism should be placed in context. Writing in *A Documentary History of Slavery in North America* (1976), Willie Lee Rose observed: "The memoirs, letters, and autobiographies of the slaveholding class also contribute to the historian's understanding of the slave system. The inquiring historian will find listings of the most valuable of these in Blassingame, *The Slave Community,* pp. 242-44."[18] Now, I must confess that I have not, since my graduate school days, cited every source I use in my writing. Consequently, only about twenty-seven of the published planter's records in the bibliography are cited in the notes.

Engerman joins Owens in questioning my use of sources. Both of them insist I mistakenly characterized the planters as monolithic in their view of the plantation. By taking "monolithic" out of context, they make me say things I never intended nor said. Owens and Engerman should remember that in that same preface from which they quote I said that "masters varied so much in character."

Engerman expressed surprise that I did not utilize the WPA interviews more extensively. I read my first slave narrative in 1955 and my first WPA interview in 1960. When I embarked on the research for *The Slave Community,* it took me almost five years to learn how to use the narratives. Then, I confidently tackled the twentieth-century interviews. With much more surprise than Stanley Engerman, I found the interviews impenetrable mysteries. Looking for guidance, I assiduously read all of the pre-1972 studies of slavery. I found none. I came away from my initial reading of the interviews dismayed over their apparent weaknesses. At the same time, I was convinced they were valuable sources if one could discover the key to unlock the treasures they contained.

The omission of the interviews was a confession of my inability to develop a reasonable critical apparatus for evaluating and determining their reliability as well as a reflection of my intellectual timidity and methodological conservatism. While I find neither of these attitudes defensible today, we might gain some perspective if we review some of the historical attitudes regarding slave sources that were current before 1972. After reading reviews and the general studies of slavery, a literary scholar, William W. Nichols, concluded in a 1971 *Phylon* essay that historians had summarily dismissed the narratives: "There may be convincing evidence to show that most slave narratives are unreliable, but that evidence has not been published. The very fact that the narratives could be so generally treated as though they had been systematically discredited makes me wonder if scholars have been viscerally reluctant to confront ex-slaves' views of themselves and their past."[19] Given such assessments, I felt I was swimming against the tide by using the narratives extensively; the even more questionable interviews represented the additional weight that could have sunk my efforts to bring the slave onto the historical stage to speak for himself.

I considered the patterns of life of the autobiographers carefully when generalizing about slave life. But residence, occupation, and size of plantation cannot be related to personalities as clearly as Engerman implies. Frequently the autobiographies do not present such information; when they do, their most salient feature is variability: the autobiographers were enslaved in many states on different plantations and held many jobs in their life times.

Engerman feels that my evaluation of black autobiographies was "overly optimistic." In taking the offensive against the cascade of preemptory negatives usually issued against the use of slave testimony, we must ask certain questions. How many scholars of slavery subject the diaries and autobiographies of whites to *any* test? If so, why did Ulrich B. Phillips and other scholars use the bowdlerized and deliberately distorted diary of Mary B. Chesnutt? Most scholars only apply two "critical" tests to the narratives. First, they reject those having abolitionist editors. Second, they treat as unreliable those narratives containing views and incidents they "feel" were probably untrue. Both of these "tests" are so subjective that they can hardly be considered "critical."

Serious critiques of the narratives must be based on a sysematic examination of the documents. The assertions of each narrator must be tested against those of his peers as well as those of his master. Is there internal consistency in the account? Do independent sources corroborate any of the details in the story? Did the narrator give essentially the same account of his bondage on different occasions? These were some of the questions I tried to answer when evaluating the narratives. Given subsequent research, I may not have been optimistic enough: Some narratives that I rejected as unreliable in 1972 I now know are trustworthy.

Making few claims to being a cliometrician, I reluctantly respond to Engerman's questions about quantitative methods and the strictures of Gutman. Writing in *The Black Family in Slavery and Freedom,* Herbert Gutman alleged that for one of his tables on the breakup of slave families in Mississippi, "Some of this material is used by John Blassingame in *The Slave Community* . . . and especially the table on page 90. Blassingame's analysis is very different from that in this study. The data reported in the table on p. 90 are inaccurate." Confused by the maddening archival and U.S. Army practice of filing similar documents in different ways, Gutman was misled: The two of us did not use the same material. I used the unbound original "Marriage Certificates" for four counties in Tennessee, one parish in Louisiana, and Adams County, Mississippi covering the period 1864-1866, while Gutman, according to his footnotes used: "Bound Volumes of Marriage Registers, 1864-1865, Davis Bend, Natchez, and Vicksburg, Mississippi, manuscript copies, Mississippi Freedmen's Bureau, Mss., volumes 43-45, Record Group, 105, National Archives."[20] My Mississippi data was for Adams County only; Gutman's included Adams *and* Warren counties.

Peter Ripley, in his seminal study, *Slaves and Freemen in Civil War Louisiana* (1976), used the same marriage certificates as I did for Concordia Parish, Louisiana. He found a total of 454 black couples whose unions were broken. I found 450 such couples. The difference comes, I believe, from Ripley's counting all couples, while I counted only those united before the Civil War began. Although I applaud Engerman's notation of the differences in the figures, I must remind him that there is a margin of error in all statistics. And since even the Census Bureau concedes a margin of error in all of its gross figures, he should at least concede Ripley (or me) a margin of 0.9 percent. Of all the broken families, Ripley found that 35.7 percent resulted from forcible separations by masters. My figure was lower because it was based on all unions, broken and unbroken, and came to 29.2 percent.

While sharing Engerman's caution regarding the applicability of quantitative techniques to many aspects of slavery, I believe we can determine with more precision than we have the nature of the slave's diet, housing, and clothing. Similarly, systematic study will yield more plausible estimates of interstate sales, morbidity and mortality, birth rates, punishment, insanity, miscegenation, productivity, and runaways. Far more than has been the case in the past, quantitative studies must take on a comparative flavor. How did the indices vary depending on the size of plantations? Did the South differ significantly from slaveholding regions in Latin America or South Africa? Beyond this rather limited range of questions, however, we must abandon either quantification or generalization. But whatever the limitations of our data, we should not abandon, as Engerman implies, attempts to determine who the typical slaves were. Although I may suffer from a "trained incapacity" to view things in any other way, I believe most of the questions we ask about slavery are not subject to statistical proof. Even in an age of computers, this should not disturb us. After all, "Statistical truth is no truer truth than linguistic truth."

Ralph Carter and John Clarke rightly challenge some aspects of my treatment of Africa. To respond briefly, I agree that Curtin probably underestimated the number of Africans brought to the New World. The African trail is a treacherous one; the specific areas of impact are difficult to locate with any degree of certainty. Still, I admit that I did not have enough appreciation of the Ashanti proverb: "Ancient things remain in the ears." If I had, I would have recognized that a much larger segment of the slaves' proverbs, folktales, sexual attitudes, material culture, and religious practices came directly from Africa than I presented in 1972. The preservation of these cultural elements led eventually to the Africanization of American culture, especially in music, language, and dance.

What impact, Carter asks, did Africa have on American whites? First, traditional African slavery affected the evolution of the institution of slavery in the United States. Second, much of the southern white man's folklore was a modification of African lore. The language, sexual beliefs, and religion of American whites also received the impress of Africa. The links, however, remain to be worked out by scholars.

Rather than proceed down the largely unmarked African trail in 1972, I tried to explore an equally significant cultural terrain: the interrelationship between antebellum blacks and whites. With Ralph Ellison I believed that "Southern whites cannot walk, talk, sing, conceive of laws or justice, think of sex, love, the family or freedom without responding to the presence of the Negroes."[21] At the same time, I felt that a full exposition of the interpenetration of the slave's culture into the white man's would detract from my major objective: a delineation of cultural manifestations in the quarters.

Many of the critics suggest some conceptual errors in my treatment of the slave family. The most significant of these, they claim, were my infrequent allusions to sexual immorality in the quarters. Rejecting Earl Thorpe's suggestion that the words "loose morality" be placed in quotation marks, I will confront the matter directly. This entire question should not, however, be blown out of proportion. The main thrust of my argument was that the slaves generally had monogamous unions held together by affection rather than by law and that the family contributed to the bondsmen's self-esteem and survival.

On one level, and standing alone, some of my comments on slave sexual mores seem anachronistic. Sometimes equating premarital intercourse with "casual liaisons" and "loose morality," I may have unconsciously projected some of the elements of the conventional bourgeois moral-immoral dichotomy in sexual behavior onto the slave. Concomitantly, I did not relate the socialization process to slave morality.

In his closely reasoned essay James Anderson asserts that Herbert Gutman demonstrated "that slaves were far more moral in their sexual behavior" than I depicted them. Herbert Gutman, discussing the "prenuptial intercourse" common in the quarters, has contended that such practices were indicative of slave norms that differed from those of whites. Although this is partially true, it is false to argue that the slaves had complete autonomy in establishing such mores.

The "group pressures" and church punishment of adulterers and fornicators mentioned by Gutman indicate that some slaves also adopted the white man's norms and treated "prenuptial intercourse" as "immoral." For example, when the South Carolina slave, Harry Macmillan, appeared before the American Freedmen's Inquiry Commission in 1863, he responded to the commissioners' questions in the following fashion:

Q. Colored women have a good deal of sexual passion, have they not? they all go with men?

A. Yes, Sir, there is a great deal of that. I do not think you will find five out of a hundred that do not; they begin at 15 and 16..

Q. Do they know any better?

A. They regard it as a disgrace and the laws of the Church are against it.

Q. They sometimes have children before marriage?

A. Yes, Sir; but they are thought less of among their companions, unless they get a husband before the child is born, and if they cannot the shame grows until they do get a husband. Some join a Church when they are 10 years old and some not until they are 20; the girls join mostly before the men, but they are more apt to fall than the men. When ever a person joins the Church, no matter how low he has been, he is always respected. When the girls join the Church after a while they sometimes become weary and tired and some temptation comes in and they fall. Sometimes the Masters, where the Mistress was a pious woman, punished the girls for having children before they were married. As a general thing the Masters did not care, they like the colored women to have children.[22]

The essential issue is not whether slaves were "moral in their behavior." Rather, it is how they defined morality. This question, as Anderson notes, I did not clearly answer. The slave's moral code was a complex one. While admonishing his children not to steal from other blacks, for instance, a father might feel perfectly justified in advising them to "take" from his master. The slave was neither an abandoned sexual hedonist nor a neurotic puritan glorifying the frigid woman. Definitions of sexual morality in the quarters varied, as they do in most communities, according to age and religious beliefs.

As a result of the conflict between his African cultural heritage and his Christian beliefs, the slave had an ambivalent attitude toward sex. "Prenuptial intercourse" and "casual liaisons" existed in an uneasy alliance with biblical and societal pronouncements against such "immoral" practices. Macmillan's use of the words "shame," "disgrace," and "fall" in referring to antenuptial fornication is inexplicable unless we recognize this tension. Christianity, with all of its perverse repression of the sexual instinct, was a reality in the slave quarters. The genius of the slaves was that they did not agonize over the contradictions between beliefs and practices the way their masters did. I noted this in 1972 when I wrote that blacks were freed "from the insuperable guilt complexes that enslaved nineteenth-century white Americans in regard to sex."

Unlike Gutman, however, I am not convinced the slaves were entirely free of the sexual restraints confining American whites. Some slave parents began at an early age to teach their children about sex; others urged them to "be good" and never engage in sexual intercourse before marriage. Minnie Folkes, a former Virginia slave whose testimony is included in *Weevils in the Wheat,* typified the impact of the second practice:

I married when I wuz 14 years old. So help me God, I didn't know what marriage meant . . . I slept in bed—he on his side an' I on mine fer three months an dis ain't no lie . . . he never got close to me 'cause muma had sed 'Don't let nobody bother yo' principle'; 'cause dat wuz all yo' had. I 'bey my muma, an' tol' him so, and I said to go an' ask muma an' ef she sed he could get close to me hit waz alright.[23]

For African-born slaves there was no link between sex, sin, and evil as in European thought. Acceptance of Christian beliefs, however, caused the slaves some conflict over sexual behavior. Older slaves and parents taught certain prohibitions to the young: voluntary miscegenation, sexual intercourse without affection, adultery, and polygamy. There were obligatory demands on sexual partners. Each was to satisfy the physical and emotional needs of the other. A man who made a woman pregnant had to offer to marry her. At the same time, since the ideal was union based on love, the woman could refuse such an offer. Although older slaves frowned on premarital sex, especially for very young girls, they felt antenuptial sex would occur. Basically, the slaves recognized the nonhuman quality of sexual abstinence.

Some elements of the discussion of the slave family are difficult to follow. Owens, for example, argues that the study was "rarely shaped by realistic doses of joys and sorrows." Then he rejects the linkage of "sexual conquest," the ignorance of slave mothers, high mortality of black children, and the "idyllic" existence of the few who survived. Nowhere in the book did I argue, as Owens asserts, that most planters encouraged monogamy in the quarters or that the slave's respect for monogamous unions came primarily from whites.

Owens and Rawick are also confused about the impact of "sexual conquest" and the "reckless pursuit" of paramours in the quarters. I noted in 1972 that "the courtship patterns in the quarters differed, in many respects, from that of whites." (p. 85) Accommodated within the culturally defined norms of the quarters, neither the "pursuit" nor the "conquest" had the dire con-

sequences Owens or Rawick perceived. Neither is wholly contradictory to a sense of community nor sensitivity to women and children. And while both "pursuit" and "conquest" may offend the
sensibilities of twentieth-century man and woman, they represented
realities in the quarters. Owens should recall that in addition to
characterizing the family as a survival mechanism, I noted that it
provided love, role models, values, companionship, sexual gratifi-
cation, and self-esteem and performed "many of the traditional
functions of the family."

Some of our confusion over the nature of the slave family could
probably be avoided by placing it firmly in the comparative framework suggested by Carter. Systematic exploration of antebellum divorce petitions would yield, for instance, a great deal of data on the
interrelationship between black and white families. Sex ratios
among whites clearly had some impact on the black family as well
as on the sexual frustrations of the white woman. Comparisons
may suggest but will not provide answers. The slave was, after all,
in a special situation. His name, for example, was often a very
fragile link in a kinship network or base for identity. Speaking in
1853, the former bondsman, David Holmes, said: "slaves never
have any name. I'm called David, now; I used to be called Tom,
sometimes; but I'm not, I'm Jack. It didn't much matter what
name I was called by. If master was looking at any one of us, and
call us, Tom, or Jack, or anything else, whoever he looked at was
forced to answer."[24]

Much of the criticism has centered on my use of Harry Stack Sullivan's theories. Genovese finds the theoretical framework
"dreary" and "unilluminating," while Rawick feels it is a "parody" of the oppressed. Since I find psychology inherently exciting,
I can only plead limited writing skills as an explanation for making
it "dreary." Genovese's searching scrutiny of interpersonal theory
suggests some exciting new areas of exploration. He realizes, however, that I did not "apply" the theory to explain slave behavior.
When theory and evidence diverged, I reported what was in the
sources.

A closer reading of interpersonal theorists would show that many
limitations Genovese perceives do not exist. Hundreds of pages in
The Complete Works of Harry Stack Sullivan focus on childhood.

Anxiety, fear, pain, and loneliness, according to Sullivan, appear at some point in childhood. So do intimacy, love, security, and tenderness. Sullivan recognized that the socialization process, even under ideal circumstances, contained contradictory elements. Selective inattention and selective memory operate in significant ways in the formation of our self-systems: Often we remember more of the love than the fear. In spite of the terror Genovese finds in childhood, we must not forget the other factors Sullivan felt contributed to self-esteem.

The most salient element of interpersonal theory is *variability*. The theory encompasses deference, whether based on love, respect, or fear. Love and terror as facets of childhood development are also included. My statement about parents treating children as lovable was part of a general discussion of self-esteem. Even if we concede all of Genovese's qualifiers, the statement still stands. Compared to the terror most children find in a threatening world, home is a haven. Still, the horrifying stories of battered children are reminders that some persons' self-concepts are deformed because of the treatment they received from their parents. The omnipresent psychiatrist's couch is another. In spite of the couch, the essential point remains: A person's most enduring self-concept is a result of his or her interaction with parents.

Since I cannot answer all of the questions without restating the theoretical framework in great detail, it might be more fruitful to try to explain why I used psychology as an analytical tool in spite of my own reservations about it. Basically, my justification for resorting to interpersonal theory was that with its focus on significant others, power relationships, self-esteem, dominance, variability, situational factors, and perception, it allows us to ask many more questions about the master-slave relation than any other theory.

Did my use of Sullivan lead to a *parody* of the psychology of the oppressed as Rawick claims? Only in the sense that every attempt at historical re-creation is a "parody." Even so, I am not unaware of the weaknesses of psychology as a tool for studying blacks. The recent writings of black psychologists indicate that most psychological theories have limited applicability to blacks for a number of reasons. First, the theories were derived largely from observations of middle-class whites. Second, they are generally designed to explain pathological rather than normal behavior. Even granting these limitations, we must recognize that Sullivan had more contacts with blacks than Freud did.

Sullivan not only had black patients in New York and Washington, but he collaborated with black scholars studying black life and culture in the 1930s. He worked, for example, with the black sociologist Charles S. Johnson in examining the personality development of Southern rural black youth. He interviewed blacks in Nashville, Tennessee, and he wrote an appendix for Johnson's classic, *Growing Up in the Black Belt: Negro Youth in the Rural South* (1941). Later, Sullivan cooperated with the incomparable black sociologist, E. Franklin Frazier, interviewed about twenty blacks in Washington, D.C., and supplied material that Frazier incorporated in his study, *Negro Youth at the Crossways: Their Personality Development in the Middle States* (1940). In addition, Sullivan drew one element of his theory, the concept of tension, directly from the writings of the black philosopher, Albert M. Dunham, Jr.

Three significant factors emerge from a reflection on Sullivan's relation with and knowledge of blacks. First, two outstanding black scholars felt he was sensitive and objective enough to provide insights into their studies of Afro-Americans. Second, the young blacks he interviewed had a positive reaction to him as a person. One of them gave this evaluation of Sullivan: "I've never known a white man like him. In fact, he was so kind and friendly like I thought he was a Negro . . ."[25] Third, Sullivan appreciated the complexity of black personality development and the role of the psychiatrist in studying it. Summarizing his views of the black situation in 1940, Sullivan wrote:

When the techniques of intensive study of interpersonal relations have been substituted for those of a detached and generally preoccupied professional man, the presumptively "typically Negro" performances have been resolved into particular instances of the "typically human." On the one hand, the social distance of the Negro and the white ordinarily conceals the personal facts; also, the Negro, well-trained in the almost infrahuman role, finds certain utilities in playing it out.

It is evident that, if we are to develop a real approximation of national solidarity, we must find and cultivate a humanistic rather than a paternalistic, and exploiting, or an indifferent attitude to these numerous citizens of our commonwealth. As a psychiatrist, I have to speak particularly against using them as scapegoats for our unacceptable impulses; the fact that they are dark-skinned and poorly adapted to our historic puritanism is really too naive a basis for projecting most of our privately condemned faults upon them. They deserve to be observed as they are, and the blot of an American interracial problem may thus gradually be dissipated.[26]

Despite my high regard for Sullivan's work, I have never proposed any single theory as the only methodological approach. But if slavery was in any sense a power relationship, then Goffman's and Sullivan's theories can be illuminating. As Genovese has correctly pointed out, it makes little sense for historians to debate which of the two psychological theories is the better. Being an eclectic, I can conceive of using Freudian theory as an analytical tool. But I believe that it might tell us more about planter than slave behavior.

In any re-examination of psychological theory, we must consider the growing body of literature by black psychologists because they have begun to suggest alternative theories to explain the unique techniques blacks developed to cope with slavery and oppression. For instance, James Comer, in *Beyond Black and White,* wrote:

Slavery, discrimination and abuse were traumatic. . . . In some blacks . . .[the] debilitating relationship to the white power structure interfered with adequate personality development. Frustration led to apathy and withdrawal that destroyed potential and ruined lives. But major adaptive pathways were available that did not include a close relationship with oppressive and abusive whites. There were physical and creative outlets that the white world could not obstruct. And there was the mechanism of religion. These provided blacks with the sense of well-being that more whites achieved by controlling the world around them.[27]

The Slave Community was one attempt to describe the adaptive pathways and outlets enabling blacks to cope with and transcend bondage. Like Ralph Ellison, I found the slaves "outside the groove of history, and it was my job to get them in, all of them."[28] The critiques show that I did not entirely succeed. I neither raised nor answered all of the significant questions. Moreover, in some cases I may have added confusion where clarity reigned before. My only hope is that it was creative confusion.

Some of the confusion in and about the text could not be resolved by the reviewers or the critics. Throughout the pages of the critiques I have been considered the illegitimate intellectual son of Stanley Elkins; his spirit allegedly resonates throughout the book. Since Elkins based his theory on the work of his predecessors, it is unfair to try to make him the scapegoat for the myopia of American historians. The ghost of U.B. Phillips haunts all of us. Nineteenth-century racism haunts all of us. But none of these either created or sustained my interest in slavery. Though not a lineal intellectual descendant of Elkins, like most scholars of my generation, I had to confront him. Among the most innovative of historians, Elkins raised the level of debate over the character of slavery by cogently presenting the scattered musings of previous scholars in a logically constructed theory buttressed by his reading of psychological theory and analogies. With the wisdom born of hindsight, we may feel that the questions he asked were too limited in range. Still, he asked many of the right ones.

Stanley Elkins and the theories he presented were still very much alive when I began writing *The Slave Community*. It may be true, as Genovese charges, that I allowed those theories to set the terms of my discussion. What I tried to do was to redefine and expand Elkins's propositions. "It is not easy," say the Yoruba, "to confess envy when stating a case against an adversary." Still, I acknowledged my appreciation for Elkins's methodological innovations by utilizing them when I felt they were appropriate. At the same time, my focus on slave culture and family life does not parallel that of Elkins. His concern with comparisons, institutional breakdown, and historiography are not replicated in *The Slave Community*. By utilizing autobiographies I resorted to sources Elkins positively rejected. Elkins relied almost exclusively on secondary sources, while I made extensive use of primary sources.

It is interesting, given the connection the critics see between *The Slave Community* and *Slavery* to look at what Elkins has said about my work. The December 1975 issue of *Commentary* contained a witty review essay in which Elkins devoted a few paragraphs to my study of slavery. After briefly summarizing the main argument of *The Slave Community,* Elkins wrote:

As it happened, Blassingame's work was not received with much enthusiasm, though not because of its basic argument, which was already familiar and had by this time come to be accepted in principle. It was rather that reviewers thought his conclusions not as original as he claimed them to be, and that he had neglected to exploit a large mass of readily available evidence—the WPA interviews with former slaves—of the very sort that should have been most pertinent to his case. But a more serious difficulty lay in Blassingame being so locked in debate with a previous version of slave personality, and so repeatedly denying its legitimacy, that he never quite got around to explaining what *did* go into the making of this culture, or what its distinctive character was, or how it got that way. It seems to have been entirely a culture of resistance, but there is surprisingly little interest shown in the nature of what was being resisted. . . . In a society where men are enslaved by other men, human relationships must at least be taken as something special, and its human products—on both sides—as special too. Whereas the slave, at the end of Blassingame's book, 'was no different in most ways from most men. The same range of personality types existed in the quarters as in the mansion.' If slavery in practice made no more difference than that, perhaps the entire subject of slavery is less important than we thought.[29]

Invited to respond to Elkins's remarks by the editor of *Commentary,* my first reaction was, "The artful dodger!" Then, remembering how strong is the temptation to protect one's turf at all costs, I decided not to write anything. After all, Stanley Elkins decided long ago not to debate the issue of slavery. Since 1959 David B. Davis, George Rawick, Eugene Genovese, Earl Thorpe, Leslie Owens, Edmund Morgan, Gwendolyn Hall, Peter Wood, Carl Degler, Julia Floyd Smith, Leslie B. Rout, Robert Starobin, Warren Dean, Franklin W. Knight, Harold Davis, Frederick Bowser, Harry Hoetink, John Lombardi, Orlando Patterson, Richard Price, Cyril Packwood, Thomas Skidmore, Florestan Fernandez, Robert Toplin, Robert Conrad, Leslie Bethell, and José Rodrigues have written dozens of books based on extensive research in primary sources in five different languages undermining every element of Elkins's theory without causing him to modify it.

The historiographical debate over Stanley Elkins's *Slavery* forms an important chapter in twentieth-century intellectual history. It also teaches us a crucial lesson. Harsh criticism may develop in the object of our criticism a bunker mentality, a paralyzing inability to flow with the new current he or she may have started. This has been illustrated repeatedly in the ebb and flow of our study of slavery. We fall all too easily into the common error mentioned in the Hausa proverb: "Faults are like a hill: you stand on your own and talk about those of other people."

If we are to continue to expand our knowledge of the complexities of slavery, we cannot evade our critics, take refuge in appendices acknowledging the existence of new works without confronting them in "revisions," or ignore the larger meanings of the debate. Taking these caveats seriously, I should note that some of the criticisms leveled against my work have transcended the issues raised by *The Slave Community*. Others have been contradictory. The larger issues should be addressed and related to the future agenda for slavery scholars. Several of the critiques suggest that racism has been so endemic to the study of slavery that in our own enlightened times scholars are overreacting to it. In our zeal to rescue the slave from unflattering stereotypes, we have failed to deal with his blemishes. As human beings interacting with others, blacks were not totally autonomous. As oppressed people, they were not always heroic. The liberal consensus on slavery has consistently ignored key areas of the slave experience.

We have never systematically examined indigenous slavery in traditional African societies. Characteristically, most Africanists have focused on Moslem slavery. As important as such studies are, it is the traditional West African institution that will tell us most about the ways Africans adjusted to and influenced the evolution of slavery in the Americas. All too often we have looked at blacks who enslaved other blacks in an effort to exonerate the white master.

The nature of American slavery has eluded liberal scholars because we have been too preoccupied with whites enslaving blacks. Perhaps it is now time for us to compare one form of racial slavery to another. What of the many American and European whites the Africans enslaved? Did the personality of whites deteriorate under the shock of enslavement? Were the whites docile or

rebellious? How quickly did they adopt African cultural norms or
language?

At the same time that we explore the reactions of whites enslaved
in Africa, we must reexamine white servitude in the Americas.
Many of our speculations about the paternalism of the southern
planter will be meaningless until we ascertain how he treated the
white indentured servant. Did he sexually exploit European
women? Did he torture and overwork his white brother? Were
there traces of the "slavish personality" in the behavior of the indentured servant? Did white indentured servants resist servitude
more or less than black slaves did during the colonial period? To
what extent was the white indentured servant a believer in and a
practitioner of the Protestant work ethic? Did he adopt the aris-
tocratic ethos of his master?

When examining colonial servitude, we should avoid overempha-
sis on periodization. The recent tendency toward exaggerating the
differences between colonial and nineteenth-century slavery threat-
ens to entangle us in an unending effort to split smaller and smaller
hairs. No historian denies the importance of change over time. But
we must also remember to look for central tendencies remaining
constant in different chronological eras. Unless we want to return
to a time when most of our history was simple narrative, we will
frequently have to present a "static" view of slavery while noting
evolutionary processes.

Central tendencies when identified on southern plantations must
be followed in other institutions and other locales. We can learn
something by comparing southern to South African society. But
how much more could we discover about the uniqueness of the
world the slaveholders made by comparing it with the world northern mill owners made? There were some similarities in the
behavior, attitudes, and philosophies of New England factory
owners and southern slaveholders. They also often characterized
their "people" in similar ways. Did factory operatives identify with
the owners out of fear or respect? Did they demonstrate a commitment to the Protestant work ethic?

One of the central tendencies of plantation life that must be reex-
amined is religion. The syncretism of African and Anglo-American
beliefs, the conflicts between conjurers and black preachers, the use

of religion as a mechanism of social control and as the genesis of resistance, the relation between acculturation and religion, and the black preacher as leader of his flock deserve more attention than I gave them in 1972. The same is true of the ways slaves influenced white religious beliefs and practices.

While the treatment of slave religion should be expanded, I would not make it as central to slave life as some scholars have. Not every slave spent every day in prayer, and surely there were many who felt like the bondsman in Elma Stuckey's poem, "That Is It":

> I holler hallelujah,
> I jump up and I shout,
> Ain't gettin' on my knees no more,
> Done just 'bout wore 'em out.

> Things go 'long about the same,
> I try to do what's right,
> I can't please Marse and can't please God,
> I reckon He is white.

> I always prayed to the Lord
> That things be turned about,
> Ain't gettin' on my knees no more,
> Done just 'bout wore 'em out.[30]

By and large, historians are overly conservative in their choice of sources. Nowhere is this conservatism more apparent than in the study of slavery. In the latter half of the nineteenth century, we examined statutes. Then, in the early years of the twentieth century, U. B. Phillips and others pioneered the utilization of plantation records. By the 1970s we had discovered, if not totally accepted, slave autobiographies, folklore, songs, and interviews. And thanks to Herbert Gutman, Stanley Engerman, Robert Fogel, and others, we are now reluctantly entertaining the use of statistics. With the exception of planter records, the most impressive feature of our agonizingly slow movement toward the use of new sources has been the depth of resistance to them in the historical guild. Amazingly, scholars who have barely seen narratives, folktales, or census data characterize them as unreliable sources. Perhaps all of us are too conservative. Confronted with an admittedly imperfect source or method, we turn all too quickly to those we consider "safe." Newspapers are sacred because historians have traditionally mined them. But those of us who have examined nineteenth-century journals or read Lucy Salmon's revealing *The Newspaper and the Historian* (1923) feel that newspapermen were as often in league with the devil as they were with God. None of the other records we rely on so heavily is infallible: Diarists can be deceiving and planters can be perfidious.

I confess that I am, in the words of Engerman, "optimistic" about the ability of historians to overcome the limitations of practically all sources. That is, after all, what we have been trained to do. At the same time, I am dismayed that slavery scholars seem to have so little confidence in the training they have received. Too many of us lack the boldness and innovative spirit Phillips displayed in 1910, when he compiled runaway ads, statutes, contracts, letters, diaries, court cases, slave narratives, travel accounts, newspapers, and petitions and published them in *Plantation and Frontier Documents*. Imitation requires no special talent. Plantation records fading from constant use by historians may still have something to tell us, but they must be supplemented by sources whose validity is not hallowed by unexamined tradition. We must at least be willing to consider the testimony of those witnesses our less enlightened predecessors damned to perdition.

The next assignment for slavery scholars is to exhume the abolitionist. After the slave, the abolitionist has received the least respect from historians as a witness. We have rejected abolitionist testimony about the peculiar institution because the reformers were allegedly too prejudiced, emotional, guilt-ridden, and mentally unbalanced. Strangely, the abolitionists are among the few victorious reformers who have been subsequently defeated by historians. The truth they presented was too painful. Admitting all of the possible limitations of abolition documents (differing in no way from other documents scholars use), I do not believe historians are so intellectually bankrupt, so ignorant of critical tests and the rules of evidence that they cannot extract useful information from such sources.

My own respect for abolitionist documents is a direct outgrowth of four years of collecting and annotating the papers of Frederick Douglass. In our search for Douglass papers we have read practically all of the abolitionist journals. Several facts of interest to slavery scholars emerged from these readings. Abolitionists, for example, compiled the largest body of slave documents in the nineteenth century. The anti-slavery newspapers contained letters, speeches, and interviews of planters and slaves and accounts of southern and Latin American travelers that can be found nowhere else. Anti-slavery societies subscribed to practically every newspaper published in the South and collectively had the largest clipping service in the United States. They clipped stories about runaway slaves, pro-slavery sermons, legislative debates, black resistance, free blacks, nonslaveholding whites, lynchings, miscegenation, plantation rules, planter wills, and manumission from southern newspapers and published them in such abolitionist journals as the *Liberator, National Anti-Slavery Standard,* and the *Anti-Slavery Bugle* or in such books as Theodore Dwight Weld's *Slavery As It Is* (1839).

"We have lived a humble life, having no historians except abolitionists," the former slave William Wells Brown asserted in an 1863 speech. Continuing, he said: "we have been oppressed at the South, and despised at the North. The literature of the country has ignored us, except when it abused us. But a new time has come."[31] While the abolitionists were not the slave's only historian, they had an antiquarian's interest in collecting documents and a lawyer's sensibility in evaluating evidence. Editors and reporters, for instance, made every effort to verify slave interviews before they published them in abolitionist journals. Similarly, the way vigilance committees investigated the fugitives who came to them for aid would put many contemporary police departments to shame. While delighting in obtaining evidence from southern newspapers, abolitionist editors welcomed "I was there" reports. Not content with relying on secondhand testimony, many abolitionists penetrated the Cotton Curtain, observed the peculiar institution, and sent regular reports to anti-slavery journals. Consequently, eyewitness accounts of plantation slavery from the pens of abolitionists abound in these journals. Many of these reports are as revealing as those of Frederick Law Olmsted, who followed in the footsteps of abolitionist correspondents.

A dispassionate view of abolitionist documents gives us some cause for optimism in relying on them. Weld's masterful compilation of sources is still unmatched in number and variety. Information in Issac Hopper's "Tales of Oppression" serialized in various journals between 1840 and 1842 that Daniel Meaders of Yale University examined, has been corroborated by census data, legal records, contemporary newspapers, and manuscripts. The speeches, letters, interviews, and autobiographies from abolition newspapers in *Slave Testimony* were corroborated using similar sources.

Even more important is our scrutiny of abolitionist documents in our research on the Douglass Papers Project. If our annotation is any test, the credibility of these much maligned men and women is far higher than historians have generally realized. Neither gullible recorders nor unprincipled reporters, the abolitionist journalists left a massive repository of valuable material about slave life and culture.

Perhaps the most important service the abolitionist journalists performed for the historian was the collection of rare sources of information on white southerners. Reports of agricultural societies, schools, colleges, and churches are significant indices of southern life. Most surprising and revealing to me, however, were the hundreds of letters southern whites wrote to abolitionist journals. Some of them are what I would call "planter confessions"—admissions of guilt and oppression. Others are strident defenses of the peculiar institution. White women, nonslaveholders, and overseers also wrote about their experiences.

Other reform organizations also did yeoman service for the historian of slavery. Among the most significant of them was the American Colonization Society (ACS). Its long-running journal, *The African Repository*, contains thousands of letters from planters, slaves, free blacks, and freedmen. Essays and extracts from speeches and reports of southerners appear frequently. The manuscript letters from masters and slaves in the archives of the ACS constitute the largest single repository of such material and is a key to analyses of manumission and planter ideology. There is, for example, considerable evidence of planter guilt in these letters. On the other side of the reform spectrum was the American Missionary Association (AMA). The *American Missionary*, its journal, contains a wealth of hitherto unexploited data on slave family life, music, and religion. Like the ACS, the AMA had a good clipping service, collected much material on slavery from southern sources, and received many letters from southern whites.

Running the gamut from anti- to pro-slavery, the reformers compiled extensive records that the innovative scholar can utilize to increase our understanding of slavery. We must, however, approach these records as cautiously as we do other documents. But criticism and "optimism" should not be treated as completely antagonistic. When missionary, colonizationist, or abolitionist records pass the tests usually applied to historical documents, we should not be afraid to use them.

We should also show greater courage in exploring the psychological dimensions of slavery. Historians have drawn masterful portraits of the economic, political, and intellectual world the slaveholders made while remaining abysmally ignorant of their socio-psychological habitat. The pioneering studies of Earl Thorpe, *Eros and Freedom* (1967) and the *Old South: A Psychohistory* (1972), have been unfairly pilloried by people who understood neither the medium nor the message. Thorpe has asked questions that must be answered. If we stress the reciprocal relationship between master and slave, we cannot understand the personality development of one without putting the other on the couch. We have essayed to psychoanalyze the bondsman even while claiming he could never tell the analyst about his dreams, traumas, and relationships with his parents and significant others. The planter, on the other hand, has left a massive array of the personal documents, life histories, interviews, and confessions that form the staples of the evidence needed by the psychoanalyst. By common agreement this is "superior" data. Without endorsing Thorpe's methodological apparatus, I believe historians must now systematically examine the personality development of the planter.

We have witnessed the beginning of a revolution in the study of slavery in the last few years. "Roots" and other media events symbolize an increasing ability of the American people to consider the complexities of the peculiar institution. Central to this new awareness has been the growth of Black Studies. However much they resisted them initially, the strident demands of black students in the late 1960s had an impact on scholars. Thanks to the students, the questions we consider today are not the same ones we considered in 1960. If we are to go on to the next plateau in the study of slavery, we must deliberately turn to Black Studies for guidance. The most significant benefit of this would be much more systematic interdisciplinary studies.

There are no magic formulas for studying slavery. My critics have, however, pointed the way toward a clearer understanding of the institution and its meaning for America. Whether or not I answered their questions, the critics have forced me to reassess my conviction that the slaves, constituting a majority of the inhabitants on the plantation, represented the most important subjects for the historian and were their own best interpreters. Analogies, stereotypes, and plantation records may provide some insights. But in the final analysis, we must ask the victim how he was victimized and the survivor how he survived.

"In all the books that you have studied you never have studied Negro history have you? If you want Negro history, you will have to get [it] from somebody who wore the shoe, and by and by from one to the other you will get a book," a former slave told an interviewer in 1929.[32] In *The Slave Community* I tried to keep faith with those bound in chains and to expand the central cast of characters who acted out the drama of slavery. It was the beginning, not the culmination, of my exploration of bondage.

NOTES

1. Robert Hayden, *Angle of Ascent* (New York, 1975), p. 32.

2. Thomas Hobbes, *Leviathan* (New York, 1964 [1651]), p. 85.

3. Benjamin Drew, *The Refugee* (Reading, Mass., 1969), p. 29.

4. Lucy Davidowicz, *The War Against the Jews, 1933-1945* (New York, 1975), p. 220.

5. Elma Stuckey, *The Big Gate* (Chicago, 1976), p. 37.

6. Georg Hegel, *The Philosophy of Right* (London, 1942), p. 239.

7. ———, *The Phenomenology of Mind* (New York, 1967), pp. 238-39.

8. Frederick Douglass, *My Bondage and My Freedom* (New York, 1855), pp. 435-36.

9. Albert Camus, *The Rebel* (New York, 1956), p. 270.

10. Robert Starobin, ed., *Blacks in Bondage: Letters of American Slaves* (New York, 1974), p. xii.

11. Clement Eaton, *The Mind of the South* (Baton Rouge, 1967), pp. 170-71.

12. Drew, *Refugee*, pp. 201-02.

13. Kenneth M. Stampp, "Slavery—The Historian's Burden," in Harry P. Owens, ed., *Perspectives and Irony in American Slavery* (Jackson, Miss., 1976), p. 166.

14. Charles C. Jones, *The Religious Instruction of the Negroes in the United States* (Savannah, 1842), 110-11.

15. Edward Pollard, "The Romance of the Negro," *American Missionary* 15 (November, 1871), 242.

16. Martin R. Delany, *Blake, or the Huts of America* (Boston, 1970), pp. 110, 126.

17. Paulo Freire, *Pedagogy of the Oppressed* (New York, 1970), p. 29.

18. Willie Lee Rose, ed., *A Documentary History of Slavery in North America* (New York, 1976), pp. 531-32.

19. William W. Nichols, "Slave Narratives: Dismissed Evidence in the Writing of Southern History," *Phylon* 32 (Winter, 1971), 407

20. Herbert G. Gutman, *The Black Family in Slavery and Freedom, 1750-1925* (New York, 1976), p. 569.

21. Ralph Ellison, *Shadow and Act* (New York, 1964), p. 123.

22. John W. Blassingame, ed., *Slave Testimony: Two Centuries of Letters, Speeches, Interviews, and Autobiographies* (Baton Rouge, 1977), p. 382.

23. Charles L. Perdue, et al., eds. *Weevils in the Wheat: Interviews with Virginia Ex-Slaves* (Charlottesville, Va., 1976), pp. 95-96.

24. Blassingame, *Slave Testimony*, p. 297.

25. Harry S. Sullivan, *The Complete Works of Harry Stack Sullivan* 2 (2 vols., New York, 1953-56), p. 98.

26. Ibid., pp. 105-07.

27. James P. Comer, *Beyond Black and White* (New York, 1972), pp. 174-75.

28. Ralph Ellison, *Invisible Man* (New York, 1972), p. 335.

29. Stanley Elkins, "The Slavery Debate," *Commentary* 60 (December, 1975), 45.

30. Stuckey, *Big Gate*, p. 61.

31. *Liberator,* June 5, 1863.

32. Fisk University, *Unwritten History of Slavery* (Nashville, 1945), pp. 45-46.

JOHN W. BLASSINGAME

Appendix
Using the Testimony of Ex-Slaves: Approaches and Problems*

Historians of the South's Peculiar Institution have been engaged in a perennial debate about the reliability of various sources. Conceding the virtual impossibility of finding the completely objective observer, many of them insist that every class of sources should be investigated. Stanley M. Elkins presented the most convincing argument on this point in 1959 when he wrote that eyewitness accounts of slavery "were both hostile and sympathetic in nature. It is perhaps best that each kind be given equal weight, as evidence in the judicial sense must always be, and the best presumption probably is that none of these observers was lying about the facts as he saw them. Different facts impressed different people, of course. . . . Much is gained and not much is lost on the provisional operating principle that they were all telling the truth."[1]

Unfortunately, few historians have acted on the principles outlined by Elkins. While examining practically all kinds of accounts written by white eyewitnesses, they have largely rejected those accounts written by ex-slaves. Ulrich B. Phillips led the way in his *Life and Labor in the Old South* (1929) when he declared that "ex-slave narratives in general . . . were issued with so much abolitionist editing that as a class their authenticity is doubtful."[2] Most

*Editor's Note: This article first appeared in the *Journal of Southern History* 41 (November 1975), 473-92. Copyright [1975] by the Southern Historical Association. Reprinted by permission of the managing editor.

scholars have followed Phillips in refusing to read the accounts of former slaves. Only three of the sixteen state studies of plantation slavery published between 1902 and 1972 drew even moderately on slave testimony. Among the general studies of slavery, only Frederick Bancroft, in *Slave-Trading in the Old South* (1931), used the testimony of former slaves extensively.[3]

A number of scholars have challenged Phillips and contend that in order to understand slavery from the vantage point of blacks, one must carefully study black testimony and suggest ways it can be used.[4] Historians need to know, for example, how to analyze interviews that were conducted with former slaves in the twentieth century. Which of the published autobiographies can be verified by independent sources? Which of them are least reliable? What kinds of questions can and cannot be answered by resorting to the accounts of former slaves? How many of the stories were written by the blacks themselves? Who edited the published narratives?

The fundamental problem confronting anyone interested in studying black views of bondage is that the slaves had few opportunities to tell what it meant to be a chattel. Since the antebellum narratives were frequently dictated to and written by whites, any study of such sources must begin with an assessment of the editors. An editor's education, religious beliefs, literary skill, attitudes toward slavery, and occupation all affected how he recorded the account of the slave's life.

Generally, the editors of the antebellum narratives were an impressive group of people noted for their integrity. Most of those for whom biographical data were available were engaged in professions (lawyers, scientists, teachers, historians, journalists, ministers, and physicians) and businesses where they had gained a great deal of prior experience in separating truth from fiction, applying rules of evidence, and accurately portraying men and events. Many of them were either antagonistic to or had little or no connection with professional abolitionists. This was especially true of Samuel Atkins Eliot and David Wilson. Eliot, the editor of Josiah Henson's first narrative, was a musicologist and essayist who had served successively as state legislator, mayor of Boston, and congressman (1850-1851). When Eliot voted for the Fugitive Slave Law, he was denounced by abolitionists. Solomon Northup's editor, David

Wilson, was a New York lawyer, state legislator, occasional poet, and former school superintendent. He had no relationship with abolitionists.[5]

Often, whites edited narratives because their interest in slavery was aroused by sensational trials involving kidnapped or fugitive blacks. For example, Harper Twelvetrees, a London manufacturer, copied John Anderson's story almost verbatim from the stenographic report of a Canadian extradition hearing. Similarly, when the New York free Negro Solomon Northup was rescued from slavery in Louisiana, he attracted the attention of one of his neighbors, David Wilson.[6]

Five of the editors, William George Hawkins, Joseph C. Lovejoy, James W. C. Pennington, Thomas Price, and William Greenleaf Eliot, were noted ministers in the United States and England. The most famous of them was William G. Eliot. Ubiquitous reformer and philanthropist, Eliot served a long tenure as pastor of a St. Louis congregational church, was president of the city's school board, and founded Washington University at St. Louis. During the antebellum period Eliot frequently castigated "fanatical abolitionists" and adhered rigidly to his belief in gradual emancipation.[7]

Many whites edited the narratives because of their interest in history. In fact, nine of the editors had published historical works before 1860. The editors who wrote one historical work during the antebellum period included Samuel A. Eliot, Pennington, and Price.[8] Other editors might properly be treated as amateur or professional historians and biographers. Numbered among them were James S. Loring, Henry Trumbull, David Wilson, Joseph C. Lovejoy, Charles E. Lester, and Charles Campbell.[9]

One of the most prolific was Charles E. Lester. A presbyterian minister, consul, and reporter, he published twenty-seven books during his lifetime and translated a number of French and Italian works into English. Lester's *The Life and Voyages of Americus Vespucius* went through several editions between 1846 and 1903.[10] Undoubtedly the most highly qualified of the historian-editors was a southerner, Virginia's Charles Campbell. School principal, newspaper editor, and essayist, Campbell edited the papers of Theodorick Bland, Jr., and the military records of the American

Revolution and wrote a book on the colonial history of his state. One of Campbell's contemporaries characterized his work as "remarkable for its research and accuracy."[11]

Some of the abolitionist editors also had impressive credentials. This is especially true of those editors with considerable journalistic experience: Louis Alexis Chamerovzow, Isaac Tatem Hopper, and James W. C. Pennington. Chamerovzow had edited various journals and served as secretary of the British and Foreign Anti-Slavery Society before he edited the narrative of John Brown. Thomas Cooper's account was edited by Hopper, the implacable Quaker prison reformer who had served as coeditor of the *National Antislavery Standard* and was one of the foremost penologists of his time. Pennington, the editor of J. H. Banks's narrative, was a former Maryland slave who had spent sixteen years as an editor and investigative reporter for several black newspapers.[12]

Many of the procedures the editors adopted are now standard in any biographical study or oral-history project. Generally, the ex-slave lived in the same locale as the editor and had given oral accounts of his bondage. If the fugitive believed that the white man truly respected blacks, they discussed the advisability of publishing his account. Once the black was persuaded to record his experiences for posterity, the dictation might be completed in a few weeks or be spread over two or three years. Often, the editor read the story to the fugitive and asked for elaboration of certain points and clarification of confusing and contradictory details. When the dictation ended, the editor frequently compiled appendices to corroborate the ex-slave's narrative. The appendices consisted almost entirely of evidence obtained from southern sources: official reports of legislatures, courts, governors, churches, and agricultural societies, books written by southern whites, or newspapers edited by them. If any of those among the editor's friends who first heard the narrative doubted its authenticity, they sometimes interrogated the fugitive for hours.[13]

A comparison of the narratives with other works written by the editors reveals few essential differences between the techniques they employed. Charles Campbell approached Isaac Jefferson's narrative with the same detachment that he used in editing the papers of Theodorick Bland. The appendices, poems, and letters contained in Joseph C. Lovejoy's biographies of his brother and of the Reverend Charles T. Torrey are similar in character to those included in his edition of the narrative of Lewis G. and Milton Clarke. The same pattern prevails in various historical works and the narratives edited by Wilson, Lester, Loring, Price, and others.[14]

One indication of the general reliability of the edited narratives is that so few of them were challenged by antebellum southerners. The first exposé was of the narrative of James Williams, which Alabama whites proved was an outright fraud. The only other antebellum attack on a narrative involved the autobiography of Charles Ball. In Ball's case, however, the charges cannot be substantiated. A comparison of the narrative with antebellum gazetteers, travel accounts, manuscript census returns, and histories of South Carolina shows that Ball accurately described people, places, rivers, flora and fauna, and agricultural practices in the state. Since the only narrative included in U. B. Phillips's justly acclaimed *Plantation and Frontier Documents* was that of Charles Ball, it may have been more reliable than the antebellum critics were willing to concede.[15]

Of course, many of the more reliable narratives contain elements that cannot be attributed to the blacks. Certain literary devices that appear in the accounts were clearly beyond the ken of unlettered slaves. First, many of the narratives contain long dialogues that could only represent approximations of the truth. Sometimes it is obvious that the editors fleshed out the sparse details supplied by the fugitives to heighten the dramatic effect of the dialogues. Second, the abolitionist editors often included direct appeals to their white readers. Many of them also penned long digressions on the duplicity of northerners in maintaining slavery. Similarly, the most complicated philosophical, religious, and historical arguments were sometimes attributed to the slaves to show that bondage violated divine law and the natural rights of man.[16] On occasion a narrative contained so many of the editor's views that there was little room for the testimony of the fugitive. Sometimes the accounts were so romantic and focused so heavily on the flight from bondage that they were more akin to Indian-escape literature than slave autobiographies. These features are so prevalent in the narratives of Elleanor Eldridge, Sally Williams, Jane Blake, and others that they generally reveal few of the details of slave life.[17] There can be little doubt that the abolitionists interjected some of their own ideas into the narrtives. Apparently, however, a majority of them faithfully recorded the factual details they received from the former slaves.

If it is conceded that many of the abolitionist editors were honest but biased men, the major task of the historian, then, is to find ways to separate their rhetoric from the sentiments of the slaves. The first step in this direction is to compare the antebellum narratives with some of the best autobiographies written by former slaves after the Civil War. Although they are sometimes rather romantic or devote few pages to their life on the plantation, the accounts published during the postbellum period are in many ways the most significant and reliable of the lot. The pain of the whip had generally faded enough for the former slaves to write about bondage with less passion than their antebellum predecessors.[18] Another way of identifying elements added by white editors is to compare the first edition of a narrative with each revised version. The first edition of most narratives is often the one with the fewest distortions.[19]

Even when one is able to identify and discount abolitionist rhetoric in the accounts of fugitive slaves, the "facts" supplied by the blacks may seem false. The only way such doubts can be removed is to try to verify the details of the account by examining independent sources. Fortunately, a plethora of antebellum sources enables historians to ascertain whether the abolitionist editors distorted the accounts of the fugitives. Several of the blacks, for example, made and wrote numerous speeches and letters antedating the publication of their narratives. When these records are compared with the published accounts, it is obvious that many of the editors tried to write the details of the fugitive's life as he dictated them. This is especially true of the narratives of Lewis G. and Milton Clarke,[20] Josiah Henson,[21] William and Ellen Craft,[22] and Henry Box Brown.[23] A number of scholars have investigated judicial proceedings, manuscript census returns, diaries and letters of whites, local records, newspapers, and city directories and have proven that the narratives of Solomon Northup, John Brown, Olaudah Equiano, and others were authentic.[24]

Many blacks who had purchased their freedom, been manumitted, or escaped from bondage wrote autobiographies without the
aid of white editors. A comparison of the narratives of such well-
known blacks as William Wells Brown, Frederick Douglass, Henry
Bibb, James W. C. Pennington, Jermain Loguen, Austin Steward,
and Richard Allen with their antebellum letters, speeches, sermons,
and books reveals so many similarities in style that there can be no
doubt about either the authorship or authenticity of their accounts.
Even such obscure men as John Thompson, Noah Davis, Solomon
Bayley, and G. W. Offley have left enough records to establish
their authorship of their autobiographies.[25] Similarly, more than 90
percent of the sixty-seven narratives published after the Civil War
were written by the blacks themselves.

Although most of them are authentic, the published narratives
constitute a limited sample of the total slave population in a
number of ways. First, there are many more accounts of slavery in
the upper than the lower south (and practically none for Florida,
Arkansas, and Texas). Second, and most important, black women
wrote less than 12 percent of the narratives. Third, the percentage
of fugitives among the narrators was much higher than the percentage of blacks who escaped from slavery. While less than 5 percent
of the bondsmen successfully followed the North Star to freedom,
fugitives wrote about 35 percent of all narratives. (The others were
written by slaves who purchased their freedom, were manumitted,
or were freed after the Civil War began.) Finally, an overwhelming
majority of the narrators were among the most perceptive and
gifted of the former slaves.

Because of the high proportion of exceptional slaves among the
black autobiographers, many scholars insist that more of the
average slaves should be heard and point to the 2,194 interviews
with ex-slaves compiled by the Works Progress Administration between 1936 and 1938 as the chief source for such testimony.
Deposited in the Library of Congress, the collection was rarely used
until Greenwood Press published it in 1972. Even before the interviews were published, Benjamin A. Botkin and Norman R. Yetman
had made a convincing case for their use. George P. Rawick and
Eugene D. Genovese have added their own enthusiastic endorsement of Botkin's and Yetman's views. According to these scholars

the WPA interviews are much more representative of the total slave population, less biased, and less distorted than the published narratives of former slaves.[26] Since there are few systematic analyses of the interviews, it is difficult to assess the validity of their claims.

One obvious shortcoming of any study based on the WPA data, however, is that few American historians have been trained to use interviews. Because of his traditional fascination with the written word, the American historian, when confronted with the oral lore represented by the WPA interviews, has no methodological tools that are applicable to them.

Social scientists have pinpointed several problems in interpreting oral lore which are especially evident in the WPA interviews.[27] The first and most important question one must raise about these sources is whether the interview situation was conducive to the accurate communication and recording of what the informants remembered of slavery. In this regard, it should be noted that black interviewers was virtually excluded from the WPA staffs in all of the southern states except Virginia, Louisiana, and Florida. Discrimination in employment led to a distortion of information; during the 1930s caste etiquette generally impeded honest communication between southern blacks and whites.

John Dollard, Hortense Powdermaker, Allison Davis, and many other social scientists who studied the South during the 1930s give vivid pictures of the milieu in which the WPA data were collected. In the context of the 1930s the oft-repeated declaration of WPA officials that they were not interested in "taking sides" on contemporary racial problems seriously limited their ability to obtain accurate information from southern blacks.[28] Traditionally, any white man who is not "with" black folks is inevitably viewed as being "against" them. Anyone who doubts this should read the essay by Wiliam R. Ferris, Jr., on the problems he encountered while collecting oral lore in Mississippi in 1968. During his interviewing Ferris found:

It was not possible to maintain rapport with both Whites and Blacks in the same community, for the confidence and cooperation of each was based on their belief that I was "with them" in my convictions about racial taboos of Delta society. Thus when I was "presented" to Blacks by a white member of the community, the informants regarded me as a member of the white caste and therefore limited their lore to non-controversial topics.

> Blacks rarely speak openly about their society with Whites because of their vulnerability as an oppressed minority. . . . As the group in power, Whites can afford to openly express their thoughts about Blacks, whereas the latter conceal their feelings toward Whites as a means of self-preservation.[29]

The black man's vulnerability to white oppression was painfully evident in the Depression South. From 1931 to 1935, for example, there were more than seventy lynchings in the South; nine blacks who had committed no crime were killed, and twenty-five were lynched for minor offenses. Many of the black informants lived in areas where labor contracts were negotiated in jails, debt was perpetual, travel was restricted, and the threat of violence made peonage a living hell. Historian Pete Daniel, after an exhaustive study of southern peonage, concluded: "The violence that attended peonage sent tentacles of dread throughout the entire black community."[30] Since many of the former slaves still resided in the same areas as their masters' descendants and were dependent on whites to help them obtain their old-age pensions, they were naturally guarded (and often misleading) in their responses to certain questions. Frequently the white interviewers were closely identified with the ancien régime; on occasion they were the grandsons of the blacks' former masters.

The answers to many of the questions on the WPA interview schedule could neither be divorced from the dependent position of the aged blacks nor the contemporary state of race relations in the South. Since attitudes toward the past were often so intertwined with the present in the minds of both informants and interviewers, there was a high premium placed on giving the "right" answers to such question as: "Was your master kind to you?" "Now that slavery time is ended, what do you think of it?" "Was your master a good man?" "Which was best, slavery or freedom?"[31] Not content with these and other leading questions indicating the kinds of replies they wanted, many of the interviewers refused, initially, to accept the "wrong" answers. This was especially the case when the former slaves described their masters as cruel and said that life on the plantation was characterized by unusually hard work. A Georgia interviewer, for example, was disturbed by the responses of Nancy Boudry to her questions:

> Nancy's recollections of plantation days were colored to a somber hue by overwork, childbearing, poor food and long working hours.
> "Master was a hard taskmaster," said Nancy. . . . "I had to work hard, plow and go and split wood jus' like a man. Sometimes dey whup me. Dey whup me bad, pull de cloes off down to de wais'—my master did it, our folks didn' have overseer."
>
> "Nancy, wasn't your mistress kind to you?"
> "Mistis was sorta kin' to me, sometimes. But dey only give me meat and bread, didn' give me nothin' good—I ain' gwine tell no story. . . ."
>
> "But the children had a good time, didn't they? They played games?"
> "Maybe dey did play ring games, I never had no time to see what games my chillun play, I work so hard. . . ."[32]

The white staff of the WPA had mastered so little of the art and science of interviewing that many of them found it impossible to obtain trustworthy data from their informants. The whites disregarded a fundamental rule of interviewing that Ferris noted in 1968: "As a white collector, rapport with Blacks was particularly delicate and required constant sensitivity to the feelings of informants."[33] Many of the WPA interviewers consistently referred to their informants as darkeys, niggers, aunteys, mammies, and uncles. Reminiscent as these terms were of rigid plantation etiquette, they were not calculated to engender the trust of the blacks. Rather than being sensitive, the white interviewers failed to demonstrate respect for the blacks, ignored cues indicating a tendency toward ingratiation, and repeatedly refused to correct the informants' belief that the interviewer was trying to help them obtain the coveted pension. Not only did most of the whites lack empathy with the former slaves, they often phrased their questions in ways that indicated the kinds of answers they wanted.

Every recorded interview had two authors, the person who asked the questions and the one who answered them.[34] Often the white interviewer-author's actions and demeanor led to distortions and limitations of what the black informant-author told him. Many of the blacks played it safe; they claimed that they remembered very little about slavery and gave one- or two-page interviews. Even the informants who gave the longest, most candid interviews refused to talk about certain things. One frustrated Kentuckian, for example, reported: "In interviewing the different negroes in this community I have not found a single negro that could admit [,] if I asked the direct question [,] that they are the least bit superstitious."[35] Sometimes it was impolitic, if not dangerous, for the ex-slave to tell all that he remembered. This is especially evident in the folk songs and tales. Although practically every intensive study of these cultural elements reveals much antiwhite sentiment, rarely does this attitude surface in the WPA collection. Many of the secular songs are lullabies or hunting songs; the white-hating trickster slave Jack almost never appears in the tales. The blacks were carefully editing what they told whites; generally, they told them only children's tales and songs. One indication of this is the difference between the tales recorded during the same period by the black folklorist J. Mason Brewer and those by the WPA. Taken from the same class of informants, the tales Brewer recorded have a relatively high antiwhite content and many Jack or John stories.[36]

A second weakness of the WPA interviews is that many of them are not verbatim accounts. The informants' stories were often edited or revised before they were typed and listed as official records. Even when the former slave's views are purportedly typed in his own words, the interview may have been "doctored," certain portions deleted without any indication in the typescript, and his language altered. Consequently, the interviews are not, as Norman R. Yetman claimed, "almost exclusively verbatim testimonies" in which blacks "describe in their own words what it felt like to be a slave." Indications of deliberate distortion and interpolation of the views of the WPA staffers pose a serious challenge to historians who rely on the interviews.[37]

The best evidence on the alteration of interviews appears in the records of Roscoe E. Lewis and a Georgia interviewer, J. Ralph Jones. In 1936 and 1937 Jones conducted five interviews that were returned to the state office of the WPA. Three of the five transcribed by the state office are virtually identical to the copies that Jones retained. The other two were significantly reduced in length and seriously distorted.[38]

Jones's interviews with Rias Body and Washington B. Allen were edited to delete references to cruel punishments, blacks serving in the Union Army, runaways, and blacks voting during Reconstruction. Jones had two interviews with W. B. Allen, and the second one is recorded in practically identical words in his record and the WPA typescript. The WPA typescript of the first interview, however, lists Allen's date and place of birth incorrectly and does not include 1,700 words that appear in Jones's record of the interview. About half of the section excluded from the WPA typescript referred to slave traders, the religious life of the slaves, the tricks they played on the patrollers, and the songs they sang. While the typescript refers to the kind treatment Allen received from his owners, Jones's records show that he spent a great deal of time talking about the hard work and cruel floggings characteristic of the plantation.[39] The WPA transcript gives the impression that Allen spoke in dialect, using such words as "fetched," "de," "dis," "chilluns," and "fokes." But in his records Jones observed that Allen "uses excellent English. . . ."[40]

J. Ralph Jones's experience was not unique. The same kinds of distortions appeared in the typescripts of the Virginia WPA. Nine of the Virginia informants included in the Library of Congress collection were also quoted in the 1940 publication, *The Negro in Virginia*. Roscoe E. Lewis, the editor, had the original report of the interviews in his possession, and seven of the nine informants he quoted presented views excluded from the typescripts of their accounts. According to the excerpts quoted by Lewis, between one and twelve hundred words of the original interviews were excluded from the typescripts of the accounts of Fanny Berry, Georgianna Gibbs, Charles Grandy, Della Harris, Mobile Hopson, Richard Slaughter, and Eliza[beth] Sparks. The typescripts are poor summaries of the ex-slaves' comments. Songs and religious sentiments were frequently left out of the WPA typescripts. Indications of cruel punishments, forced marriages, family separations, ridicule of whites, and the kindness of Union soldiers appeared in the records cited by Lewis but often do not appear in the WPA typescripts.[41]

Although the facts are not entirely clear, it is obvious that many of the WPA interviews were altered after the dictation ended. The national office of the WPA encouraged this in regard to the language patterns of the blacks when it urged state directors to record dialect uniformly. This may have accounted for dialect being ascribed to former slaves who spoke English perfectly. But how can one account for the discrepancies between the interviews Jones and others recorded and those the WPA staff typed? Were two out of every five interviews in Georgia and other southern states distorted in the same way? While there are no definitive answers to these intriguing questions, historians must ponder them when they try to use the WPA interviews.

A third factor that led to distortion of the WPA interviews was the average age of the informants; two-thirds of them were at least eighty years old when they were interviewed. And, since only 16 percent of the informants had been fifteen years or older when the Civil War began, an overwhelming majority of them could only describe how slavery appeared to a black child. Because all of the blacks were at least seventy-two years removed from slavery, there was no sense of immediacy in their responses; all too often they recalled very little of the cruelty of bondage. A good way of determining the impact of age on the responses of former slaves is to compare the WPA interviews with the hundreds conducted by northern journalists, soldiers, missionaries, and teachers during and immediately after the Civil War. These informants were still close to bondage, and consequently they remembered far more of the details of slavery than the WPA respondents.[42]

Were the WPA informants, as Yetman claimed, representative of the total antebellum slave population? Apparently not. Since the average life expectancy of a slave born in 1850 was less than fifty years, those who lived until the 1930s might have survived because they received better treatment than most slaves. Taken at face value, there seems to have been a bias in many states toward the inclusion of the most obsequious former slaves. This is especially true when most of the informants had spent all of their lives in the same locale as their former master's plantation. Since the least satisfied and most adventuresome of the former slaves might have migrated to northern states or cities after the Civil War, the WPA informants may have been atypical of antebellum slaves. Geographically, the WPA collection is also a biased sample. Although 920,266 of the South's 3,953,760 slaves (23 percent) lived in Virginia, Missouri, Maryland, Delaware, and Kentucky in 1860, only 155 blacks from these states were included among the 2,194 published interviews (7 percent of the total). Consequently, the upper south (and especially the border states) is underrepresented. On the other hand, while Arkansas and Texas had only 293,681 or 7 percent of southern slaves in 1860, the 985 black informants in these states constituted 45 percent of all former slaves interviewed by the WPA.[43]

Most of the interviews are so limited in focus or are so short that it requires considerable skill to extract reliable information from them. In the South Carolina volumes, which contain some of the longest interviews, only 18 percent of the accounts are more than five pages long. Because of the brevity of the interviews it is often impossible to resolve internal inconsistencies, reconcile tone with "facts," separate rumor from direct observations, fathom subtle nuances, verify uncertain chronology, or determine the extent of "structural amnesia" and the manipulation of data to conform to the conditions existing in the 1930s. Since the major objective of the WPA project was to record folklore, other topics relative to plantation slavery often received little attention.

Although there are probably other weaknesses and limitations of the interviews that could be noted, the historian's major concern must be with determining ways to utilize them. One of the cardinal principles in interpreting oral lore is that the investigator must have an intimate knowledge of the informant's group, tribe, or race. According to the Africanist Jan Vansina, "members steeped in the culture itself, and sometimes only the more sensitive among them" are in the best position to study oral lore; "it is preferable that study of traditions be entrusted to people who belong to the society itself."[44] But whether black or white scholars study the WPA interviews is not as important as the approaches they take. They should begin by mastering the skills of the linguist and then systematically examine the internal structure of the interviews, the recurrence of symbols and stereotypes, the sequence of episodes, and the functions they serve.

Given the staffing policies of the WPA, some effort must be made to determine the relationship between the sex and race of interviewers and the reliability of the accounts. Generally, the stories are most revealing when the informant and the interviewer were of the same sex; black interviewers obtained more reliable information than white ones; and white women received more honest responses than white men. Fortunately, a majority of the former slaves in most states were interviewed by white women: 60 percent in North Carolina; 80 percent in Arkansas; and 90 percent in Georgia. The reverse, however, was true in South Carolina, where 78 percent of the former slaves were interviewed by white men.

There are also other important variations in the collections. Although the Arkansas staff interviewed more blacks than any of the others, a larger percentage of them had never actually been slaves. For example, about 40 percent of the Arkansas informants were born during or after the Civil War. (Many of them were in their forties or fifties in 1938.) All things considered, the Georgia collection is one of the most reliable of the WPA volumes: Most of the informants had actually been slaves (though not as old as the South Carolina blacks) and were interviewed by white women. The Georgia staff also made an effort to evaluate the interviews they collected. These evaluations were cautious and generally in accord with the data contained in the interviews. Louise Oliphant, for instance, asserted, "There are many ex-slaves . . . who have vivid recollections of the days when their lives were inseparably bound to those of their masters. . . . Mistreatment at the hands of their masters and the watchdog overseers is outstanding in the memory of most of them." On the other hand, Ruby Lorraine Radford discovered that "out of about thirty-five negroes contacted [,] only two seemed to feel bitter over memories of slave days. All the others spoke with much feeling and gratitude of good old days when they were so well cared for by their masters." Unlike most white interviewers, Radford did not accept such declarations as indicative of planter paternalism. Instead, she tried to correlate them with the average age of the informants and concluded that "most of the slaves interviewed were too young during the slavery period to have experienced any of the more cruel punishments, though some remembered hearing tales of brutal beatings."[45]

The interviewing skill of the Georgians differed greatly from that of many other white southerners. Consequently, it is mandatory to compare the stories collected by black interviewers with those collected by whites. The key questions in this comparison are those that involve life in the quarters and the treatment of slaves (frequency of floggings, adequacy of food, character of masters, etc.). The portrait given by South Carolina informants is a good example of those recorded by all-white interview staffs. According to South Carolina blacks, most of them were well treated, bountifully fed and clothed, and rarely overworked by kind masters. Most of them longed for the old plantation days. Although a great deal of this can be attributed to the general propensity of man to view his childhood through rose-colored lenses, most of it was due to caste etiquette and the actions and attitudes of the white interviewers.

The former slaves who talked to black interviewers presented an entirely different portrait of their treatment from what they told white interviewers. Black scholars at Hampton Institute, Fisk University, and Southern University conducted approximately nine hundred interviews with ex-slaves between 1929 and 1938. The interviews they received run directly counter to the South Carolina image of planter paternalism. More important, none of the volumes of interviews conducted by whites reveal as much about the internal dynamics of slave life as these 882 accounts. The informants talked much more freely to black than white interviewers about miscegenation, hatred of whites, courtship, marriage and family customs, cruel punishments, separation of families, child labor, black resistance to whites, and their admiration of Nat Turner. If one begins with the testimony collected by the predominantly black WPA staff at Hampton, by John B. Cade in Louisiana, and by Ophelia Settles Egypt in Tennessee and uses them as the standard of accuracy, many of the general distortions in the WPA collection can be eliminated.[46]

In spite of the skewed sample, the distortions, and the biases, the WPA interviews reveal much about the nature of slavery. Given the average age of the informants when they were freed, for instance, their stories contain a great deal of information about the childhood experiences of slaves. And, given the interests of interviewers, they contain a large repository of folklore. Using only those slaves who were at least fifteen years old in 1860, it is possible to compile some limited statistics on the separation of families, the age at which children started work, the occupations of slaves, and the extent to which overseers and drivers were used. The most reliable information can be compiled by asking questions that differ from those asked by the white interviewers. In this way some of the distortions caused by the interview situation can be overcome. Since the memory of the harshness of the antebellum plantation was inversely related to the former slaves' geographical distance from it, it is necessary to compare the stories of informants still living on or near those plantations with those of blacks who had migrated and resided in other states. It is significant, for example, that former South Carolina slaves who were interviewed in Georgia had a far different view of bondage than those who were interviewed in South Carolina.[47] Such comparisons as this improve the accuracy of data compiled from the WPA interviews.

On certain topics the WPA interviews are incomparable sources. They probably contain, for example, more religious and secular songs than any other single source. Similarly, the interviews contain much genealogical data on black families not found anywhere else. The WPA collection is also a rich source of information on black speech patterns. There are, however, many problems involved in the use of such data.[48]

Uncritical use of the interviews will lead almost inevitably to a simplistic and distorted view of the plantation as a paternalistic institution where the chief feature of life was mutual love and respect between masters and slaves. A more sophisticated examination using the skills of the linguist, statistician, folklorist, behavioral scientist, anthropologist, and Africanist will uncover the complexity of life on the plantation. Such systematic studies of oral lore combined with critical examinations of published narratives will enable scholars to write more revealing and accurate portrayals of slavery.

Many scholars, while granting the desirability of studying both kinds of black testimony, still wonder which of them is the best kind of historical evidence. The WPA interviews are so numerous and now so much more accessible than the published narratives that at first glance they would appear to have the edge. On the other hand, the narratives, while part of the black oral tradition, are literary records and easier for most historians to study. Then, too, if all the narratives that have been published in newspapers, magazines, church minutes, and court records were collected, they would probably outnumber the WPA interviews. Actually, the two sources are complementary: the interviews include the women (50 percent of the total) and "average" slaves who did not publish their stories; the narratives include the blacks from the border states missing in the interviews; and the preponderance of WPA informants from Texas, Arkansas, and Florida makes up for the paucity of narrators from these states.

By and large, the topics covered in the interviews and the narratives are identical. Both kinds of testimony may be biased. The narrative has, however, three great advantages over the interview. First, the average narrator was twenty-eight years younger than the average WPA informant when their stories were recorded. Second, an overwhelming majority of the narrators were over twenty years of age when they obtained freedom and could thus tell what slavery was like for adults as well as for black children. Third, all of the book-length narratives were far longer than the WPA interviews. As a consequence of these differences, personality traits appear in sharp relief in the narratives, while often being obscured in the interviews.

Although there can be no definitive answer to the question, there is a way to demonstrate some of the advantages mentioned above. One former Kentucky slave, Peter Bruner, wrote a narrative (1918) and was interviewed by the WPA (1936). A careful reading of the two stories reveals many of their similarities. But there are so many contradictions in the two accounts that it is obvious that (1) Bruner concealed some things from the interviewers, (2) the transcription was inaccurate, or (3) Bruner by 1936 had forgotten many of the details he included in his 1918 narrative.

In both the 950-word interview and the 54-page narrative Bruner recalled his cruel master, the floggings he received, and his numerous attempts to escape. But in the interview he revealed nothing about his parents or the development of his attitudes, character, or personality. In the interview Bruner and his master have a one-dimensional quality; both have complex personalities in the narrative. Besides these elements, Bruner's narrative includes many other things that he did not reveal to the WPA interviewer: his addiction to alcohol; blacks who helped runaways and resisted floggings; the amusements (gambling, drinking, dueling) of the planters and their oppression of poor whites; introspective revelations about his feelings about being enslaved; the development of his attitudes toward work, slaveholders, and poor whites; and the Weltanschauung of the slave.[49]

In the final analysis, the methodological skills possessed by the historian and the questions he wants to answer will determine whether he uses the narratives or the interviews. Where skills and interests intersect, he will use both. In either case, the approach must be a critical one and take into account the following declaration of Solomon Northup:

There may be humane masters, as there certainly are inhuman ones—there may be slaves well-clothed, well-fed, and happy, as there surely are those half-clad, half-starved and miserable. . . . Men may write fictions portraying lowly life as it is, or as it is not—may expatiate with owlish gravity upon the bliss of ignorance—discourse flippantly from arm chairs of the pleasures of slave life; but let them toil with him in the field—sleep with him in the cabin—feed with him on husks; let them behold him scourged, hunted, trampled on, and they will come back with another story in their mouths. Let them know the heart of the poor slave—learn his secret thoughts—thoughts he dare not utter in the hearing of the white man; let them sit by him in the silent watches of the night—converse with him in trustful confidence, of "life, liberty, and the pursuit of happiness," and they will find that ninety-nine out of every hundred are intelligent enough to understand their situation, and to cherish in their bosoms the love of freedom, as passionately as themselves.[50]

If scholars want to know the heart and secret thoughts of slaves, they must study the testimony of the blacks. But since the slave did not know the heart and secret thoughts of masters, they must also examine the testimony of whites. Neither the whites nor the blacks had a monopoly on truth, had rended the veil cloaking the life of the other, or had seen clearly the pain and the joy bounded by color and caste. The perceptions of neither can be accepted as encapsulating the totality of plantation life. Consequently, whether one focuses on the slaves or the master, one must systematically examine both black and white testimony. But, just as there are some topics on which only the masters can provide reliable information, there are some questions that only the slaves can answer. In this regard, scholars should always remember the perceptive observation of Frederick Douglass that a free man "cannot see things in the same light with the slave, because he does not, and cannot, look from the same point from which the slave does." Because of these differences in perceptions scholars who have studied a variety of sources have concluded that "there are questions about the slave system that can be answered only by one who has experienced slavery. How did it 'feel' to be owned? What were the pleasures and sufferings of a slave? What was the slave's attitude toward his owner, toward the white man's assumption of superiority, toward the white man's God? Did the slaves want to be free? Did they feel it was their right to be free?" The individual and collective mentality of the slaves, the ways they sought to fulfill their needs, the experiential context of life in the quarters and in the fields, and the black man's personal perspective of bondage emerge only after an intensive examination of the testimony of ex-slaves.[51]

NOTES

1. Stanley M. Elkins, *Slavery: A Problem in American Institutional and Intellectual Life,* 2nd. ed. (Chicago, 1968), 3.

2. Ulrich B. Phillips, *Life and Labor in the Old South* (Boston, 1929), 219.

3. Harrison A. Trexler, *Slavery in Missouri, 1804-1865* (Baltimore, 1914); Chase C. Mooney, *Slavery in Tennessee* (Bloomington, 1957); J. Winston Coleman, Jr., *Slavery Times in Kentucky* (Chapel Hill, 1940); and Frederick Bancroft, *Slave-Trading in the Old South* (Baltimore, 1931), cited many interviews and narratives in their studies.

4. Benjamin A. Botkin, "The Slave as His Own Interpreter," Library of Congress, *Quarterly Journal of Current Acquisitions* 2 (November 1944), 37; Richard Hofstadter, "U.B. Phillips and the Plantation Legend," *Journal of Negro History* 29 (April 1944), 109-24.

5. Josiah Henson, *The Life of Josiah Henson, Formerly a Slave, Now an Inhabitant of Canada.* Narrated by Himself [to S. A. Eliot] (Boston, 1849); Solomon Northup, *Twelve Years a Slave,* edited by Sue Eakins and

Joseph Logsdon (Baton Rouge, 1968), ix-xiv; Claude M. Fuess, "Samuel Atkins Eliott," *Dictionary of American Biography* (23 vols. and index, New York, 1928-1973; cited hereinafter as *DAB*) 6: 81-82.

6. Harper Twelvetrees, ed., *The Story of the Life of John Anderson, the Fugitive Slave* (London, 1863); Frederic Boase, ed., *Modern English Biography* (6 vols., London and Edinburgh, 1965) III, 1055; Northup, *Twelve Years a Slave,* ix-xiv.

7. Lunsford Lane, *The Narrative of Lunsford Lane* . . . [edited by William G. Hawkins] (Boston, 1848); William G. Eliot, *The Story of Archer Alexander from Slavery to Freedom,* March 30, 1863 (Boston, 1885); Apleton's Cyclopaedia of American Biography* (6 vols., New York, 1886-1889) 3, 121; Charlotte C. Eliot, *William Greenleaf Eliot: Minister, Educator, Philanthropist* (Boston and New York, 1904), 126-51; Frank J. Bruno, "William Greenleaf Eliot," *DAB* 6, 82-83.

8. Thomas Price, *The History of Protestant Nonconformity in England from the Reformation Under Henry VIII* (2 vols., London, 1836-1838); Frank J. Bruno, "William Greenleaf Eliot," *DAB* 6, 82-83; A. Everett Peterson, "James W. C. Pennington," *DAB* 14, 441-42.

9. Henry Trumbull, *History of the Discovery of America* (Brooklyn, [1810]); Chloe Spear, *Memoir of Mrs. Chloe Spear, a Native of Africa,* [edited by James S. Loring] (Boston, 1832); Robert Voorhis, *Life and Adventures of Robert Voorhis,* [edited by Henry Trumbull] (Providence, 1829); James S. Loring, "The Franklin Manuscripts," *Historical Magazine* 3 (January 1859), 9-12; Israel R. Potter, *Life and Adventures of Israel Ralph Potter* (1744-1826), [edited by Henry Trumbull] (Providence, 1824); James S. Loring, *The Hundred Boston Orators Appointed by the Municipal Authorities and Other Public Bodies* . . . (Boston, 1852); Joseph C. Lovejoy, *Memoir of the Rev. Charles T. Torrey* . . . (Boston, 1847); Owen and Joseph C. Lovejoy, *Memoir of the Rev. Elijah P. Lovejoy* (New York, 1838).

10. Allan Westcott. "Charles Edwards Lester," *DAB* 11, 189-90.

11. Isaac Jefferson, *Memoirs of a Monticello Slave, as Dictated to Charles Campbell* . . . edited by Rayford W. Logan (Charlottesville, 1951), 3-8; Edward A. Wyatt, IV, *Charles Campbell, Virginia's "Old Mortality"* (Charlottesville, 1935).

12. James W. C. Pennington, *A Narrative of Events of the Life of J. H. Banks, an Escaped Slave* . . . (Liverpool, 1861); John Brown, *Slave Life in Georgia* . . .edited by Louis A. Chamerovzow (London, 1855); Isaac Tatem Hopper, *Narrative of the Life of Thomas Cooper* (New York, 1832); Rufus M. Jones, "Isaac Tatem Hopper," *DAB* 9, 224; A. Everett Peterson, "James W. C. Pennington," *DAB* 14, 441-42.

13. Lewis G. and Milton Clarke, *Narratives of the Sufferings of Lewis and Milton Clarke* . . . [edited by Joseph C. Lovejoy] (Boston, 1846), 192-41; Moses Roper, *A Narrative of the Adventures and Escape of Moses Roper* . . . edited by Thomas Price (London, 1840), 121-84.

14. See for example: Northup, *Twelve Years a Slave*, [edited by David Wilson] (Auburn and Buffalo, 1853); Peter Wheeler, *Chains and Freedom: or, The Life and Adventures of Peter Wheeler* . . ., [edited by Charles E. Lester] (New York, 1839), v-20.

15. Charles Ball, *Slavery in the United States: A Narrative of the Life and Adventures of Charles Ball, a Black Man* . . ., [edited by Thomas Fisher] (New York, 1837); Edwin J. Scott, *Random Recollections of a Long Life, 1806 to 1876* (Columbia, S. C., 1884), 9-10, 31-32, 95-98; John M. Bateman, comp., *The Columbia Scrapbook, 1701-1842* (Columbia, S. C., 1915), 20, 31-34, 53; Helen K. Hennig, ed., *Columbia, Capital City of South Carolina, 1786-1936* (Columbia, S. C., 1936), 10, 67-70, 315, 374; Robert Mills, *Statistics of South Carolina* . . . (Charleston, 1826), 688, 713-14; John Drayton, *A View of South Carolina* . . . (Charleston, 1802), 104, 111, 116-49); William G. Simms, *The Geography of South Carolina* (Charleston, 1843), 122-27; Ulrich B. Phillips, ed., *Plantation and Frontier Documents: 1694-1863* (2 vols., Cleveland, 1909) 2, 59-67; James Williams, *Narrative of James William. An American Slave* . . . [edited by John G. Whittier] (Philadelphia, 1838).

16. Henry Box Brown, *Narrative of Henry Box Brown* . . . (Boston, 1849), 1-3.

17. Jane Blake, *Memoirs of Margaret Jane Blake* (Philadelphia, 1834); Elleanor Eldridge, *Memoirs of Elleanor Eldridge* (Providence, 1838); Sally Williams, *Aunt Sally; or, The Cross the Way to Freedom* (Cincinnati, 1858). Other unreliable narratives include Aaron, *The Light and Truth of Slavery* (Worcester, Mass., n.d.); Reginald Rowland, *An Ambitious Slave* (Buffalo, 1897); John H. Simpson, *Horrors of the Virginian Slave Trade* . . . *The True Story of Dinah* . . . (London, 1863); and Smith H. Platt, *The Martyrs, and the Fugitive* . . . (New York, 1859).

18. See: Henry C. Bruce, *The New Man. Twenty-nine Years a Slave. Twenty-nine Years a Free Man* (York, Pa., 1895); Louis Hughes, *Thirty Years a Slave* (Milwaukee, 1897); Jacob Stroyer, *My Life in the South* (Salem, 1889); Elizabeth H. Keckley, *Behind the Scenes* (New York, 1868).

19. Josiah Henson, *An Autobiography of the Reverend Josiah Henson,* edited by Robin W. Winks (Reading, Mass., and other cities, 1969), v-xxxiv.

20. Jean Vacheenos and Betty Volk, "Born in Bondage: History of a Slave Family," *Negro History Bulletin* 36 (May 1973), 161-66.

21. Robin W. Winks, *The Blacks in Canada: A History* (Montreal, New Haven, and London, 1971), 178-84, 195-204.

22. Mifflin W. Gibbs, *Shadow and Light: An Autobiography* (Washington, 1902), 12-13; *Chambers's Edinburgh Journal,* 2nd ser., 15 (March 15, 1851), 174-75; William Craft, *Running a Thousand Miles for Freedom . . .* (London, 1860).

23. *Liberator,* June 8, 1849; July 11, 1850; Gibbs, *Shadow and Light,* 13-14; *Non-slaveholder* 4 (May 1849), 107.

24. Northup, *Twelve Years a Slave*, edited by Eakins and Logsdon; John Brown, *Slave Life in Georgia,* edited by F. Nash Boney (Savannah, 1972); Philip D. Curtin, ed., *Africa Remembered: Narratives of West Africans from the Era of the Slave Trade* (Madison, Milwaukee, and London, 1967), 60-98.

25. See for example: Wilson Armistead, *A Tribute for the Negro* (Manchester, 1848), 519-22; Bayley, *Narrative of Some Remarkable Incidents in the Life of Solomon Bayley . . .* (London, 1825).

26. Eugene D. Genovese, "Getting to Know the Slaves," *New York Review of Books,* September 21, 1972, pp. 16-19; Norman R. Yetman, "The Background of the Slave Narrative Collection," *American Quarterly* 19 (Fall 1967), 534-53. Unless otherwise indicated, all references to the WPA interviews are to George P. Rawick, ed., *The American Slave: A Composite Autobiography* (19 vols., Westport, Conn., 1972).

27. For suggestive critical essays see: Lewis A. Dexter, *Elite and Specialized Interviewing* (Evanston, 1970), 119-62; *American Journal of Sociology* 62 (September 1965), entire issue; Stephen A. Richardson, et al., *Interviewing: Its Form and Functions* (New York and London, 1965).

28. Yetman, "The Background of the Slave Narrative Collection," 534-53; Allison Davis, Burleigh B. Gardner, and Mary R. Gardner, *Deep South: A Social Anthropological Study of Caste and Class* (Chicago, 1941); Bertram W. Doyle, *The Etiquette of Race Relations in the South: A Study in Social Control* (Chicago, 1937); John Dollard, *Caste and Class in the Southern Town* (New Haven and London, 1937); Hortense Powdermaker, *After Freedom: A Cultural Study in the Deep South* (New York, 1939).

29. William R. Ferris, "The Collection of Racial Lore: Approaches and Problems," *New York Folklore Quarterly* 27 (September 1971), 261-62.

30. Pete Daniel, *The Shadow of Slavery: Peonage in the South 1901-1969* (Urbana, Chicago, and London, 1972), 29; Charles S. Johnson, Edwin R. Embree, and W. W. Alexander, *The Collapse of Cotton Tenancy* (Chapel Hill, 1935); Arthur F. Raper, *Preface to Peasantry: A Tale of Two Black Belt Counties* (Chapel Hill, 1936); Charles S. Johnson, *The Shadow of the*

Plantation (Chicago, 1934); Commission on Interracial Cooperation, *The Mob Still Rides: A Review of the Lynching Record, 1931-1935* (Atlanta, 1936).

31. Rawick, ed., *The American Slave* 3, Pt. 3, 237, 253-54; Pt. 4, 82, 86; 17, 41, 303.

32. Ibid., 12, Pt. 1, 113-14.

33. Ferris, "The Collection of Racial Lore," 271.

34. On informant-interviewer interaction see Lewis A. Dexter, "Role Relationships and Conceptions of Neutrality in Interviewing," *American Journal of Sociology* 62 (September 1956), 153-57.

35. Rawick, ed., *The American Slave* 16 (Kentucky), 99.

36. J. Mason Brewer, "Juneteenth," Texas Folklore Society, *Publications* 10 (Austin, 1832), 9-54; Brewer, "John Tales," ibid., 21 (Austin, 1946), 81-104.

37. Norman R. Yetman, ed., *Voices from Slavery* (New York, Chicago, and San Francisco, 1970), 1; Rawick, ed., *The American Slave* 1, xvii-xviii.

38. J. Ralph Jones, "Portraits of Georgia Slaves," *Georgia Review* 21 (Spring-Winter 1967), 126-32, 268-73, 407-11, 521-25; 22 (Spring and Summer 1968), 125-27, 254-57; Rawick, ed., *The American Slave* 12. Pt. 1, 9-16, 86-90; Pt. 2, 17-27, 13; Pt. 3, 14-15; Pt. 4, 205-11.

39. Jones, "Portraits of Georgia Slaves," 21, 268-73, 407-11; Rawick, ed., *The American Slave* 12, Pt. 1, 9-16, 86-90.

40. Jones, "Portraits of Georgia Slaves," 21, 271.

41. Writers' Program, Virginia, *The Negro in Virginia* (New York, 1940), 31-33, 57, 65-71, 82, 92-95, 143-44, 154-55, 170-71, 201-202, 302; Rawick, ed., *The American Slave* 16 (Virginia), 1-6, 15-16, 21-26, 31-41, 46-54. Lewis contributed a preface to *The Negro in Virginia,* but he was not formally designated editor of the volume.

42. Yetman, "The Background of the Slave Narrative Collection," 534-53. For examples of interviews conducted by northerners during and immediately after the Civil War, see: Laura S. Haviland, *A Woman's Life-Work: Labors and Experiences of Laura S. Haviland* (Chicago, 1887), 439-49; and George H. Hepworth, *The Whip, Hoe and Sword; or, The Gulf-Department in '63* (Boston, 1864), 152-59.

43. U. S. Bureau of the Census, *Negro Population 1790-1915* (Washington, 1918), 57.

44. Jan Vansina, "Once upon a Time: Oral Traditions as History in Africa," *Daedalus* 100 (Spring 1971), 456. See also Vansina, *Oral Tradition: A Study in Historical Methodology* (Chicago, 1965).

45. Rawick, ed., *The American Slave* 13, Pt. 4, 291, 309, 326.

46. Ophelia Settles Egypt interviewed 100 former slaves; John B. Cade

and his associates, 482; and Roscoe Lewis and Hampton Institute blacks, 300. Yetman, "The Background of the Slave Narrative Collection," 534-53.

47. Rawick, ed., *The American Slave* 13, Pt. 3, 233-35, 288-94.

48. Ibid., 1, 176.

49. Ibid., 16 (Kentucky), 88-90; Peter Bruner, *A Slave's Adventures Toward Freedom,* (Oxford, Ohio [1918]).

50. Northup, *Twelve Years a Slave,* edited by David Wilson, 206-207.

51. Frederick Douglass, *My Bondage and My Freedom* (New York, 1855), 339; Writers' Program, Virginia, *The Negro in Virginia,* 27.

Index

About the Contributors

MARY F. BERRY is Assistant Secretary of Education at the Department of Health, Education and Welfare. She has held the positions of Provost of the division of Behavioral and Social Sciences at the University of Maryland, College Park, and Chancellor at the University of Colorado, Boulder. A noted historian and lawyer, Dr. Berry is author of *Black Resistance, White Law: A History of Constitutional Racism in America* (1971), and *Military Necessity and Civil Rights Policy, 1861-1868* (1977).

GEORGE P. RAWICK is Lecturer in the Department of History of the University of Missouri, St. Louis. He is author of *From Sundown to Sunup: The Making of the Black Community* (1972) and editor of the multivolume *The American Slave: A Composite Autobiography* (1970).

EUGENE D. GENOVESE is Professor of History at the University of Rochester and author of *The Political Economy of Slavery: Studies in the Economy and Society of the Slave South* (1961), *The World the Slaveholders Made: Two Essays in Interpretation* (1969), and *Roll, Jordan, Roll: The World the Slaves Made* (1974).

EARL E. THORPE is Professor of History at North Carolina Central University and author of *The Mind of the Negro: an Intellectual History of Afro-Americans* (1961), *Eros and Freedom in Southern Life and Thought* (1966), *The Central Theme of Black History* (1969), *Black Historians: A Critique* (1971) , and *The Old South: A Psychohistory* (1972).

LESLIE HOWARD OWENS is Associate Professor of History at the University of Michigan, Ann Arbor, and author of *This Species of Property: Slave Life and Culture in the Old South* (1976).

RALPH D. CARTER is Assistant Professor of History at Rutgers University and author of several articles on Afro-American slavery.

STANLEY ENGERMAN is Professor of Economics and History at the University of Rochester and co-author with Robert Fogel of *Time on the Cross: The Economics of American Negro Slavery* (1974).

JOHN HENRIK CLARKE is Professor of Black and Puerto Rican Studies at Hunter College and author and editor of numerous books, including *History and Culture of Africa* (1969), *William Styron's Nat Turner: Ten Black Writers Respond* (1968), and *Marcus Garvey and the Vision of Africa* (1976).

JAMES D. ANDERSON is Assistant Professor of Education at the University of Illinois, Urbana, and author of several articles on the history of education in America.

JOHN W. BLASSINGAME, author of *The Slave Community,* is Professor of History at Yale University. He is also author of *Black New Orleans, 1860-1880* (1973), editor of *Slave Testimony: Two Centuries of Letters, Speeches, Interviews, and Autobiographies* (1977), and editor of the Frederick Douglass Papers.

AL-TONY GILMORE is Director of Afro-American Studies and Associate Professor of History at the University of Maryland, College Park. He is author of *Bad Nigger! The National Impact of Jack Johnson* (1975).